Immigration and Population

Immigration and Population

Stephanie A. Bohon
Meghan Conley

polity

First published in 2015 by Polity Press

Polity Press
65 Bridge Street
Cambridge CB2 1UR, UK

Polity Press
350 Main Street
Malden, MA 02148, USA

ISBN-13: 978-0-7456-6415-6
ISBN-13: 978-0-7456-6416-3(pb)

A catalogue record for this book is available from the British Library.

Library of Congress Cataloging-in-Publication Data

Bohon, Stephanie.
    Immigration and population / Stephanie A. Bohon, Meghan E. Conley.
        pages cm
    ISBN 978-0-7456-6415-6 (hardback) -- ISBN 978-0-7456-6416-3 (paperback) 1.
Emigration and immigration--Social aspects. 2. Population geography. 3. Demography.
I. Conley, Meghan E. II. Title.
    JV6225.B6487 2015
    304.8--dc23
                                          2014022762

Typeset in 11/13 Sabon by
Servis Filmsetting Limited, Stockport, Cheshire

For further information on Polity, visit our website:
politybooks.com

To the tired, the poor, the huddled, the wretched, and the homeless who have journeyed to US shores for nearly 250 years.

Contents

Figures, Tables, and Boxes

Figures

Tables

Text boxes

Acknowledgements

No book could be completed without the support of many people. We are indebted to Peter Fernandez and to Michael Jarrett, who died a few months prior to the completion of this project. Their constant encouragement sustained us. We would also like to thank Dr. Jon Shefner and the faculty of the Department of Sociology at the University of Tennessee, who provided considerable instrumental support. We are grateful to the staff at Polity, especially Commissioning Editor Jonathan Skerrett, and Editorial Assistant Elen Griffiths, who gave us guidance on the direction of our writing and patiently handled our lives' disasters. Finally, we gratefully acknowledge the helpful comments of Dr. Bridget Gorman (Rice University), Dr. Rebecca Clark (NICHD), and Dr. Carmel Price (Furman University).

1

The Demography of Immigration

Reyna works at a grocery store in a small town in the Appalachian Mountains. An immigrant of Turkish descent, she entered the United States about 10 years ago. Although her foreign accent is unmistakable, Reyna speaks fluent English, and she is polite and pleasant to her customers. Having worked her way up from an entry-level position, she is currently training to manage her own store in the grocery's chain, and she has just purchased her first home.

Much about Reyna's story epitomizes the classic stereotype of the hardworking immigrant striving for a better life in a new country. At the same time, her story also illustrates today's complicated global web of international migration, in which place of birth and ethnic identity often differ and immigrants sometimes have experiences of living in three or more countries. For example, Reyna often returns to Turkey to visit relatives, but she was not born in Turkey, nor has she ever lived there. Reyna was born in Germany, where Turks are the largest ethnic minority and comprise about 5 percent of the German population (Şen 2003). Reyna is one of nearly 43 million immigrants living in the United States and one of nearly 49 million Americans who are associated with German–US immigration either by immigrating directly from Germany or by being the descendants of German immigrants. Yet, she is not German. She is one of only a relatively small number of US immigrants of West Asian / Middle Eastern descent (United Nations 2011).

The story of people like Reyna underscores that there is no

universal "immigrant experience" in today's globalized world; rather, there are as many immigrant experiences as there are immigrants. Despite this, there are important trends in immigration, and immigrants share several characteristics. First, many people today live in a country other than the one where they were born. Most of these immigrants reside in the developed world (nearly 128 million in 2009) in the 34 wealthiest countries that comprise the Organization for Economic Co-operation and Development (OECD). OECD countries are home to nearly 60 percent of all immigrants. In fact, about 9 percent of the population of OECD countries is comprised of immigrants, although immigrants comprise only 3 percent of the world's total population (United Nations 2011). Most immigrants migrate to developed countries from other developed countries; increasingly, however, immigrants are also migrating to developed countries from developing countries (OECD 2007). The developing world is also home to a smaller but still sizable number of immigrants (just over 86 million in 2009: United Nations 2011). This book focuses exclusively on immigration to developed countries, especially emphasizing the United States, which is the world's biggest immigrant receiver.

Second, immigration typically flows along network lines shaped by cultural, geographic, and historical conditions (Gurak and Caces 1992; McKenzie and Rapoport 2010). Thus, many people from the Middle East immigrate to the European Union, especially France and Germany, but far fewer Middle Easterners immigrate to the United States (Foad 2010). At the same time, many Asian immigrants settle in English-speaking countries, and there are large East and Southeast Asian populations in the United Kingdom, United States, Canada, and Australia. *Network migration* also explains why immigrants end up in some parts of a host country instead of others. For example, in the early 1900s, the demand for sheepherders resulted in the migration of many people from the Pyrenees Basque Country of Spain and France to southern Idaho; today, Idaho is home to the largest population of Basque people outside of their homeland (Bieter and Bieter 2004).

Third, immigrants are not the same as those they leave behind (Kennedy, McDonald, and Biddle 2006; Belot and Hatton 2012).

2

The process of immigration is difficult and it requires considerable financial, intellectual, and physical capital, as well as a willingness to take risks. For example, immigrants tend to be slightly better educated than the non-immigrants they leave behind (Feliciano 2005). Also, the further immigrants migrate, the greater the *selection effect* (ibid.). A selection effect is a term social scientists use to describe groups who behave differently from others because they are different (Jasso 1988; Rumbaut 1997a). Among immigration scholars, selection refers to systematic differences between the group of people from a country who emigrate and those who stay at home. These differences include measurable qualities, such as educational attainment and income, as well as traits that are difficult to quantify, such as ambition, risk-aversion, and optimism. For example, few young people in India have a college education (World Bank 2012), whereas 80 percent of Indian immigrants and their descendants living in the United States do (KewalRamani et al. 2007).

Fourth, differences in the liberalness of immigrant laws results in some countries receiving large populations of immigrants, while other countries are home to relatively few. Germany, for example, hosts as many immigrants (nearly 11 million in 2009) as eight of its border countries (Netherlands, Denmark, Poland, Czech Republic, Austria, Switzerland, Luxembourg, and Belgium) combined (United Nations 2011). Still, Germany has far fewer immigrants than the United States and Russia (Freeman 2006). The United States – the world's largest immigrant-receiving country – was home to more than 40 million immigrants in 2010 (Grieco et al. 2012). In contrast, Japan and Korea accept relatively few immigrants (United Nations 2011).

Although the United States has more foreign-born residents than any other country in the world (United Nations 2013), it does not have the highest proportion of immigrants relative to the general population. About 13 percent of US residents are immigrants, outpacing the foreign-born percentages in France and Italy, where immigrants account for 11.1 and 8 percent, respectively, of the total population (Vasileva 2011). Still, more than 16 percent of Germany's population is foreign-born, while a whopping 42.4 percent of Luxembourg's population is foreign-born (OECD 2013).

In fact, as a percentage of the total population, the foreign-born population of the United States is comfortably in the middle of the OECD countries. Luxembourg, Australia, Switzerland, Israel, New Zealand, Canada, Belgium, Spain, Ireland, Germany, Estonia, Austria, and Sweden all have a greater proportion of foreign-born residents than the United States (ibid.). The biggest immigrant receivers – in terms of their proportion in the general population – are in the Middle East, and some Middle Eastern countries have more immigrants than natives (United Nations 2011). The biggest proportionate receivers are, in order, Qatar (87 percent immigrant), the United Arab Emirates (70 percent), Kuwait (69 percent), Jordan (46 percent), and the occupied Palestinian territory (44 percent).

Types of immigration

Although "immigrant" refers generally to those who live in a country outside of their country of origin, some countries identify a broad array of immigrant statuses. For example, immigrants in the United States can be *lawful permanent residents* – those who are allowed to reside and work permanently in the United States; *conditional permanent residents* – those who have applied for, but not yet received, lawful permanent residence; and refugees and asylees. The United States also offers several types of non-immigrant visas – such as student, visitor, and certain employment visas – which temporarily authorize people to study, visit, or work in the country under certain circumstances, but not to remain for long periods of time. In some countries, including the United States, some immigrants have the opportunity to become citizens. This process is known as *naturalization.*

Immigrants can also be *unauthorized* or *irregular*, meaning that they lack permission to be in their host country. The term *unauthorized* is the official term used by US government agencies; the United Nations uses the term *irregular* in its publications, but the two terms are synonyms. In 2011, the unauthorized population in the United States totaled an estimated 11.1 million people – including approximately 1 million children under the age of

The Demography of Immigration

Table 1.1   Type of immigrants by legal status and motivation to migrate

Legal status	
Authorized	
Naturalized	An immigrant who has been granted citizenship in his/her host country
Lawful permanent resident	An immigrant who is allowed to work and reside permanently in his/her host country
Conditional permanent resident	An immigrant who has applied for, but not yet received, lawful permanent residence or asylum
Non-immigrants	Immigrants holding visas to visit, study, or engage in work in their host country for a specified period of time
Unauthorized	
Irregular	An immigrant who does not have permission to reside in his/her host country

Motivation	
Voluntary	
Economic	A person who immigrates for reasons of work
Family reunification	A person who immigrates in order to form a family or to join family members
Involuntary	
Refugees	A person seeking shelter in a host country in order to escape political violence, environmental devastation, or other life-threatening conditions
Asylees	A person living in a host country who has been granted permission to do so based on meeting refugee criteria
Trafficked	A person coerced or forcibly taken into a host country for illicit purposes

18 – and comprised 3.7 percent of the total US population (Hoefer, Rytina, and Baker 2012). In contrast, countries in the European Union host approximately 1.9 to 3.8 million irregular immigrants (Morehouse and Blomfield 2011), despite the fact that the European Union is more populous than the United States. The vast majority of unauthorized immigrants in the United States originate from Latin America. As of 2010, approximately 58 percent (6.5 million) of unauthorized immigrants in the United States originated from Mexico, while another 23 percent came from other countries in Latin America (Hoefer, Rytina, and Baker 2012). In contrast, the vast majority of irregular migrants to Europe in recent years have originated from Afghanistan, Albania, Iraq, the Palestinian territories, and Somalia (Morehouse and Blomfield 2011). Although the sending countries have not changed, in recent years, the numbers of unauthorized or irregular status migrants have declined in both the United States and Europe.

Countries admit immigrants for three reasons: labor market needs, the perceived value of family reunification, and humanitarian concerns (Cobb-Clark 2003). These criteria are prioritized differently across time and place, so the type and number of immigrants received can differ considerably from country to country and over time. Immigrants contribute to foreign economies by filling vacant jobs. Thus, many countries design immigration policies to give preferential admission to immigrants who can provide labor for jobs that natives cannot fill. For example, many chemists working in the United States, including many who received advanced degrees from US universities, are from countries such as China, Germany, and the Philippines (National Research Council 2007). The majority of immigrants moving from developing to developed countries are *economic* (or *labor*) *migrants* (Martin, Abella, and Kuptsch 2006). These are people whose decision to immigrate is primarily motivated by the desire to improve their economic situation by obtaining a better or higher-paying job. Most immigration between developed countries is also labor migration; transnational corporations may move workers overseas or white-collar workers might take advantage of opportunities abroad in their field.

Legal consequences of unauthorized status in the United States and Europe

In the United States, unauthorized status is largely treated as a violation of civil immigration law, rather than criminal law. This means that unauthorized immigrants may face civil penalties in the form of removal and restrictions on or exclusion from future lawful entry for their unauthorized presence in the United States. However, their unauthorized presence is not in itself a violation of criminal law, and thus it is not subject to criminal penalties. In other words, unauthorized immigrants who are apprehended may be detained and removed (i.e., deported), but they do not face criminal penalties simply as a result of living in the United States with unauthorized status.

In Europe, irregular migration is addressed by individual member states. That is, different countries in Europe have different policies and legal approaches to addressing resident irregular migrants. Austria, for example, offers few opportunities for regularization and deals strictly with irregular migrants, primarily using voluntary repatriation and forced return (deportation) to address its population of irregular migrants. France and Italy have also utilized mass expulsion against their Roma populations (Severance 2010). The Commissioner for Human Rights of the Council of Europe (2010) has noted an increase in the criminalization of irregular migrants in the member countries of the European Union, both at border crossings and as a result of their presence.

Most countries recognize that family immigration often occurs in stages, and that it is socially desirable and ethical to reunite family members. Thus, countries admit immigrants for the purpose of family reunification (Suárez-Orozco, Todorova, and Louie 2002; Cobb-Clark 2003). There are many reasons that families become separated during the migration process. Often, one family member is admitted into another country first as an economic migrant, and he or she can use their position, once established, to bring other family members with them. Some people immigrate in order to form families through marriage (DeJong, Root, and Abad 1986).

In the United States, people seeking entry through family reunification are prioritized based on their relationship to the person already living in the country. Generally speaking, the immigration process is quicker and easier for those whose family members are US citizens than for those whose family members are foreign-born and non-naturalized. Additionally, the spouses, minor children, and parents of US citizen adults have priority over siblings and adult children (Hendricks 2008). That is, there are no limits on the number of visas allocated annually to the spouses, minor children, and parents of US citizens. However, there is an annual cap on the number of visas allocated to the adult children and siblings of US citizens; there are also annual limitations on visas allocated to the spouses and children of lawful permanent residents (Bergeron 2013).

Some immigrants must move to survive as a result of conditions in their home country. For example, people may be forced to leave countries experiencing extreme and prolonged economic deterioration, such as double-digit unemployment, in order to provide for themselves and their families. However, these immigrants are usually classified as voluntary labor migrants, rather than economic refugees (Harris 1993). In contrast, those who are displaced from their homes due to political conditions – such as war – or environmental conditions – such as earthquakes or tsunamis – are considered to be *involuntary migrants*. As of 2008, humanitarian concerns for these immigrants have prompted nations to house more than 15 million foreign-born people (United Nations 2011). When displaced people cross an international border, they are sometimes called *refugees* or *forced migrants* (Teitelbaum and Weiner 1995). Asylum is a legal protection granted to refugees by their host country; however, because of national security concerns and political relationships between countries, some involuntary migrants are denied asylum and sent back to their home country, even though this action might lead to their imprisonment, torture, or death (Stanley 1987). Returning refugees to their home country when it is not safe – an action called *refoulement* – violates international law. Nonetheless, more than half of the refugee-receiving countries monitored by the United Nations were suspected of violating international treaties on non-refoulement in 2005 (United Nations High Commissioner for Refugees 2006).

Since it is not uncommon to deny asylum to some refugees, immigration scholars often distinguish between refugees (i.e., forced migrants) and *asylees* (i.e., forced migrants whose refugee status is officially recognized by their host country). Although international law establishes criteria for refugees, countries interpret these criteria through different lenses; likewise, the terminology is inconsistently applied. For example, the US government refers to those who have met US asylum criteria as *refugees* if they apply for asylum from outside of the United States and *asylees* if they apply for asylum after arriving in the United States or one of its ports of entry (Martin 2010).

A third group of involuntary migrants are those who are brought to a country against their will. In the United States, many African Americans are the descendants of those who were forcibly transported to North America from Africa as part of the transatlantic slave trade. Today, scholars estimate that about 900,000 people living in foreign countries have been *trafficked* into the sex trade or in forced labor through kidnapping or coercion, although the extent of human trafficking worldwide is difficult to estimate (Gozdziak and Collett 2005). Although this book focuses primarily on voluntary migrants, it is important to note that the distinction between voluntary and involuntary migration is often blurred by political exigencies.

The demography of immigration

Demography is the interdisciplinary study of population change, and population scientists (called *demographers*) can be sociologists, geographers, economists, biologists, historians, epidemiologists, statisticians, and other social scientists. Although a small subset of demographers holds advanced degrees in demography, most who call themselves demographers are self-labeled. Other scholars who do not self-identify as demographers may be labeled as such because they work as demographers, they publish in demography outlets, or their work is widely used by demographers. This diverse group of scholars is united by a deep interest in *demographic processes* and (to a much lesser extent) a set of statistical techniques for studying these processes. The demographic processes are the three events – fertility, mortality, and migration – that influence a population's size or composition.

It may seem odd to talk of a demography of immigration, since migration (which includes population movements between and within countries) is one of the three demographic processes. Certainly, any study of immigration can rightly be called *demography*. However, the demographic perspective on immigration is distinct from how non-demographers view immigration, in that the demographic perspective focuses on larger trends among immigrant groups, rather than on the experiences of a single immigrant or a small group of immigrants. Demographers also tend to favor quantitative methods of study over ethnographic methods, although some demographers do engage in ethnographic work. Demographers usually prefer objective measures (e.g., years of education completed, age, or place of settlement) over subjective measures, like attitudes or orientations. Thus, when demographers study immigrant assimilation, they often use statistical techniques to examine the magnitude of differences between immigrant groups and natives on measurable outcomes such as annual earnings, type of housing occupancy, or employment rates. Social psychologists, on the other hand, focus more closely on the individual experiences of immigrants as they attempt to negotiate social conditions in their new country.

This book focuses on immigration as a population process, so we present immigration through a demographic lens. As such, we focus on two interrelated points about immigration as demography. First, we consider the role that immigration plays in the understanding of other population processes in which demographers have a paramount interest. These processes include population composition (chapter 2), fertility (chapter 5), aging (chapter 6), and health and mortality (chapter 7). We closely scrutinize these processes and how they are complicated by immigration. Second, we focus on the understanding of immigration and the measurement of how immigrants impact societies based on findings from demographic research. Thus, we also explore topics that interest demographers beyond basic demographic processes, such as immigrant labor (chapter 3), immigrants and the environment (chapter 4), and immigrant education (chapter 8). This is hardly an exhaustive examination of the demography of immigration. However, we hope to provide an overview of the largest topics within demography and the biggest issues related to immigration that can be approached through demographic knowledge.

Immigrants and anti-immigrants

How well immigrants fare in a host country and how well their descendants are accepted in their new land varies greatly from country to country and often depends on where immigrants originate. Some countries, such as Australia, the United States, and Canada, consider themselves a land of immigrants, and new immigrants to these countries can expect to find Australians, Americans, and Canadians who have the same ancestry as they do. However, in many other countries, the ethnic origin of immigrants is very important. For example, Germans make a distinction between *Spätausiedler* – immigrants who are considered German by ancestry, despite being born in other countries – and *Zuwandern* (all other immigrants). In Norway, a child born to two immigrant parents is also considered an immigrant.

The United States receives more immigrants than any other nation in the world, and there is a popular saying that everyone comes from somewhere else. It is a common practice among US residents to ask one another where they "came from," and many will respond with two or three ethnicities (e.g., English-Scots-Irish), often referring to countries they have never visited and about which they know very little. With the possible exception of American Indians, who themselves crossed the Bering Strait from Asia at least 13,000 years ago, there is no such thing as an "ethnic American." Whereas American Indians currently comprise less than 2 percent of the US population, immigrants have comprised at least 10 percent of the US population for most of the twentieth century and all of the twenty-first (Gryn and Larsen 2010). Most US residents are either immigrants, children of immigrants, or grandchildren of immigrants. In fact, some of the most famous Americans, including Alexander Graham Bell, Albert Einstein, Enrico Fermi, and Henry Kissinger, were immigrants.

Despite the self-conception of the United States as a "melting pot" and the close connection that nearly all Americans have to their immigrant ancestors, the reality is that many US residents want immigration to be stopped or severely curtailed (Bauer, Lofstrom, and Zimmermann 2000; Haubert and Fussell 2006). The discrepancy between the real value that immigrants provide and the perception of natives that immigrants are harmful is not limited to the United States. There is a sizable and growing body of work on anti-immigrant sentiment across Europe as well (McLaren 2003; Schneider 2008; Hjerm 2009). Across Europe, Canada, Australia, and the United States, there is a tendency for residents to over-estimate the number of immigrants in their country and to misidentify many immigrants as unauthorized or irregular (Appave and Laczko 2011). The fact that many countries benefit from immigration while the citizenry reviles immigrants poses a considerable policy challenge. Appave and Laczko (2011: xiii) note:

> Societies with a rich diversity of skills and experiences are better placed to stimulate growth through their human resources, and migration is one of the ways in which the exchange of talent, services and skills can be fostered. Yet migration remains highly politicized and often negatively perceived, despite the obvious need for diversification in today's rapidly evolving societies and economies.

The Demography of Immigration

The global recession and rising economic insecurity have contributed to an escalation in immigrant scapegoating. Legislators and policymakers in the United States, for example, have created and implemented a record number of state and local anti-immigrant bills in recent years, including English-only policies for business practices and drivers' written tests, the criminalization of Sharia law, eligibility verification for state entitlement programs, citizenship verification for the issuance of birth certificates, and citizenship verification for attendance at public colleges and universities, among others. Federal policymakers in the United States have also made several failed attempts to criminalize unauthorized immigration and end *birthright citizenship* – or the practice of granting citizenship to those born in the United States – for the children of immigrants, a point we discuss further in chapter 5.

Beyond legislative restrictions on immigration, immigrants have also been the targets of violence. In the United States, the Southern Poverty Law Center (SPLC) has documented an escalation in the number of anti-immigrant hate groups (Beirich 2011). The number of nativist extremist organizations, which actively target individual immigrants and immigrant families, has nearly doubled since 2008, reaching a total of 319 documented groups in 2010 (ibid.). Reflected in this rise in extremist hate groups and anti-immigrant nativism is an increase in the number of violent assaults and hate crimes targeting immigrants – particularly Latinos and Muslims. In Europe, Koopmans and his colleagues (2005) have noted a similar rise in violence against immigrants, particularly those who are racial, ethnic, and religious minorities.

Much of the anti-immigrant sentiment stems from the belief that some groups – usually the most numerous immigrant groups – will never fully fit into their new society, a point we discuss further in chapter 2. However, it is important to note that which immigrant group is considered unassimilable has changed dramatically over the centuries (Kao, Vaquera, and Goyette 2013). Irish, Italians, and Poles were once considered too poorly educated, too unhealthy, and too different to fit into the United States. Today, however, their descendants are "undifferentiated Americans" (Alba 1990), meaning that they are indistinguishable from other white people living in the United States. Much of the anti-immigrant rhetoric about these European immigrants that appeared in newspapers in the early 1900s is now being repeated to describe immigrants from Latin America and Asia, who comprise 53.1 and 28.2 percent of the US foreign-born population, respectively (Grieco et al. 2012), suggesting that immigrant groups often follow a similar path from rejection to acceptance; only the country of origin changes. As Espenshade (1995: 201) notes:

> little has changed in how immigrants are perceived. At least since the 1880s, immigrants have been assumed to take jobs away from and to lower wages of native workers, to add to the poverty population, and to compete for education, health and other social services . . . All that seems to have changed are the origins of migrants and the terms used to describe them.

Despite the fact that the descendants of earlier "unassimilable" immigrants have been completely absorbed into the US mainstream, it is too simplistic to think that Asian and Latino immigrants will follow the same path to absorption in the United States as European immigrants who entered at the beginning of the twentieth century. The 400-year history of Africans and their descendants in the New World – a group brought to the Americas as slaves – suggests that this racial minority has never been fully absorbed into the United States in the same way as Italian, Slavic, Irish, and Greek immigrants. Although African Americans are viewed as fully American, they continue to have lower average levels of income, employment, education, wealth, and occupational status compared to whites, including white immigrants (Shuey and Wilson 2008). The ways in which race and racism complicate the immigrant experience is an important theme that recurs throughout this book.

Immigrant assimilation and adaptation

In 1910, almost a third of all residents in many major US cities were immigrants (Hirschman 2005); then, as now, one of the

14

largest immigrant receiving cities was Chicago. Sociologists at the University of Chicago in the 1920s were greatly interested in the processes by which these immigrants were being absorbed into the native population of the city. Robert Park and Ernest Burgess stand out among these Chicago School scholars who believed that, over time and generations, immigrants would be completely absorbed and indistinguishable from the rest of the US population. In 1921 they published their *contact hypothesis*, theorizing that immigrant contact and interaction with the native population ultimately results in the acquisition of the language of the host country and intermarriage with host-country natives, resulting in eventual and complete absorption into the mainstream.

Park and Burgess' (1921) theory, which is now referred to as *straight-line assimilation*, argues that the process of becoming "American" occurs in four stages: contact, conflict/competition, accommodation, and assimilation. Essentially, immigrants enter a country and have contact with the native population, who respond largely with curiosity. As the immigrant group grows, conflict emerges between native and immigrant groups as they compete for jobs and other scarce resources such as housing. As contact between the two groups continues, however, friendships form, and the native group begins to accommodate immigrants and their children, and eventually the descendants of immigrants lose their ethnic differences and are completely absorbed into the mainstream. Park (1928) acknowledges that the process will be lengthier for some groups than for others. He specifically points to the likely difficulties that Japanese immigrants faced because of the "racial uniform which classifies [them]" (ibid.: 890). Other Chicago School sociologists (especially Wirth 1928; Warner and Srole 1945; Gans 1962) accepted Park and Burgess' contact hypothesis and elaborated on straight-line assimilation theory over the next half-century.

Sociologists have long considered assimilation to be a multi-faceted process involving several dimensions (see Gordon 1964; Hirschman 1983). These dimensions include cultural, structural, marital, identificational, receptional, and civic assimilation. In other words, immigrants are considered to be fully assimilated

when their descendants' culture, their choice of marital partners, their educational attainment, their earnings, and their
occupational prestige are indistinguishable from those of natives.
Additionally, immigrants' descendants are assimilated if they do
not experience prejudice or discrimination and there are no power
struggles between immigrant and native groups.

Straight-line assimilation suggests that assimilation has occurred
when an immigrant group has become assimilated in all of the
important dimensions of social life. This is not to say that the
descendants of immigrants never exercise their "ethnic options"
(Alba 1990; Waters 1990). For example, as many as a million
people – many of whom claim some Irish descent – attend Boston's
annual St. Patrick's Day parade each year, wearing T-shirts and
buttons that proclaim "Kiss me, I'm Irish!" Few of these people
give much thought to their Irish heritage the rest of the year.

Although straight-line assimilation effectively explains the
immigrant experience of mostly white and European immigrants
who entered the United States in the early 1900s, historical events
during the twentieth century radically changed immigration, and
these changes forced scholars to re-evaluate the Chicago School
views of assimilation. During the mid twentieth century, events
such as the Great Depression and two World Wars virtually ended
Europe–United States immigration flows, and the enactment of
strict immigration policies restricted flows even further. When
immigration to the United States resumed after 1965, the new
immigrant flows were primarily comprised of Asians and Latinos,
shifting the ethnic composition of immigrants.

Post-1965 immigrants to the United States are often called
new immigrants, but this label oversimplifies and homogenizes
differences in the experiences of immigrants such as those from
Mexico and China. Chinese immigrants have been entering the
United States since the mid-1880s, and, in fact, halting the flow of
immigration from China was the first step that the United States
took historically to reduce immigration. Labeling Chinese immigrants as "new" ignores this nearly 200-year history and places
newly arriving Chinese in the same group as Chinese Americans
who have been in the United States for generations and who may

have little in common with newcomers. Similarly, Mexicans have a long history in the United States that belies their "newness." Some Mexicans settled in the United States long before there was a United States, and some US states, like California and Texas, used to be part of Mexico. Nonetheless, it is commonplace in the United States to use the terms "Latino" and "Asian" synonymously with "immigrant," especially in places where Latinos and Asians have not traditionally settled. This has created a myriad of difficulties for US-born Latinos and Asians living in states like Arizona, where police are allowed to interrogate people on the suspicion that they are unauthorized immigrants (Campbell 2011).

Because they are racial minorities, Asian and Latino immigrants to the United States are unlikely to have the same assimilation experience as white European immigrants (Louie 2004). Indeed, these two groups demonstrate widely divergent outcomes, particularly with regard to education. Latinos living in the United States have the lowest level of educational attainment and the highest level of both high school and college attrition of all major ethno-racial groups (Kaufman, Alt, and Chapman 2001), while Asians are better educated than non-Latino whites (Williams 2003). Some immigration scholars suggest that these differences result from different immigrant histories (Ogbu 1978, 1991) and different cultural motivations (Takagi 1998; Schuck 2003) that lend themselves to *oppositional culture* for many Latinos and *model minority status* for Asians. The concept of an oppositional culture suggests that groups that are discriminated against (including many immigrant groups) disengage from societally accepted means of achieving – like earning a college degree – because they will not receive the same returns on their investment as whites. In contrast, some groups – especially Asian immigrant groups – over-invest in education and other means of human capital accumulation because they fear discrimination (Sue and Okazaki 2009 [1990]). Some researchers have even suggested that Asian immigrants excel because of their attachment to Confucian or other traditional values (see Louie 2004; Kasinitz et al. 2008).

Chua and Rubenfeld (2014) have suggested that the children of Asian immigrants thrive because they are exposed to a "triple

New immigrant destinations

For most of the twentieth century, the majority of immigrants settled in the same places, but over the last three decades, migration streams have changed significantly, and the settlement patterns of immigrants have diversified. Since the 1980s, Latino and Asian immigrants have dispersed throughout the United States to *new destinations*, particularly in the Southeast and Midwest regions. Based on Census data of the absolute size and growth levels of immigrant populations across multiple destinations in the United States, Singer (2004) has documented the rise of new immigrant gateways throughout the nation. In this typology, those destinations broadly considered to be *established* gateways have historically higher-than-average rates of immigrant population growth and an overall large immigrant population in absolute numbers. The metropolitan areas that comprise these established gateways include places like Chicago, New York, San Francisco, Los Angeles, and Miami. In Europe, cities like London are also established gateways.

Emerging gateways, which are now generally referred to as new destinations, are places that have had a low percentage of foreign-born persons until at least the 1970s, as well as a relatively small foreign-born population in absolute numbers, followed by an exponential increase in both the percentage and absolute numbers of the immigrant population after 1980. In the United States, examples of emerging gateways include Atlanta, Las Vegas, and Washington, DC. Most of these metropolitan areas became new gateways for immigrants in the 1990s. In Europe, cities like Madrid are also new destinations.

package" of cultural forces that run counter to what they define as modern American culture. The three elements of this package – a superiority complex, insecurity, and impulse control – interact to inspire the determination to prove oneself successful through sacrifice and hardship. According to Chua and Rubenfeld (ibid.), this formula explains the success of model groups as varied as Mormons, Jews, Cuban exiles, and immigrants from Asia and certain countries in the West Indies and Africa.

Cultural theories to explain different immigrant outcomes have generally fallen into disfavor as continuing evidence substantiates the primacy of race and class in predicting educational attainment and economic outcomes (cf. Ainsworth-Darnell and Downey 1998; Tyson, Darity, and Castellino 2005; Harris 2011). Research by Louie (2004), for example, demonstrates that Chinese Americans see schools as places where hard work is rewarded. However, despite being at the top of the educational hierarchy (which, in a race-neutral society, should guarantee placement at the top of the occupational hierarchy), few Asians are in the top professional ranks of US corporations.

Group membership does matter, but not necessarily because of culture. Immigrants are more likely to live near and associate with co-ethnics (Light and Bonacich 1988; Pérez 1992; Zhou 1992; Portes and Stepick 1993), and the characteristics of the co-ethnic population may influence immigrant outcomes. A Chinese immigrant to the United States, for example, will spend a lot of time surrounded by well-educated people because of their association with other Chinese immigrants and Chinese Americans. Thus, Chinese immigrants may be socialized to aspire to high levels of education. Such associations explain why Cuban immigrants and their descendants have high levels of educational attainment when other Latino groups have much lower levels of educational achievement, on average (Portes and Stepick 1993; Bohon, Kirkpatrick Johnson, and Gorman 2006).

Nonetheless, it is important that culture is not discounted entirely. As Kasinitz and his colleagues (2008: 84) note: "[We] must also give full credence to the different cultural repertoires and beliefs emerging from the different backgrounds from which the group comes, which are reinforced, undermined, or modified in the new environments in which people find themselves." These scholars caution, however, that cultural explanations for differences in immigrant outcomes must be viewed as "highly contingent on social structure" (ibid.: 18). For example, language is an important cultural marker, but some groups acquire new languages faster than others because of the similarities or differences between their native language and the language of their host country or because settlement conditions provide fewer or more opportunities to use their native language. For these reasons, Spanish-speaking immigrants learn English faster than immigrants who speak Asian languages, but children of Latino immigrants acquire English more slowly than children of Asian immigrants (Goldenberg 2010). Additionally, acquiring a new language too quickly can be detrimental if immigrants lose their native language in the process, since bilingual students demonstrate better educational outcomes than monolingual students (Portes and Rumbaut 2006).

Many factors combine to explain immigrant assimilation, but is assimilation important to immigrants? Immigration scholars in the last few decades have recognized that assimilation does not necessarily translate into success for immigrants; at the same time, many immigrant groups succeed without assimilating. Because of this, most demographers today advocate for viewing immigrant adaptation through a framework of *segmented assimilation* rather than straight-line assimilation. The segmented assimilation model recognizes that immigrants have different conditions of exit and entry, they settle in a variety of situations, and they face an array of structural barriers to integration. These differences lend themselves to differential outcomes over time. Immigrants isolated in impoverished neighborhoods with poor-quality schools may have fewer opportunities to succeed. On the other hand, residential isolation among immigrants may also protect immigrants from the values or behaviors of natives that may impede success (Zhou and Bankston 1994, 1998). Segmented assimilation theory emphasizes that one of the most important factors affecting an immigrant's later-life success is the *context of reception* (Portes and Zhou 1993), and whether or not that context is welcoming to newcomers. These contexts include policies aimed at easing or hindering immigrant incorporation (cf. Conley 2013) and neighborhood characteristics such as socioeconomic status and crime levels. We discuss segmented assimilation theory and its limits in more detail in chapter 2.

For immigrants who have low levels of education and cannot speak the language of their host country, the presence or absence of *mobility ladders* also matters. Mobility ladders are factors that move immigrants up and down the socioeconomic scale. These include types of jobs in which low-skilled workers can start at an entry level and work up to more skilled white-collar positions. Unfortunately, since the 1970s, fewer of these types of jobs are available (Ortiz 1986; Dunne, Roberts, and Samuelson 1989) in the places where immigrants tend to settle (Rumbaut 1994).

Assimilation is also a slippery concept. In the United States, American culture is fluid as it is continually molded by the changing array of immigrants entering the country. Thus, it is difficult to determine what it means to be assimilated. As Kasinitz and his colleagues (2008) quite rightly point out, if everyone is eating burritos, should we label this cultural assimilation for Chinese Americans and cultural retention for Mexican Americans?

Many scholars also recognize that assimilation – even if it leads to upward mobility – is not and should not be a laudable goal (see Glazer 1993). To assimilate necessarily entails the nearly complete shedding of one's ethnic identity in favor of an identity wholly linked to the culture of the host country. This may not be ideal for several reasons. For example, there are great advantages to being bilingual (Cho 2000; García 2005), and becoming an "American," for example, may mean accepting unhealthy personal habits such as eating more fat and less fiber, and driving more instead of walking (see chapter 7). Some scholars advocate for *cultural hybridization* whereby the children of immigrants take on the best characteristics of their place of settlement and retain the best characteristics of their parents' culture (Soysal 1994; Appadurai 1996; Sassen 1996). Thus, *adaptation* (see Gibson 2001) is generally viewed by demographers as the most desirable outcome for immigrants.

Adaptation is the process of changing in order to survive and thrive in a new environment. Adaptation differs from assimilation in that it implies that the immigrant and his or her children can take on the good and/or necessary habits, practices, and values of their host country while maintaining the good from their country of origin. Because some dimensions of assimilation can be harmful, demographers focus less on immigrant assimilation and more on adaptation. The work on immigrant adaptation considers the degree to which immigrants achieve parity with natives on key outcomes like educational attainment, earnings, employment rates, and housing quality, while giving little consideration to the development of attitudes and beliefs of the host population.

Hochschild has long argued that the focus on immigrant parity with natives is a short-sighted means for measuring immigrant success (see especially Hochschild and Mollenkopf 2009). She calls for a reconceptualization of successful immigrant settlement based on life satisfaction. In this understanding, immigrants are successfully incorporated into their host society when they are pleased with their lives in their new countries, can achieve their goals, and are able to acquire the goods, services, and social positions they desire. We agree with this position in principle, but these factors are extremely difficult to measure. Thus, in this book, we concentrate on more traditional measures of immigrant adaptation that focus on parity with natives on measurable outcomes.

2

Assimilation, Adaptation, and Integration

According to Park and Burgess (1921: 735), assimilation is the "process of interpenetration and fusion in which persons and groups acquire the memories, sentiments, and attitudes of other persons and groups and, by sharing their experience and history, are incorporated with them in a common cultural life." In this definition, assimilation is the process by which distinct groups and cultures merge into a shared culture. In the United States, this is closely related to the concept of the nation as a "melting pot" – the idea that multiple and distinct cultures blend over time, becoming increasingly similar and virtually indistinguishable in terms of norms, values, behaviors, and characteristics. This differs from *cultural pluralism* (Kallen 1924), the idea that ethnic groups retain and elaborate their own cultural and ethnic heritages, in which society is often conceptualized as a "salad bowl."

Classical assimilation theory, which is sometimes referred to as straight-line assimilation, implies a linear process whereby increasingly assimilated immigrant generations are increasingly successful in the host society (Rumbaut 1997b). In this model, the children of immigrants will eventually integrate successfully into mainstream culture, regardless of their racial and ethnic characteristics. The assimilation process will supposedly enable each successive generation to be upwardly mobile in their educational and occupational attainment, be more integrated into mainstream society, and show less ethnic distinctiveness in language use, residential concentration, and intermarriage patterns.

There is considerable evidence of successful assimilation of successive immigrant generations. For example, Citrin and his colleagues (2007) tested several measures of assimilation for Latino immigrants in the United States. They found that the descendants of Latino immigrants, beginning with the *second generation* – or the children of immigrants – rapidly acquire English and begin to lose Spanish. Moreover, the children and grandchildren of Latino immigrants have English-language policy preferences that more closely resemble the policy preferences of US-born whites and blacks. Whereas first-generation Latino immigrants strongly oppose policies that would make English the official language of the United States and strongly support bilingual education practices, their children and grandchildren express less opposition toward English-only policies and less support for bilingual education practices. Citrin and his colleagues also found that Latino immigrants have similar levels of patriotism to US-born whites (and higher levels of patriotism than US-born blacks). Finally, their research found that each successive generation is more likely to define themselves primarily as Americans, rather than with an ethnic identifier (Hispanic or Latino, for example), whereas first-generation Latino immigrants are more likely to define themselves primarily by their country of origin. Given these findings, Citrin and his colleagues suggest that Latino immigrants do not challenge the country's national identity.

Other studies reveal similar findings related to immigrant assimilation. Waters and Jimenez (2005), noting four primary benchmarks of immigrant assimilation – socioeconomic status, spatial concentration, language assimilation, and intermarriage – find that immigrants today increasingly resemble the US-born population over time in each of these characteristics. Additionally, Parrado and Morgan (2008) find that Latina immigrants in the United States have comparable levels of fertility to US-born white women.

Demographers and others have engaged in a long and lively debate over how assimilation works and whether or not it is ideal (cf. Gordon 1964; Portes and Böröcz 1989; Gans 1992a, 1997; Glazer 1993; Massey 1994; Alba and Nee 1997; Rumbaut 1997b;

Zhou 1997a). Some critics argue that the earliest applications of classical assimilation theory have implied a one-way, Anglo-centric process of integration by which immigrants and other minorities abandon their cultural and ethnic heritage in favor of that of the dominant (and usually white) host society (Brown and Bean 2006; Kasinitz et al. 2008). However, Alba and Nee (1997), seeking to reclaim the terminology under the name of *new assimilation theory*, point to Park and Burgess' (1921) original use of the terms *interpenetration* and *fusion*, suggesting that distinct cultures affect one another and blend with one another in order to create a new shared culture. Similarly, Bean and Stevens (2003) argue that assimilation implies the *convergence* of cultural and ethnic groups, rather than minority groups being subsumed by a dominant culture. Nevertheless, as a result of its complicated history, many avoid the term *assimilation*, preferring instead to use terms such as *integration, adaptation*, and *incorporation* to refer to the ways that immigrants and host societies change and accept one another.

Gordon (1964) differentiated between what he termed *structural assimilation* – the process by which minority group members come to have primary interactions with dominant group members, including through intermarriage – and *acculturation*. Acculturation is the process by which minority groups – in this case, immigrants – adopt the patterns of the majority group – the host society. In this sense, acculturation operates as a one-way process; the immigrant acculturates to the dominant host society, but, according to Gordon, the host society largely does not change in response to the influx of immigration. Gordon notes, however, that the host society may change in some superficial ways, such as through "minor modifications in cuisine, recreational patterns, place names, speech, residential architecture, sources of artistic inspiration, and perhaps few other areas" (Gordon 1964: 100).

Assimilation and acculturation suggest not only the extent to which immigrants merge with their host societies, but also the extent to which host societies accept immigrants. Still, Rumbaut (1997b) argues that the straight-line model of assimilation is problematic because it implies progressive improvement as immigrants increasingly resemble their host societies, which in turn suggests that immigrants have some type of deficit or pose a problem to the host society until they are assimilated. On the contrary, however, research has demonstrated that acculturation is often detrimental to the health and well-being of immigrants and their children (Gilbert 1987; Kaplan and Marks 1990; Marks, Garcia, and Solis 1990; Rumbaut 1997b; Caetano and Clark 2003; Flores and Botanek 2005; see also chapter 7).

Additionally, not all scholars are optimistic about the prospects for immigrant assimilation, even if it is considered desirable. Frey (1997), for example, suggests that the concentration of immigrants in particular destinations results in a condition akin to *demographic balkanization* – the spatial segregation of the population by race, ethnicity, class, and age. More than two-thirds of immigrants in the United States cluster in just six states, and half of all immigrants reside in just five metropolitan areas (Singer 2004). According to Frey (1997), the spatial concentration of immigrants in these areas will create a bifurcated nation – one that is deeply multicultural and content with its immigrant population, and another that is primarily comprised of white and black US-born residents and more conservative on issues related to immigration and multiculturalism. This demographic balkanization will result in, among other conditions, concentrated poverty in immigrant receiving destinations and a segmented labor force in which immigrants occupy the lowest-skilled and lowest-paying jobs in the formal and informal economy (see chapter 3). It is important to note, however, that immigrants since the 1990s not only have dispersed to new gateway cities, but also are settling in new nations (like Spain).

Spatial assimilation is the process by which immigrants, over time and generations, move into homes that are geographically closer to natives until there is no longer a noticeable physical distance between the places where immigrant groups settle and where natives settle (Massey 1985). For example, today, only about 6 percent of residents in New York's Little Italy neighborhood claim Italian heritage; in 1950, more than half did (Roberts 2011). The diffusion of immigrants and their descendants into multi-ethnic neighborhoods generally has positive consequences. Having many non-immigrant and non-coethnic neighbors is associated with greater human and financial capital and greater use of the host country's dominant language (cf. South, Crowder, and Chavez 2005).

Of course, the concentration of immigrants in a single location is not always detrimental. Work on *ethnic enclaves* – places with local labor markets marked by immigrant-owned businesses and their co-ethnic employees – suggests that there are conditions under which immigrants can fare very well (Portes and Stepick 1993). For example, Cuban immigrants to the United States are, on average, highly successful. The majority of Cuban immigrants and Cuban Americans are also heavily concentrated in South Florida, but their high socioeconomic status and continuing upward mobility suggest that fears about demographic balkanization (Frey 1997) can be overstated.

The theory of *segmented assimilation* (Portes and Zhou 1993) suggests that immigrants have three possibilities for integration based on disparities in human and social capital. The first path, upward assimilation into mainstream white society, most closely resembles the classical theory of straight-line assimilation. Other immigrant groups may find a second path – upward mobility while maintaining their distinct cultural and ethnic identity (Waters et al. 2010). However, immigrants may also experience a "bumpy" road toward assimilation, as Gans (1992a) has noted, with the process of assimilation resembling a long and winding path with no predictable end. Some immigrant groups may even tend toward a third path of downward assimilation into a permanent underclass, as assimilation eludes even the children and grandchildren of immigrants. In some cases, the children of immigrants may embrace attitudes and behaviors that are considered oppositional to the mainstream society (Portes and Zhou 1993). As Portes and his colleagues (2005: 1000) note, "the central question is not whether the second generation will assimilate to American society, but *to what segment* of that society it will assimilate" (emphasis in original).

Portes and Zhou (1993) posit two primary barriers to successful integration for the children of immigrants, resulting from the characteristics of the host society and new generations of immigrants. First, earlier generations of immigrants to the United States were primarily of European descent, making it easier for them to be eventually accepted into mainstream US society. Recent immigrants, however, are primarily comprised of racial and ethnic minorities and are therefore likely to be confronted with the persistent effects of racism, which may impact their educational, occupational, and economic mobility (Portes 1997; Zhou 1997b; Rumbaut 2005; Haller, Portes, and Lynch 2011). Second, the rapid deindustrialization of the United States since the 1950s has altered economic opportunities for recent immigrants by providing little possibility for upward mobility. The US labor market has split along economic lines, with highly paid professional positions at one end and menial low-wage occupations at the other. As a consequence, some immigrants and their descendants may find that their pathway to assimilation is blocked by structural factors, particularly in relation to their racialization as minorities. Thus, according to Portes and his colleagues (2005: 1006):

> Children of Asian, black, mulatto, and mestizo immigrants cannot escape their ethnicity and race, as defined by the mainstream. Their enduring physical differences from whites and the equally persistent strong effects of discrimination based on those differences, especially against black persons, throws a barrier in the path of occupational mobility and social acceptance. Immigrant children's identities, their aspirations, and their academic performance are affected accordingly.

Of course, this pessimistic view – that descendants of poorly educated immigrants from developing countries who face widespread racial discrimination will never achieve parity with the dominant groups, regardless of time or generation – is rejected by many scholars. Perlmann (2005), for example, compared current Mexican immigrants to the United States and their children to non-Jewish Southern, Central, and Eastern Europeans and their children who immigrated to the United States between 1890 and 1914. He found that the children of European immigrants achieved economic success more quickly than the children of Mexican immigrants, and not all of the difference in the speed of economic assimilation could be accounted for by changes in the overall economic structure of US society. However, Perlmann's findings led him to conclude that, although assimilation is slower for Mexican immigrants today, there is every reason to suggest that the descendants of Mexican immigrants will be economically undifferentiated from Anglos after four or five generations.

Perlmann's optimism is shared by other scholars whose work also shows that the descendants of immigrants who are poorly educated, ethno-racial minorities are often doing as well as their native counterparts (cf. Waldinger and Feliciano 2004). The results of a major study of the adult children of immigrants in New York City (Kasinitz, Mollenkopf, and Waters 2008) show that these children – despite the barriers they face – are speaking English, working in jobs no different from the children of the US-born, and successfully combining the cultures of the United States and their parents' native countries. Neckerman, Carter, and Lee (1999) suggest that race and socioeconomic status are not such big barriers to adaptation as demographers have feared, because the new second generation is creating a *minority culture of mobility* by developing strategies for labor market success in the face of discrimination. Finally, Waldinger (2007) points out that the structure of the labor market is constantly in flux, and the children of immigrants are highly adaptive. Thus, changes in the economy and changes in the racio-ethnic make-up of immigrants may not be a harbinger of a future immigrant underclass.

The impact of reception context on immigrant integration

Key to immigrant assimilation is the importance of the reception context for immigrants in the host society. How a society perceives itself and how it receives and responds to an influx of immigrants will impact how immigrants are integrated into that society (Crul, Schneider, and Leslie 2012). New-destination immigration to the

United States and the immigrant situation in France offer telling examples.

Beginning in the 1990s, Latino immigrants began to settle in the US Southeast, which historically has been home to few Latinos and immigrants (Suro and Singer 2002; Singer 2004). The rapid influx of immigrants – particularly those who are low-income and easily distinguished from the US-born by their racio-ethnic characteristics and language – has been perceived as a threat to the normalcy of life in these new destination places (Neal and Bohon 2003). In their research, Neal and Bohon (ibid.) found that the biggest predictor of anti-immigrant sentiment among Southerners was the length of time that the US-born had lived in the South and how attached they were to ingrained ideas of Southern-ness. Similarly, research has documented that the US-born in new immigrant destinations often perceive that immigrants challenge the foundations of their communities, either in terms of the racial composition – such as through an influx of brown immigrants in a destination that previously was thought of as black and non-Latino white – or in terms of their definitions of who they are as a community (Furuseth and Smith 2006; Lippard and Gallagher 2010; Massey 2008; Mohl 2003; Neal and Bohon 2003). Thus, immigrants have been negatively portrayed as a criminal element or as a burden on taxpayer resources, particularly in relation to already overburdened primary- and secondary-education school systems (Bohon, MacPherson, and Atiles 2005). Since new destinations are typically unaccustomed to immigrants and are therefore largely unprepared to meet the needs of a rapid population surge (Atiles and Bohon 2002), immigrants' use of, or demand for, any resources may be received negatively by the community (Bohon, Massengale, and Jordan 2009; Marrow 2005; Singer 2004; Stamps and Bohon 2006).

Several states in the US Southeast have responded to the influx of Latino immigrants with restrictionist legislation (see Anrig and Wang 2007). One such state is Alabama, where immigrants have noted a generalized and widespread hostility toward anyone perceived as foreign-born (Conley 2013). In 2011, Robert Bentley, the Governor of Alabama, signed into law the Beason–Hammon

Alabama Taxpayer and Citizen Protection Act, otherwise known as HB 56. Not only did HB 56 expand the roles and responsibilities of state and local law enforcement agencies in determining the citizenship and immigration status of Alabama residents, it also targeted the routine aspects of living and working in Alabama. Thus, the law required that people provide proof of citizenship or lawful immigration status prior to entering into a "business transaction" with the state of Alabama, and it rendered unenforceable any existing or future public- and private-sector contracts with unauthorized immigrants. HB 56 also mandated that school administrators determine the citizenship or immigration status of newly enrolling students. Together, these provisions made Alabama's law the most comprehensive anti-immigrant legislation in the nation.

Importantly, HB 56 was enacted in a state that hosted a relatively small population of unauthorized immigrants, even compared to other states in the US Southeast. Estimated at just 2.5 percent of the state's total population in 2010, or approximately 120,000 people – the majority of whom are Latinos of Mexican origin (Passel and Cohn 2011) – Alabama had fewer unauthorized immigrants per capita than half the states in the nation. At the same time, Alabama's share of unauthorized immigrant residents had increased dramatically, by more than 2300 percent since 1990 (ibid.), reflecting a similar pattern of Latino immigration and in-migration (i.e., the movement of people into an area from another area within the same country) throughout the southeastern United States (Suro and Singer 2002; Singer 2004). It is likely that the dramatic and visible increase of Latino immigrants who were presumed to be unauthorized – regardless of their actual status or proportion in the population – contributed to Alabama lawmakers enacting such extreme legislation (Conley 2013).

The 2005 riots in France offer another telling story about the importance of reception context for immigrant integration. For years, and particularly since the end of World War II, France has experienced a rapid influx of Muslim immigrants. During this time, the country has primarily held a classical assimilationist perspective on integration, meaning that standard policy has obligated immigrants in France to become "French" (Givens 2007). That is, immigrants in France – who are primarily racial and ethnic minorities – are expected to disregard their own cultural (and often religious) identities and adopt a singular (and secular) French identity. At the same time, immigrants are portrayed as a criminal and destructive element by the French media and politicians. In fact, former French President Nicolas Sarkozy has referred to the children of immigrants as *racaille*, a term that has been translated as "scum," but which Haddad and Balz (2006: 29) note has a "distinctly racist connotation." Immigrants in France are also legally discriminated against in housing and employment opportunities, and many complain that predominantly immigrant schools are staffed by inexperienced and under-resourced teachers (ibid.). In 2005, Paris erupted in a series of widespread and sustained riots, as immigrants protested against extreme unemployment in immigrant communities (Smith 2005). However, the riots resulted as much from immigrants' fears about their social exclusion and marginalization as from economic discrimination (Murphey 2011).

These examples demonstrate the importance of reception context for immigrant integration. In places where immigrants are not well received, or where immigrants are perceived as threatening, the implementation of certain laws, policies, and rhetoric may actually hinder the integration of immigrants into society (Portes and Böröcz 1989) and prolong anti-immigrant sentiment (Hjerm 2007). A hostile reception context may negatively affect immigrant integration, for example, by limiting access to essential resources like language acquisition programs (Citrin, Reingold, and Green 1990), by encouraging employers to target those perceived as foreign-born for additional work eligibility verification measures (Newman et al. 2012), or by compelling police and immigration agents to target those perceived as foreign-born for increased enforcement. These conditions may be particularly problematic in places that have historically lacked an immigrant presence, as these new immigrant destinations typically lack sufficient resources, as well as organizations and people familiar with immigrants, to offset the challenges of integration and produce positive messages about immigrants.

Immigrants as a threat to national identity

Immigration can dramatically alter the racial and ethnic composition of a host country. In fact, demographers have determined that immigration is the driving force behind demographic change in developed countries with low fertility rates (Coleman 2006). As the United States and countries in Western Europe have experienced a surge in immigrant settlement, particularly of racial and ethnic minorities, this has led to speculation on how immigrants will be perceived by and integrated into the host society. In particular, immigrant settlement has often challenged the conceptualization of the host nation and notions of belongingness.

Contemporary immigration has substantially increased the racial and ethnic diversity of the United States, Germany, France, Italy, and elsewhere, as the national origins of immigrants have changed dramatically over time. Germany, for example, now hosts more than 4 million people of Turkish descent – the single largest ethnic minority in the nation (Mandel 2008). The composition of Italy's immigrant population has also shifted rapidly, and the nation is now home to more than 930,000 African immigrants, who comprise 22 percent of the foreign-born population (Tragaki and Rovolis 2012). Many native Germans and Italians have perceived these rapid demographic shifts as overwhelmingly negative (Martin 1994; Horowitz 2010).

In the contemporary United States, immigrants from Latin America and the Caribbean comprise 53.1 percent of the foreign-born population (with a majority from Mexico, at 29.3 percent of the total foreign-born population), while immigrants from Asia comprise another 28.2 percent of the foreign-born population (Grieco et al. 2012). As illustrated in figure 2.1, this marks a considerable shift from the predominantly European migration of the early twentieth century (Gibson and Jung 2006). During this era, immigrants from Germany, Ireland, Italy, and other European countries comprised the majority of immigrants to the United States. In contrast, by 2010, immigrants from Europe accounted for approximately only 12 percent of

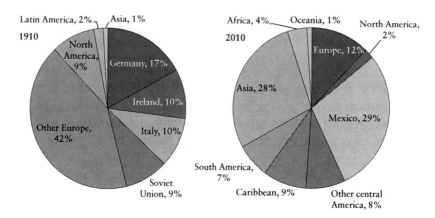

Figure 2.1 US foreign-born population by origin, 1910 and 2010

Source: compiled with data from Gibson and Jung (2006) and Grieco et al. (2012)

the foreign-born population in the United States (Grieco et al. 2012).

In the United States, these demographic shifts have not gone unnoticed. Media and social commentators have remarked on the changing "face" of the country, which calls into question how immigrants fare in a society that has long been marked by a black–white color line. As the country becomes increasingly ethnically and racially diverse, scholars have debated whether such diversity will increase tolerance for difference or whether the color line will shift from black–white to white–nonwhite (Lee and Bean 2010). In addressing this debate, Lee and Bean (2010) demonstrate that the social distance between different racial groups is fading rapidly for Asians and Latinos, who intermarry with other racial groups (including whites) at a much higher rate than blacks, suggesting that the future of the color line is not a shift from black–white to white–nonwhite but, rather, to black–nonblack.

The media have been quick to announce projections that the nation will be *majority–minority* by 2042, meaning that non-Latino whites will no longer comprise the majority of the US population. Most of this change is projected to be driven by the growth of the Latino population. Still, Parrado (2011) contends that this prediction is inaccurate, as fertility estimates for Latino immigrants are inflated (see chapter 5). Moreover, Perez and Hirschman (2009) note that these claims fail to acknowledge that many Latinos self-identify as white. The social boundaries of whiteness have also changed considerably over time and may expand to include Latinos, Asians, and others (Lee and Bean 2007). Thus, white people may continue to remain the majority in the United States for quite some time.

Nevertheless, the apparent change in the US racial and ethnic composition resulting from immigration has raised concern over how this immigration may impact the host country, not only economically but also socially and culturally. Economically, immigration advantages a host country as immigrants may offset the rapidly aging population of the host country and stimulate the economy through entrepreneurship and taxes (see chapters 3 and 6). Socially, immigrants often have strong family ties and traditional values, which natives admire and value. Additionally, countries may embrace *multiculturalism*, the idea that multiple cultures can coexist peacefully and to the benefit of the host country. Residents of New Zealand and Canada, for example, hold strong positive associations regarding immigration, multiculturalism, and cultural diversity (Ward and Masgoret 2008). People may also value the "cultural novelty" of immigrants (Shutika 2008), or the perception that immigration to their area makes them "cosmopolitan" (Haubert and Fussell 2006).

Although immigration provides many advantages to the host society, it is often perceived as deeply threatening. Mayda (2006: 5) argues that immigration may "feed cultural and national-identity worries, driven by the belief that the set of values and traditions that characterize the receiving country's society are threatened by the arrival of foreigners." In fact, perceptions of *cultural threat* – the idea that immigrants present a symbolic threat to the identity and culture of the host society (Newman 2013) – may be more salient than perceptions of *economic threat* – the worry that immigrants take jobs from natives (Citrin, Reingold, and Green 1990; Sniderman, Hagendoorn, and Prior 2004; Sides and Citrin 2007).

Do Latinos constitute a racial group?

Omi and Winant (1994) theorize race as a dynamic social construct, rather than a static characteristic of one's identity. In other words, one's racial identification – in terms both of how a person self-identifies and of how others identify that person – may change in response to a variety of social conditions and situations. For example, different countries identify and categorize race differently. Thus, immigrants often find that their racial identification changes when they enter a new country. As Kao and her colleagues (2013) note, many Chinese, when entering the United States, are surprised that they now belong to the same racial group as Southeast Asian Indians, who have a markedly dissimilar history, culture, and phenotype.

In the United States, Latinos, too, confront a variety of possibilities in their racial classification and often perceive that they do not conform to the country's recognized racial categories. Although they share a geographical region of origin, Latinos do not share a single *phenotype* – or appearance – resulting in part from the existence of indigenous peoples and the history of colonization of Latin America. Latino immigrants, in particular, often self-identify by their country of origin. Non-Latinos may lump together these individuals of varying ethnic and indigenous origins into an overarching *panethnicity* – such as Latino or Hispanic – though US-born people of Latin American origin are also likely to self-identify as Latino or Hispanic (Hitlin, Brown, and Elder 2007). Latinos may also adapt their racial self-identification in different contexts (McConnell and Delgado-Romero 2004). Thus, as Rodríguez (2000: x) notes, "In the United States today, a person may be Puerto Rican or Mexican on a personal level, Latino on an instrumental level, and Hispanic to the government. Some people might classify this person as black, white or Asian. Others think of Latinos as a brown race, and still others, as a multiracial ethnic group."

The US Office of Management and Budget (OMB) sets the standards by which federal agencies collect data on race and ethnicity. Currently, the OMB recognizes the following groups as races: (1) white; (2) black or African American; (3) American Indian or Alaska Native; (4) Asian; (5) Native Hawaiian or Other Pacific Islander; and (6) Some Other Race (Office of Management and Budget 2003). Latinos (or Hispanics) are not considered a racial group. Instead, "'Hispanic or Latino' refers to a person of Cuban, Mexican, Puerto Rican, South or Central American, or other Spanish culture or origin regardless of race" (Humes, Jones, and Ramirez 2011: 2). Thus, in the collection of race and ethnicity data, US residents are first asked whether or not they are Latino, and, if so, they are asked to report whether they are Mexican, Puerto Rican, Cuban, or some other Hispanic ethnicity. Then they are asked to report a race. The Census Bureau and other data collection agencies recognize that this classification of Latinos is somewhat problematic because it places the group into a strange racio-ethnic hybrid that is confusing to many survey respondents, especially those who consider "Hispanic and Latino" to be their race. In fact, in both the 1990 and 2000 Censuses, more than 95 percent of people who selected the "Some Other Race" category also self-identified as Hispanic or Latino (Lee and Bean 2004).

It is clear that immigration poses a perceived threat to a nation's identity. However, many of these perceptions have been dismissed as alarmist. For one, despite the apparent surge in immigrant settlement in recent decades, it is important to note that the foreign-born population in the contemporary United States, as a percentage of the total population, is actually lower than it has been in the past. As a percentage of the total US population, the proportion of foreign-born residents of the United States was actually higher in the late nineteenth century and early twentieth century than it is today, and accounted for 14.7 percent of the total US population in 1910 (Singer 2013).

Additionally, the United States in particular has had a long and complicated history with every immigrant cohort, and alarmism over the nation's changing immigrant characteristics has been the rule rather than the exception (Higham 1955; Feagin 1997; Jaret 1999; Hing 2004). In the early twentieth century, European immigrants to the United States, especially those from Eastern and Southern Europe, were characterized as "inferior races" (Grant, quoted in Feagin 1997: 21). At the time, these immigrants were also maligned for their "refusal" to relinquish their norms, values, and linguistic preferences and be absorbed – or *assimilated* – into the dominant cultural identity of the host nation.

The concern among residents of the United States and many European countries that immigration will negatively impact the cultural and national identity of the host country is, in part, related to the racial and ethnic characteristics of immigrant newcomers (Chavez 1997, 2008; Sánchez 1997; Galindo and Vigil 2006; Mayda 2006; Sides and Citrin 2007). In the United States, fears that immigrants of diverse racial and ethnic backgrounds distort the existing culture stem from the belief that recent immigrants differ markedly from immigrants of the past. For example, Huntington (2004b) has argued that the culture of the United States has been steadily eroded by the refusal or inability of contemporary immigrants to assimilate. He (2004a, 2004b) asserts that US national identity (or the "American way of life") has for centuries revolved around a key set of foundational characteristics: adherence to an Anglo-Protestant cultural tradition, as expressed through individualism, the Protestant work ethic, and a commitment to Christian religious principles; adoption of the English language; commitment to the rule of law; and patriotic nationalism. Huntington asserts that past generations of immigrants have supported these foundational practices and have thus strengthened the nation's identity. Yet, this way of life, in Huntington's assessment, is threatened by an influx of recent immigrants who are unwilling or unable to assimilate into US society, in contrast to past generations of immigrants who wholeheartedly embraced this national identity. Thus, Huntington (2004b: 18) notes: "America's third wave of immigration that began in the 1960s brought to America people primarily from Latin America and Asia rather than Europe as the previous waves did. The culture and values of their countries of origin often differ substantially from those prevalent in America."

Focusing predominantly on the rapid influx of Latino – and specifically, Mexican – immigrants, Huntington argues that contemporary immigrants are not invested in assimilating into US society. The proximity of Mexico and Latin America to the United States, combined with the scale, illegality, concentration, persistence, historical presence, and language of Latino immigrants threatens the US national identity and the nation's future existence (Huntington 2004a, 2004b), as contemporary immigrants find it easier to maintain their own distinct cultural identities rather than assimilate into their host nation. Although most demographers disagree with his position, Huntington is not alone in his belief that the changing composition of a nation could lead to a crisis of national identity (see, for example, Brimelow 1996 and Taylor 2011), and perceptions such as these have led immigration restrictionist groups to advocate for tougher immigration policies.

Demographers agree that a rapid influx of immigrants of minority races and ethnicities usually results in ethno-racial tension between natives and foreign-born populations, although Chavez (2008) has argued that such tensions are generally exacerbated by the media and political interest groups. This ethno-racial tension has been explained, in part, through *group threat theory*. Blumer (1958) argued that racial prejudice results as a defensive reaction to perceptions of collective threat. In this theory, members of a majority or dominant group in a society fear that minority groups threaten their social position and access to scarce resources by competing for the same resources. Blalock (1967) explicitly connected the sense of group threat to an area's changing racial composition. Originally, this theory was mostly used to explain racial tensions between whites and blacks in the United States.

Applied to immigration, group threat theory suggests that a visible and noticeably increasing foreign-born population, particularly of immigrants who do not share the racial and ethnic characteristics of the majority population of the host country, contributes to the perception of group threat. This sense of group threat is especially prevalent during times of economic strain, when scarce resources appear to be even scarcer. In a study of the impact of immigration on anti-immigrant sentiment in twelve European countries, Quillian (1995) found that poor economic conditions, combined with the size of a minority immigrant group in relation to the majority group of the host society, impacted perceptions of group threat, leading to anti-immigrant and racial prejudice. Other research (cf. Espenshade and Hempstead 1996; Semyonov, Raijman, and Gorodzeisky 2006) indicates that groups that are especially vulnerable to economic strain often feel threatened by an increasing minority presence (whether immigrant or native) and express greater preference toward restrictive immigration policies. Others (Semyonov et al. 2004; Sides and Citrin 2007) note, furthermore, that feelings of threat need not be based on an actual increase in the size of the foreign-born population but merely on the *perception* of their increase. In fact, people often overestimate the size of foreign-born and minority populations, and these perceptions contribute to an increase in negative attitudes toward immigrants and minorities (Alba, Rumbaut, and Marotz 2005).

Still, the evidence supporting the relationship between a sense of group threat and the population size of racio-ethnic minorities or immigrants is more nuanced (Newman and Johnson 2012). Some research indicates that increased exposure to immigrant populations actually reduces anti-immigrant sentiment, as regular contact produces more favorable attitudes toward immigrants (Fetzer 2000; McLaren 2003). Not at all surprising is the finding that people who have immigrant friends and associates report less *xenophobia* – or fear of, disdain for, and hostility toward those labeled as "foreign" (McLaren 2003; Hjerm 2007). On the other hand, Hjerm's (2007) research on 20 European countries finds that neither the actual size nor the perceived size of the immigrant population impacted perceptions of threat overall, regardless of the nation's GDP. Hjerm attributes the differences in findings between his research and that of Quillian (1995) in part to the fact that Quillian only examined countries in Western Europe. Instead of the size of the immigrant population, Hjerm (2007) and others (cf. Koopmans et al. 2005) suggest that the political culture of the nation, its sense of national identity, and the strictness of its immigration and integration policies are all much more salient to the increase in perceived tensions between natives and immigrants.

Nevertheless, the changing racial and ethnic composition of countries has not occurred without backlash. Increases in the immigrant population, particularly of those whose racial and ethnic characteristics differ markedly from those of the host society, have been linked to a number of restrictionist policy outcomes. In the United States this includes state adoption of English-only laws (Citrin et al. 1990) and employment eligibility verification policies (Newman et al. 2012). France, which experienced a rapid rise in its Muslim immigrant population after World War II and the decolonization of Africa and Asia, and which currently hosts the largest population of Muslims in Europe, has implemented legislative reforms targeting Muslim women, such as bans that prevent Muslim women from wearing their traditional headscarves and burkas in public places (Leane 2011).

In recent years, some countries with sizeable foreign-born populations have witnessed a resurgence of *nativism* – the prioritization of native-born citizens over people who are foreign-born. In the United States, nativism has been expressed through white nationalism and anti-immigrant activism in response to the shifting racial and ethnic composition of the country (Perea 1997; Galindo and Vigil 2006; Southern Poverty Law Center 2006; Bebout 2012). The Southern Poverty Law Center, a US organization that tracks hate groups, has charted a recent and rapid escalation in the number of white supremacist and anti-immigrant groups, including *nativist extremist* organizations – which actively target individual immigrants and immigrant families – across the nation (Beirich 2011). Similarly, Koopmans and his colleagues (2005) note an increase in attacks on ethnic minorities and immigrants throughout Europe and particularly in Germany, where Turkish immigrants have been targeted by groups affiliated with the skinhead subculture.

Recent events in Greece offer another notable example of nativism and anti-immigrant sentiment. Since 2009, Greece has struggled with a severe economic depression. The imposition of strict austerity policies has increased civil unrest and dissatisfaction with governing parties and the European Union at large. At the same time, Greece has a growing immigrant population, including an increase in irregular immigration from Afghanistan, Bangladesh, Pakistan, and Iraq. In 2012, Golden Dawn, an extremist far-right party, gained several seats in the Greek Parliament. The party campaigned on an overtly anti-immigrant platform, using the slogan "Get the Stench out of Greece" (Faiola 2012). Supporters of Golden Dawn have been accused of numerous acts of violence against immigrant communities, including the stabbing and beating of several immigrants and attacks on immigrant-owned stores and market stalls and immigrant community centers. Despite this, a September 2012 poll found that nearly 22 percent of Greek respondents expressed favorable attitudes toward Golden Dawn (Migration Policy Institute 2012).

In the United States, immigration restrictionists have argued that liberalized immigration policies will change the political landscape of US society (see, for example, Camarota 2013). Others have gone further, suggesting that immigrant advocates deliberately intend to change the racial and ethnic composition of the United States in order to alter the make-up of society more broadly (Taylor 2011). In fact, immigrant advocates have even been labeled *reconquistas* – suggesting that they are involved in a seditious attempt to allow Mexico to reconquer lost ground in the United States (see, for example, Buchanan 2006). Bill O'Reilly, a conservative radio and television host, writer, and political commentator, elucidated this position on the talk radio program *The Radio Factor*:

> You have people who hate America, and they hate it because it's run primarily by white, Christian men ... And there is a segment of our population who hates that, despises that power structure. So they, under the guise of being compassionate, want to flood the country with foreign nationals – unlimited, unlimited – to change the complexion – pardon the pun – of America (quoted in Ironside 2007).

Immigrants today may, in fact, face more extreme challenges to integration – and more hostile reception contexts – compared to immigrants of the past, as a result of the changing racio-ethnic composition of immigrants, their settlement patterns, the receiving country's governmental policies, and for other reasons (Portes and Böröcz 1989). In the US context, for example, Massey (2008) points to five specific factors that threaten the integration of contemporary immigrants: (1) decreased opportunities for economic mobility resulting from the shifting economic structure of the nation; (2) decreased access to higher education and decreased educational attainment of successive immigrant generations; (3) the constancy of contemporary immigration, which facilitates the revitalization (rather than assimilation) of immigrant communities; (4) the rapid growth of unauthorized immigrants who are easily exploitable and lacking in many economic, social, and political rights; and (5) the rise in nativism and the "ethnic demonization" of immigrants by politicians, the media, and some academics. Thus, despite consistent evidence showing that immigrants continue to integrate into society, it may also be true that immigrants today do not integrate as quickly or as easily as they have in the past. If this is true, however, then the blame for the challenges to immigrant integration rests not with the immigrants themselves, as Huntington (2004a, 2004b) would have us believe, but with a reception context and structural barriers that make it difficult for the immigrants of today to fully integrate into their host societies.

3

Immigrants in the Economy

On September 1, 2010, headlines across the United States heralded a massive decline in the *stock* of US unauthorized immigrants – from 12.2 million in 2007 to 11.3 million in 2009 – and an 8 percent decline in the *flow* of unauthorized immigrants (Passel and Cohn 2010). "Stock" refers to the total number of immigrants living in a country, while flow refers to the number entering each year. These declines came after more than a decade of rapid increases in the unauthorized immigrant population in the United States. In fact, the US government estimates that more than half of all unauthorized immigrants in the United States entered between 1995 and 2004 (Hoefer, Rytina, and Baker 2012).

The decline in the number of unauthorized immigrants is largely attributed to the Great Recession. Beginning in 2007, the Great Recession resulted from a dramatic downturn in the US economy, including massive unemployment and cuts to working hours, the likes of which had not been seen since the 1940s (Elsby, Hobijn, and Sahin 2010). At the same time, economic conditions in Mexico – the country which sends the most immigrants to the United States and which accounts for nearly 60 percent of all unauthorized immigrants – improved (Hoefer, Rytina, and Baker 2012). It is difficult to compare estimates of the unauthorized immigrant population in any country over time, since estimates are often revised as new information is revealed (ibid.); however, scholars agree that the stock of unauthorized immigrants in the United States shrank during the Great Recession, and it is likely that at least some of the

Unauthorized immigrants

The United Nations Global Commission on International Migration defines migrants with irregular status as non-nationals who are living without authorization in a country due to one of eight reasons: (1) they illegally crossed a border; (2) they entered a country using false documents; (3) they provided false information in acquiring legal documents; (4) they overstayed their visas or permits; (5) they lost legal status during their stay; (6) they were born to migrants with irregular status; (7) they escaped deportation; or (8) they fall into one of the first seven conditions but are tolerated by their host country (these people are called *tolerated persons*). Not all conditions apply in all countries. For example, in the United States, children born to parents with irregular status are US citizens and are not classified as unauthorized immigrants.

Various terms are used to describe immigrants with irregular status. These terms include *illegal, undocumented, clandestine, irregular,* and *unauthorized.* Generally the terms used reflect partisan bias (see Morehouse and Blomfield 2011), with terms such as *illegal aliens* reflecting anti-immigrant agendas, and terms such as *undocumented* reflecting pro-immigrant orientations. The terms *undocumented* and *illegal* are also imprecise; the first term is inadequate because some unauthorized immigrants may possess expired or counterfeit documents, and the latter because unauthorized immigration is often a violation of civil – rather than criminal – law. Terms that incorporate the word "illegal" have broadly been criticized for their dehumanization of unauthorized immigrants. The United States government uses the term *unauthorized immigrants* in official documents. The United Nations has used *migrants with irregular status* in official reporting since 2005.

reductions in the immigrant stock are due to economic conditions (Passel and Cohn 2010; Greenstone and Looney 2012). The flow of highly skilled authorized immigrants also declined during the Great Recession. The US State Department (2013) reported that they issued 25 percent fewer H-1B visas in 2010 than they had ten years earlier. H-1B visas are temporary work permits for foreign nationals with college degrees who have specialized skills in occupations such as chemistry or medicine.

The changes in immigration stock and flows in response to changes in the economy underscore the inextricable connection between immigration and the economy. Sluggish job growth and lagging production reduce demand for immigrant workers. At the same time, immigrants are unlikely to settle in a new country if they do not expect to find good opportunities in the economic sector. Immigration scholars anticipate an increase in immigration as the US economy begins a slow recovery, businesses increase their demand for immigrant workers, and immigrants resume seeking work in the US labor market (Greenstone and Looney 2012). Indeed, a slow recovery from the Great Recession has been matched recently with a small increase in the estimated number of unauthorized immigrants in the United States in 2012 (Passel, Cohn, and Gonzalez-Barrera 2012). Figure 3.1 shows trends in unauthorized immigrant stock before and after the Great Recession.

Immigration trends resulting from the Great Recession focus attention on two questions often raised by immigration scholars and public opinion makers. First, how do immigrants impact the economy of their host country? For example, do immigrants suppress wages, and do working conditions worsen when employers hire foreign-born workers? Do immigrants take jobs from native workers, or do they create jobs? Second, how well do immigrants fare in the labor markets of their host country? That is, do immigrants earn incomes commensurate with native workers, and do they get fair returns for their human capital?

For decades, demographers have sought to understand the role that immigrants play in the labor market (Card and Raphael 2013). Immigration could be harmful to an economy if it drives up unemployment by increasing the number of people in the labor market

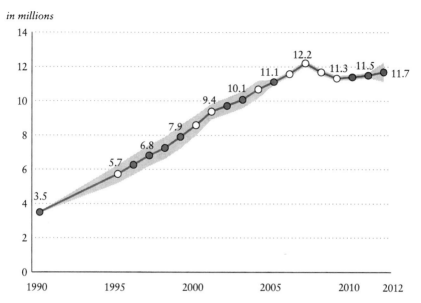

in millions

Figure 3.1 Estimates of the US unauthorized immigrant population, 1990–2012, in millions

Note: Shading surrounding line indicates low and high points of the estimated 90% confidence interval. White data markers indicate the change from the previous year is statistically significant (for 1995, change is significant from 1990). Data labels are for 1990, odd years from 1995–2011 and 2012.

Source: Pew Hispanic Research Center (reprinted with permission)

who want to work but do not have jobs. Immigrants may also be willing to work for lower wages, thus exerting downward pressure on overall wages, especially if the presence of immigrants increases the labor supply so that employers do not have to increase wages to keep their businesses staffed. Moreover, the working conditions for all low-skilled workers could potentially decline if immigrants are willing to work in poor conditions or if their immigration status makes them afraid to report employers who maintain dangerous work places. On the other hand, immigration could also improve the economy if immigrants fill important job vacancies and spend their wages in the local economy, creating a demand for new jobs. Additionally, the presence of immigrants may keep employers from outsourcing jobs to other countries. Immigrants may be necessary to staff essential jobs in industrial sectors, such as agriculture, that would otherwise face severe labor shortages.

Immigrants in the labor market

In considering the impact of immigrants on the economy, some people suggest that immigrants cause more harm than benefit (see Linton 2002; Brücker and Jahn 2011; Zavodny 2011). According to one line of reasoning, immigrants take jobs from native workers and drive down wages because they are willing to work harder for less money. This argument suggests that every job that is held by an immigrant would otherwise be held by a native worker. This position assumes that the supply of jobs is fixed. On the contrary, however, the number of jobs in a local labor market expands when more workers move into the market. A more nuanced argument against immigration is that the addition of immigrants to the labor market increases the supply of labor and drives down the cost of that labor, causing wages to decrease. Employers also substitute higher-cost native workers with lower-cost immigrant workers whenever possible in order to maximize profits, which can result in native job loss (Cohen-Goldner and Paserman 2006; Cortes 2008; Schwartzman 2008).

At the same time, others argue that immigrants are an economic boon (cf. Peri 2010; Lynch and Oakford 2013). According to this line of reasoning, the supply of jobs is not static, and population growth in any form leads to economic growth. Immigrants provide much-needed (and often low-skilled) labor, thereby producing economic expansion and higher wages for all. Moreover, immigrants may take jobs that native workers eschew, keeping these jobs from being outsourced to other countries. Immigrants are often entrepreneurial, so they create new businesses and provide more jobs for the economy. Immigrants also pay taxes at the federal and lower levels of government, yet they use few public resources. Thus, they provide a needed infusion of government funds.

Do immigrants pay taxes?

Many Americans mistakenly believe that unauthorized immigrants do not pay taxes. In fact, US federal, state, and local governments receive $162 billion annually from immigrants and their businesses in the form of taxes, and this revenue includes taxes from unauthorized immigrants (American Immigration Council 2013). The myth that unauthorized immigrants do not pay taxes is based on the mistaken assumption that all unauthorized immigrants are paid in cash "under the table" by unscrupulous employers. However, an abundance of tax data refutes this assumption. First, the Social Security Administration estimates that it receives about $13 billion annually in payroll taxes from unauthorized immigrants, who, because of their status, will never be able to reclaim this money (Gross et al. 2013). Second, many forms of taxes are linked to goods and services, rather than income, and individuals are not exempt from these sales and excise taxes. A few states, such as Alaska, New Hampshire, and Delaware, do not have sales taxes, but most of these states have few immigrants (unauthorized or otherwise). Unauthorized immigrants also pay property taxes, either directly on their properties or indirectly through rent to landowners who, in turn, pay taxes. Third, the US federal government and state governments have recently seen a large increase in tax revenues from tax returns filed using Individual Taxpayer Identification Numbers (ITIN). ITINs were designed for foreigners abroad with taxable investments in the United States. However, in 2005, there was a 40 percent increase (to 1.4 million) in the number of tax returns filed with ITINs – an increase that cannot be accounted for by investment (Institute on Taxation and Economic Policy [ITEP] 2013), which suggests that unauthorized immigrants are filing their taxes with ITINs. Certainly, some unauthorized immigrants work "off the book"; however, a recent study indicates that most people working under these

conditions make less than $13,000 a year (Valenzuela et al.
2006). These people would be unlikely to owe any income
taxes under federal and most state laws.

Overall, there is widespread agreement among immigration
scholars that immigration provides economic benefits. Immigrants
do not drive up unemployment rates or drive down wages in the
long run (Cohen-Goldner and Paserman 2006; Peri 2012). They
create jobs (Pedace 2006; Islam 2009) and stimulate investment
(Peri 2010). They pay taxes and do not receive a disproportionate share of government benefits (Lofstrom and Bean 2002). They
reduce the native poverty rate (Peri 2012). They fill jobs that
native workers will not take (Linton 2002). Additionally, immigrants appear to be absorbed into the economies of their host
countries very quickly, so they can expect relatively good returns
from their decision to migrate.

Immigration and wage suppression

Despite the mounting evidence that immigrants are a net benefit to
the economy, demographers also admit that it is difficult to develop
a good method to accurately estimate the impact of immigrants on
wages, employment, and working conditions for native workers.
To argue conclusively that immigration results in lower wages,
increased unemployment, or poorer working conditions, we would
need to speculate on how conditions would be without immigrants.
Demographers working in the field of economics approach this
issue by examining differences in wages across local labor markets
with different proportions of immigrants (see Grossman 1982).
This is called *the local labor market approach*. Studies using this
approach usually conceptualize local labor markets as metropolitan areas, states, or provinces. If a place with a high proportion of
immigrants has lower wages than a place with a low proportion of
immigrants, then it can be inferred – but not conclusively proven –
that immigrants suppress wages. The reverse is also true.

A landmark study by Chiswick (1978) using the local labor market approach revealed that immigrants fared as well as natives in the labor market. Although immigrant men tended, on average, to have less education than native men, they made up for the difference by investing heavily in on-the-job training. After a short time, the differences in wages between immigrants and natives were minimal, suggesting that immigrants do not drive down aggregate wages. Chiswick's findings were widely cited as evidence that immigrants are easily absorbed into the labor market.

Later economists (especially Borjas 1985, 1995) questioned whether Chiswick's findings could be extrapolated to the future. These economists point out that 63 percent of the immigrants in Chiswick's study were European or Canadian, in keeping with a general trend in pre-1965 immigration flows to the United States. After passage of the 1965 Hart–Cellar Act, which lifted restrictions on non-European immigration, immigration flows to the United States changed, and most new immigrants arrived from Asia and Latin America. This change in sending countries coincided with a shift in the skill characteristics of immigrants. More recent flows of immigrants consist of a large proportion of poorly educated, low-skilled workers (although, on average, the education and skill level of entering workers remain high). It is also worth noting that shifts in immigrant sending countries radically changed the ethnic composition of immigrants in the United States (see Portes and Zhou 1993) which increased the chances of immigrants facing discrimination in the labor market (Bohon 2001; McCall 2001), but few demographers working as economists consider racio-ethnic discrimination in their models.

Despite the differences between Chiswick's sample and more recent cohorts of immigrants, later findings based on local labor market techniques do not differ much from Chiswick's. The work conducted in the United States examining states or metropolitan areas overwhelmingly indicates little relationship between immigration and wages (Friedberg and Hunt 1995; Card 2001, 2007; Card and Lewis 2007), suggesting that immigrants are easily absorbed into local industries and exert little pressure on wages (cf. Card 2005). These findings are somewhat surprising, since a basic reading of supply and demand theory suggests that immigration should increase the supply of low-skilled workers, thereby suppressing the wages of native workers who lack high school diplomas. However, empirical evidence shows that the gap between the wages of high school dropouts and high school graduates has remained the same over time despite marked increases in the number of immigrants (Card 2005).

Harvard economist George Borjas and his colleagues (Borjas 2003; Borjas and Katz 2007) have criticized the local labor market approach to studying the impact of immigrants on wages and challenged the conclusion that immigrants do not depress wages. Using a *time-series approach* to study the US labor market as a whole as immigration fluctuates over time, they compared trends in wages to trends in immigration flows across the entire country. Their findings led to the conclusion that the presence of *low-skilled immigrants* significantly reduces the wages of poorly educated natives (those with only a high school diploma or less), although *high-skilled immigrants* appear to have no impact on the wages of the well-educated US-born.

The findings by Borjas and his colleagues are consistent with the *relative labor supply theory*, which suggests that increasing the supply of low-skilled workers should reduce the wages of such workers, since employers can easily substitute one (cheaper) worker for another (Cortes 2008). Immigration should not affect the wages of high-skilled workers because the substitution of immigrants to natives is imperfect. In other words, most workers can be easily trained to work on a factory line, so factory employers hire the cheapest workers; however, an accountant's skills cannot replace those of a chemist. Mass immigration is referred to in the economics literature as *supply shocks*, since the sudden presence of a large number of available workers disrupts the existing supply and demand for labor by making labor more plentiful (and cheaper). By 2000, immigrants comprised only about 13 percent of the US labor market, but they comprised 28 percent of the adult population without a high school diploma or its equivalent (Card 2005), and Borjas argues across his work that the downturn in wages for low-skilled labor starting in the 1980s

Skilled and unskilled workers

Research on immigrants in the economy often distinguishes between *low-skilled* (or *unskilled*) and *high-skilled workers*, although there is little agreement on who constitutes the membership of each group. Skill level is usually associated with education; workers without at least some college education are considered low-skilled, and those who have attended college are considered high-skilled (Ottaviano and Peri 2008). However, there is some variability between studies, with some researchers placing only high school dropouts in the low-skilled category, and others (e.g., Borjas 2003) placing high school diploma holders in the low-skilled category.

It can be misleading to refer to someone as "low-skilled" because he or she lacks a formal education. Clearly, some of the most poorly educated workers have specialized skills learned on the job (e.g., welding, masonry, and brick-laying) that people with very high levels of education do not possess. Additionally, immigrants who are unauthorized may be restricted by their immigration status to the very worst jobs in the labor market, regardless of their education (or "skill") level (Card 2005). Even highly educated immigrants may be relegated to poor jobs because their credentials are not accepted in their new country. In the aggregate, however, jobs that are dominated by people with low levels of education are jobs that do not require highly specialized skills. These are jobs such as cleaning, working on assembly lines, and lawn maintenance. Jobs classified as high-skilled do not necessarily entail specialized skills, but entry into these jobs often requires a bachelor's degree or higher level of education.

is at least partially attributable to this large supply of immigrant labor.

How can it be that immigrants have no impact on the wages of native workers at the local level, as local labor market approaches show, yet they have a great deal of impact on unskilled workers at the national level, as time-series approaches show? To reconcile these disparate findings, economists have had to adjust both models. With regard to the local labor market approach, researchers realized that native workers may leave labor markets when immigrants appear and immigrants may select some local labor markets over others because of more job opportunities (see Borjas 2006). Thus, the apparent lack of effect in the local labor market is actually an effect passed on to another market. After taking these possibilities into account, more recent findings demonstrate that immigrants *may* exert a negative impact on the wages of low-skilled native workers (Card 2001; Card and DiNardo 2000; Lewis 2005), but the effect is much smaller than asserted by Borjas.

With regard to the time-series approach, Card (2005) argues that Borjas' (2003) concept of low-skilled labor is overly simplified because he assumes that all low-skilled workers are the same. Ottaviano and Peri (2008) and Lewis (2013) extend Card's argument by pointing out that Borjas and his colleagues (especially Borjas, Grogger, and Hanson 2008) incorrectly accounted for how perfectly low-skilled immigrant workers can substitute for natives. A greater proportion of newer immigrants are more likely than the US-born or more established immigrants to have less than a high school education, but a smaller proportion of immigrants than of the US-born discontinue their education after high school. In fact, immigrants are more likely than the US-born to hold bachelor's degrees. Thus, if economists see low-skilled immigrants as a perfect substitute for low-skilled US-born workers, they must assume that employers see no difference between high school graduates, high school dropouts, and those who never attended high school. However, if employers prefer high school graduates, then the comparisons in the economic models are flawed because, among US immigrants, the group defined as low-skilled is comprised of a large proportion of people with no high school education at all and few with high school diplomas. Among the US-born, the group defined as possessing a high school diploma or less is comprised of many people with a high school diploma, almost no one with no high school education, and a small fraction of people who are high school dropouts (Card 2001, 2005).

Such differences in educational attainment matter. Research by Ottaviano and Peri (2008) shows that the labor demand for those with a high school diploma is quite different from the demand for those without a high school diploma. Their work demonstrates that an increasing supply of immigrant labor decreases the wages of native dropouts, but the depression of the wages of high school diploma holders is much more modest than Borjas (2003) predicts. Even when education levels are the same, some evidence indicates that immigrants without high school diplomas do not substitute perfectly for natives with the same level of education (Cortes 2008).

Ottaviano and Peri (2008) also criticize Borjas (2003) for incorrectly accounting for capital adjustments. Borjas argues in the title of his 2003 article that "The labor demand curve is downward sloping," meaning that the cost of labor declines as the supply of labor increases. However, economists have long assumed that labor and capital (usually technology) are often substitutable (see Arrow et al. 1961). In other words, if labor becomes too expensive, industries will adjust by replacing workers with labor-saving technology. The reverse is also true: if technology is expensive, industries will hire more workers. Ottaviano and Peri argue that Borjas did not consider changes in demand for each type of worker when supplies of other factors change. By adjusting the time-series model to allow for changes in (non-labor) capital inputs, Ottaviano and Peri show that Borjas overestimated the negative impact of immigration on the wages of low-skilled workers.

Now that these factors have been correctly accounted for in the models, the bulk of research in the United States suggests that the presence of immigrants slightly depresses the wages of low-skilled native workers, but that immigration overall is associated with an increase in the average wage of US-born workers (Ottaviano and Peri 2005, 2006, 2007; Card 2007). Thus, the question of how immigrants impact the economy should be narrowed to "Whom do they impact?" Generally speaking, highly skilled immigrants have no negative impact on the economy. In fact, highly skilled immigrants may improve the economy, just as increasing education levels of native workers improves the economy. Most of the negative impact occurs because of low-skilled immigrants, and that impact is felt mainly by the most poorly educated low-skilled natives. However, even that effect is somewhat short-lived. Research examining US workers' wages between 1990 and 2006 demonstrated that immigration negatively impacted wages of low-skilled workers but only for a short time (Ottaviano and Peri 2008). In the short run, recent immigration was associated with a 0.7 percent reduction in wages for US-born workers without a high school diploma, and a 6 percent reduction in wages for previous immigrants. In the long run, however, immigration was associated with a small (0.3 percent) improvement in wages for US-born workers without a high school diploma and a slightly larger (0.6 percent) improvement in wages for all native workers (ibid.). Thus, those most negatively impacted by immigration are other immigrants.

The small body of work that examines labor markets in other countries generally confirms these findings. For example, the phenomenon of *Spätausiedler* (i.e., people of German descent born outside of Germany in places such as Russia and Hungary) immigrating to Germany had no impact on the wages of the German-born (Glitz 2012). The author of this study speculates that this non-effect may be due to high rates of unionization in Germany, which makes it difficult for employers to hire workers at lower wage rates. However, this finding is also consistent with research in the United States on the impact of immigrants on the wages of natives, despite the fact that the United States has very low rates of unionization (Antecol, Kuhn, and Trejo 2006). Other researchers (e.g., Brücker and Jahn 2011) also find that immigration to Germany has no negative impact on German-born workers. In fact, in the long run, the immigration of high-skilled workers reduces unemployment and drives up the wages of natives by a small amount. Similarly, research on immigrants from the former Soviet Union to Israel finds no long-term effect of wage suppression for native Israelis (Cohen and Tai-Hsieh 2001; Friedberg 2001).

Labor market displacement and expansion

Labor market displacement occurs if immigrants occupy jobs that would ordinarily be filled by native workers. However, it is possible that immigrants expand the labor market. Immigrants may actually create jobs by putting more money into the economy through their spending or by creating their own businesses and hiring workers. The ability to replace one set of workers with another is called *substitutability*, while the possibility that immigrants create jobs is called *complementarity* (Islam 2009; Zavodny 2011).

One way that scholars can examine labor market displacement or expansion is by comparing unemployment rates across local labor markets with different proportions of immigrants. Scholars can also examine whether or not unemployment rates in a single labor market fluctuate with changes in immigration flows over time. Studies using these approaches generally find that unemployment rates are generally lower in places with more immigrants, suggesting that immigrants complement native workers (Islam 2009).

Most of the research on the economic impacts of immigrants is conducted in the United States, since there are far more immigrants spread across a greater number of local labor markets than in other developed countries. A few studies in other countries report results consistent with those in the United States. For example, studies of Russian immigrants in Israel (Cohen-Goldner and Paserman 2006) showed that the more than 1 million immigrants entering the country between 1989 and 2000 had no effect on native workers in terms of either unemployment or movement from one job sector to another. Research in Canada (Islam 2009) also confirms that immigrants complement, rather than substitute for, native workers.

However, many economists have speculated that the findings of immigrant–native employment complementarity may not translate to Europe, which has much higher rates of unemployment and far less *labor market flexibility*. Labor market flexibility refers to the speed with which labor markets adapt to changes in society. Labor markets that react slowly are referred to as *rigid*. European countries have far more labor market rigidity than the United States (Brücker and Jahn 2011) because they have greater regulation of businesses, more barriers to starting new businesses, and greater unionization. Thus, immigrants are unlikely to drive down wages, but they may be very likely to drive up unemployment rates.

Germany, the world's third-largest receiver of immigrants (after the United States and Russia), is a telling case. The German labor market is marked by high and persistent unemployment, high rates of unionization, and extensive regulation of businesses (ibid.). About 85 percent of all German workers have their wages set by collective bargaining agreements (Ellguth and Kohaut 2007), although about half of all workers earn more than what is required by the agreement (Jung and Schnabel 2011). Because of these factors, Germany's rigid labor market should be more greatly impacted by immigrants than the labor market of the United States.

The evidence that more labor market displacement due to immigration occurs in Europe than in the United States is mixed. Examining *Spätausiedler* returning to Germany, Glitz (2012) shows some evidence for labor displacement. For every ten ethnic German immigrants who found a job, about three German-born natives became unemployed. However, in considering all immigrants to Germany, Brücker and Jahn (2011) demonstrate that neither the unemployment rate for immigrants nor the unemployment rate for all workers was affected by immigration, despite the fact that 4 percent of the German workforce entered Germany between 1980 and 2004. Brücker and Jahn *do* find evidence for displacement, but their findings show that low-skilled, recent immigrants take jobs from low-skilled, established immigrants, not from natives.

One problem with scrutinizing unemployment rates in the local labor market to examine displacement is that this approach cannot account for the possibility that immigrants displace native workers, and the native workers, in turn, leave the local labor market for opportunities in another labor market. In this situation, the unemployment rate would remain unchanged. To adjust for this, some scholars have examined how immigrant inflows affect native outflows from labor markets (see, for example, Borjas 2006). If there is a high rate of native *out-migration* in response to an increase in immigration, it can reasonably be inferred that immigrants are displacing native workers and driving them to new labor markets.

In the United States, it is clear that states with the highest proportion of immigrants have low proportions of US-born residents. California, New York, Texas, Florida, Illinois and New Jersey were home to nearly 70 percent of the working-age immigrant population in 2000, but only a third of all US-born working-age people lived in those states (Borjas 2006). Borjas (ibid.) finds that two US-born workers will leave a state for every ten immigrants who enter, and between three and six US-born workers will leave a metropolitan area for every ten immigrants who enter. He asserts this as evidence that immigrants are displacing native workers, despite the fact that unemployment rates remain static at the state and metropolitan level.

However, that natives leave an area when immigrants enter does not mean that native out-migration is the result of immigration. Labor market restructuring could be the driving factor, a point that Borjas (2006) concedes. Other societal factors may also be at work, as is illustrated in the case of Atlanta, Georgia. In the 1990s, many immigrants moved to Atlanta to take jobs in construction. Many of these immigrants were employed in building houses in counties surrounding the metropolitan areas, and these houses were usually more expensive than immigrants could afford. Many upwardly mobile Atlantans moved into these houses outside of the metropolitan area because they found the communities of newly built homes nicer than those in Atlanta; at the same time, many immigrants clustered in impoverished neighborhoods in the inner city (Atiles and Bohon 2003). In this scenario, immigrants moved in and natives moved out, but the natives were able to move out because of immigrant labor, and immigrants were able to move into Atlanta because of the native demand to move out.

Of course, it is also possible that natives may out-migrate in response to immigration, but the phenomenon is not related to labor displacement. Many immigrants are racio-ethnic minorities, and many people live in racially segregated neighborhoods. When minorities enter predominantly white neighborhoods, there is a tendency for *tipping*: a few members of a minority group settle, and white residents leave en masse. When tipping occurs, white residents often resettle in nearby neighborhoods. However, some relocate to new cities altogether (cf. Fossett 2006; Zhang 2011).

Labor market assimilation

Work on wage suppression and labor displacement studies immigration from the perspective of workers born in the host country. When demographers consider the labor market from the perspective of immigrants, many are concerned about how well immigrants are absorbed into their host countries (Chiswick 1978; Borjas 1985, 1995; LaLonde and Topel 1992; Schoeni 1997). Thus, a great deal of demographic research examines *earnings assimilation*. Assimilation is the process whereby immigrants become indistinguishable from natives; earnings assimilation means that the earnings of an immigrant group are, on average, identical to the average earnings of a similar native group. Researchers studying immigrants in the United States usually restrict comparisons of immigrants to non-Latino white, US-born workers, since people of color tend to experience discrimination in the labor market (Antecol, Kuhn, and Trejo 2006; Kesler 2010). Some demographers divide earnings assimilation into two parts: *employment assimilation* and *wage assimilation*. Employment assimilation examines the likelihood of having a job. Wage assimilation examines how much people who have jobs earn. Wage assimilation is different from earnings assimilation because earnings assimilation uses both the earnings of people with jobs and the earnings of people who do not have jobs (and therefore have zero earnings) in the calculation, while wage assimilation excludes those without jobs.

Most of the research conducted since the late 1970s (Chiswick 1978) suggests that immigrants are eventually absorbed into the labor market; however, how quickly this happens depends on the type of immigrant and the conditions of the labor market they are entering (Bratsberg, Barth, and Raaum 2006; Kogan 2006). Comparing immigrant men in the United States, Canada, and Australia from 1980 to 1990, researchers found that the greatest earnings assimilation occurred in the United States and the least occurred in Australia (Antecol, Kuhn, and Trejo 2006). Although new immigrants entering the United States initially earned far lower wages than immigrants in Australia or Canada, adjusting for currency differences, immigrants' wages in the United States also grew at a much faster rate. In Australia, surprisingly, the reverse is true. Immigrants start with relatively high wages – in fact, average wages are higher for new immigrants than for the Australian-born – but, over time, their average wages actually decrease relative to natives', putting them more in line with native workers. In Israel, immigrants from the former Soviet Union – most of whom are highly educated – have not achieved wage parity with Israeli natives ten years after immigrating (Eckstein and Weiss 2004).

With regard to employment assimilation, in the United States, Australia, and Canada, newly arrived immigrants have much lower employment rates than natives, either because they have more difficulty finding jobs or because there are barriers to gaining employment permission (Antecol, Kuhn, and Trejo 2006). However, the likelihood of being unemployed soon after entry is much higher in the United States and Australia than in Canada. Overall, with sufficient time in the host country, immigrants in all three countries ultimately achieved rates of employment similar to those of native workers (ibid.). This is also true of former Soviet immigrants in Israel (Eckstein and Weiss 2004).

Ultimately, how well individual immigrants fare in the labor market and how quickly they are assimilated into it depends on three factors: (1) the economic conditions of the labor market entered; (2) public policies that affect the economy; and (3) the characteristics of immigrants (Cobb-Clark 2003; Kogan 2006; Kesler 2010). Labor market conditions include unemployment rates and the availability of low-skilled jobs. Evidence from the

United States suggests that the gap between immigrant and native average wages is wider when economic conditions are poor and unemployment rates are high. The gap narrows in good economic times. This is because immigrants' wages fall faster than the wages of the US-born during times of high unemployment (Bratsberg, Barth, and Raaum 2006). These trends are important to note because they imply that immigrants in the United States may be doing more poorly now – during the Great Recession and its aftermath – than in the past, but we do not yet have enough data to know for sure.

Governments can implement a range of policies that have a broad impact on immigrant earnings assimilation. Policy determines whether or not immigrants can receive assistance if they are unemployed or otherwise impoverished, how much assistance, and for how long. These policies vary widely from country to country, with the United States severely restricting immigrants' access to income support programs such as unemployment benefits (Lofstrom and Bean 2002; Cobb-Clark 2003). Governments also create laws that control the flow of immigrants and determine which immigrants are authorized to work. Immigrants working without permits have fewer job opportunities and make less money (Flippen 2012). Government policies and a country's political orientation can also affect the dispersion of wages across the economy (Nightingale and Fix 2004). Social democratic countries like Sweden tend to have high minimum wages and liberal income transfer policies that reduce income differences between the poorest and the richest. Social democratic policies that create a low wage distribution thereby reduce inequality between immigrants and natives (Kogan 2006; Kesler 2010). In contrast, economically liberal countries like the United States and the United Kingdom have large gaps between the rich and the poor.

Finally, earnings assimilation depends on immigrants' *human capital*. Human capital is an umbrella concept used to describe all of the characteristics of an individual that can be capitalized upon for higher wages or a better job (Linton 2002). Important sources of human capital for immigrants include fluency in the language or languages of the host country and high levels of education

(Cobb-Clark 2003). There is fairly consistent evidence that, since 1970, there has been a sizable wage gap between immigrants and natives in the United States, and the direction of that gap depends on human capital. Soon after entry, immigrant men without a high school diploma make about 20 percent less an hour, on average, than native men, while similarly educated immigrant women make about 10 percent less an hour than native women (Card 2005). Immigrants' earnings increase with time in the United States, but the gains are not enough to completely close the gap. At the same time, immigrants with a college degree – more than one-fifth of all US immigrants – earn, on average, about 30 percent more than natives (ibid.).

The earning potential of the children of immigrants is perhaps more interesting and more telling than the income of their parents. Second-generation US immigrants – those born in the United States to at least one immigrant parent – have a slightly higher level of education than the third or later generations – those born in the US to US-born parents. This higher education explains why second-generation immigrants are more likely to be employed and earn more money than the third and later generations (Card 2005).

The informal and secondary labor markets

Earnings assimilation should not be confused with upward mobility. Although immigrants earn wages similar to native workers, this does not mean that wages are high. In fact, the working conditions for those at the bottom of the occupational ladder have deteriorated considerably through falling real wages and more non-standard working arrangements, such as subcontracting, temporary and part-time work, and on-call employment (Kopczuk, Saez, and Song 2010; Kalleberg 2011; Flippen 2012).

Nearly everyone agrees that the best economy is one in which there is full employment and high wages (cf. Linton 2002). Under such conditions, people are able to find work, and work provides a sufficient income to meet their needs. However, such conditions are increasingly rare in developed countries. Commenting on conditions in the United States and citing Hudson (2007), Flippen (2012: 22) points out, "a large proportion of jobs that once provided good wages, stability, health insurance and pensions, and the potential for upward mobility to US workers, have been replaced by jobs that do not provide any of those things." Immigrants are experiencing wage assimilation, but for many this simply means that low-skilled natives are faring as poorly as low-skilled immigrants.

Even with this caveat, assimilation in the labor market may not be occurring, despite findings to the contrary. One difficulty researchers face when attempting to understand immigrant earnings assimilation is that many immigrants work in the *informal economy*. The informal economy is defined broadly as any work that is unreported and, therefore, untaxed and unregulated (Flippen 2012). Some of these jobs, such as the trade in illicit drugs, can be profitable, albeit illegal. Most jobs in the informal economy, however, entail work that is irregular and poorly paid, such as mowing lawns, caring for children, and cleaning. Low-wage labor in the United States is often informal or subcontracted labor (Flippen 2012; Lynch and Oakford 2013). This work is rarely captured in official statistics, because those working in the informal economy may report as not being in the labor market. Thus, analysis of the wages of immigrants tends to show an overly optimistic picture of wage assimilation, since informal workers are excluded.

Still, wages are just one benefit that people get from working, and even if immigrants achieve wage and employment assimilation, there is little evidence that they are doing as well as natives with regard to other work compensation. Good jobs supply steady work, health insurance (in the United States), and retirement benefits (McCall 2000). Good jobs also provide safe working conditions and financial assistance to employees when they are injured on the job (Kalleberg 2011). In fact, the differences between good and bad jobs are so vast that many scholars refer to the pool of bad jobs as the *secondary labor market* (see Hudson 2007; Pedace 2006).

We do not have much information about total benefits immigrants receive – or fail to receive – in the secondary labor market, but a recent study of Latino construction workers in Durham, North Carolina (Flippen 2012) offers a small snapshot of the difficulties of working in some of the economy's worst jobs. This study divides immigrants working as subcontractors from those working as employees in construction companies, under the assumption that subcontracting jobs are in the secondary labor market while company jobs are not. Although not all subcontracting work is secondary labor market work (poorly paid without benefits), much of it is (ibid.), and because of increased legal sanctions on employers who hire unauthorized immigrants, much work in the construction field has moved to subcontracting in order to insulate employers from being fined (Massey and Bartley 2005; Gentsch and Massey 2011). The study finds that Latino men working in construction lose about $2,000 a year due to layoffs, but men working as and for subcontractors lose about double that amount. Those who are unauthorized lose nearly $7,500. Furthermore, 90 percent of the men who were unauthorized and working as subcontractors received no job benefits, a situation that held for only 13 percent of the Latino immigrant men who were authorized and working for large construction companies.

Other US-based work comparing unauthorized immigrants' economic well-being to that of similarly skilled authorized immigrants supports the North Carolina study. Naturalized citizens earn about 40 percent more, on average, than non-citizen immigrants. Immigrants with work permits earn about 6 percent more, on average, than those without work authorization. Furthermore, formerly unauthorized immigrants who were granted authorized status saw a 15 percent increase in their real wages after five years. (These studies are reviewed in Lynch and Oakford 2013.) Collectively, these findings support the need for governments to reconsider restrictions on immigrants' work to achieve the goals of full employment and high wages.

Entrepreneurship, ethnic economies, and enclaves

Immigrants tend to have higher rates of self-employment than natives in many developed countries, and, over time, self-employed immigrants usually report wages on par with or higher than native workers (Blanchflower 2004). High rates of immigrant entrepreneurship may be explained by the *blocked mobility hypothesis* (see Raijman and Tienda 2000), which suggests that immigrants can escape discrimination in the labor market and ensure good wage returns on their human capital through self-employment (Liebermann, Suter, and Rutishauser 2014). Given the propensity to enter into self-employment and the generally good outcomes associated with entrepreneurship, working for oneself is often viewed by scholars as the best way for immigrants to adapt quickly to a new labor market (Maxim 1992; Portes and Stepick 1993).

Of course, not all self-employment is entrepreneurship (Budig 2006). Working in the secondary labor market or informal economy by cleaning houses, taking care of children, or mowing lawns cannot be equated with owning and operating a retail or service establishment, employing others, or being in private practice. Financial benefits and working conditions are clearly different (Lofstrom 2013). However, even self-employment in "bad" jobs can be beneficial if it is more rewarding than working for others (Raijman and Tienda 2000) or if there are few opportunities to work for someone else (van Tubergen 2005; Valdez 2006).

Despite the advantages of self-employment, some immigrant groups have much higher rates of entrepreneurship than others (Yuengert 1994). Differential rates may be explained by differences in human capital (van Tubergen 2005), ability to mobilize resources (Aldrich and Waldinger 1990), prior self-employment experience (Akee, Jaeger, and Tatsiramos 2007), and alternative opportunities in the larger labor market (Liebermann, Suter, and Rutishauser 2014).

Many demographers have long assumed that one advantage of self-employment for the immigrant community is that immigrant entrepreneurs often employ co-ethnic workers, thus speeding the workers' economic adaptation (see Xie and Gough 2011). A labor market in which co-ethnic business owners employ workers who are from their own country of origin is called an *ethnic economy*. An ethnic economy located within a city, which is separate from the city's or metropolitan area's larger labor market, is called an *ethnic enclave* (cf. Portes and Stepick, 1993; Bohon 2001). Ethnic enclaves in the United States include Chinatown in San Francisco, Los Angeles, and New York, and Little Havana in Miami.

Whether or not immigrants fare better within the ethnic economy (a position referred to as the *enclave thesis*) has been hotly debated since the 1980s. Most demographers traditionally sided with Portes and his colleagues (Portes and Manning 1986; Portes and Jensen 1992; Portes and Stepick 1993), who argue that co-ethnic hiring networks are beneficial in speeding immigrant economic assimilation. In theory, immigrants benefit from the ethnic economy for the following reasons: (1) ability to speak the language of the host country is usually unimportant; (2) employers feel an obligation to preferentially hire co-ethnic workers, while workers feel compelled to work hard for their employers; (3) cultural differences in work are muted; and (4) insofar as employers are trading in ethnically defined goods, immigrants' skills may be in high demand (see Bohon 2001). Despite these assumed advantages, most recent work (cf. Xie and Gough 2011) using a life course perspective to study wage assimilation demonstrates that immigrants may not be better off working for co-ethnic employers, and some immigrant groups may receive lower returns on their education when working in ethnic economies than when working in the larger labor market.

4

Immigration and the Environment

In April 2013, the Sierra Club – one of the largest and most influential environmental groups in the United States – stunned many when they announced their support of comprehensive immigration reform with a path to citizenship for unauthorized immigrants in the United States (Mock 2013). Sierra Club President Allison Chin and Executive Director Michael Brune explained, "If we are serious about solving the climate crisis and protecting our democracy, then we need to work with the hardworking men and women who want to play by the rules and play a part in building a healthy, safe, and prosperous future for our country." The announcement represented a reversal of the organization's long-held official position of immigration policy neutrality and the private opinions of many Sierra Club leaders that immigration is a key factor in environmentally damaging population growth (Beirich 2010; Palmer and Samuelsohn 2013).

The effect of population on the environment has long been a concern of demographers (Ehrlich 1968; Hogan 1992; Betts 2004). Thomas Malthus, whom many consider to be the first demographer (Petersen 1999), argued in 1798 that unchecked population growth would inevitably lead to famine, as the number of people to feed would outpace the food supply and human sprawl would reduce the amount of land available for cultivation. Although Malthus was not concerned with immigration, per se, his work underscores that humans are both a part of the natural environment and harmful to it. Malthus, and many who came after him, stressed the commonly held view that population growth – a significant cause of environmental strain – is the largest threat to the welfare of humans (Malthus 1798; Garling 1998; Fischer-Kowalski and Amann 2001).

An emphasis on the environmental harms caused by immigrants ignores the facts that all people can harm the environment, regardless of where they are, and that the effects will be felt around the world. The recent Sierra Club announcement, which stressed that environmental damage caused by population occurs on a global scale, reflects a broader view of the interplay of population and the environment. The announcement also acknowledges that immigrants are often more susceptible to environmental degradation, such as air and water pollution, than natives in their country of destination because immigrants are often concentrated in some of the developed world's poorest neighborhoods (Hunter 2000a; Bullard, Warren, and Johnson 2005). Some members of the Sierra Club lauded the new announcement as an important step in expanding the organization's push for *environmental justice* – a perspective that views environmental harm as disproportionately affecting the poor and disenfranchised. Others saw the announcement as ignoring a long-held Malthusian "truth" that population growth – including through immigration – is fraught with environmental harm.

The environmental impact of immigrants

Of the three demographic processes (fertility, mortality, and migration), only immigration does not affect global population growth. As Ehrlich and Ehrlich (2004: 108) point out, "Migration, whether internal or international, does not, of course, change the total number of people on the planet." However, immigration results in population redistribution, and this redistribution can potentially harm the environment in several ways.

At the most basic level, immigration increases the population size of the destination country (Orenstein 2004; Zlotnik, Bloom and Jimenez 2011). Once a population has exceeded an area's *carrying capacity* – the amount of all life that can be sustained in a given place – pollution increases, land is shifted from productive uses like agriculture to less productive uses like housing and transport, and demands for water, energy, and waste management cannot be met easily (Catton 1980; Foster 2002; Zlotnik, Bloom, and Jimenez 2011). According to Ehrlich and Holdren, two pioneers of the modern environmental movement, "if there are too many people, even the most wisely managed technology will not keep the environment from being overstressed" (1972: 376). Most demographers and ecologists agree with this sentiment (Chertow 2001; Xiao 2013). In the United States, where nearly 40 million immigrants currently account for about a third of all population growth (Patten 2012), the President's Council on Sustainable Development concluded there was a need to reduce immigration flows in order to work toward sustainability (Population and Consumption Task Force 1996).

Ecologists who believe in the necessity of population reduction for environmental sustainability are referred to as *Malthusians* (Muradian 2006) or *neo-Malthusians* (Neumayer 2006). Malthusians and neo-Malthusians believe that immigrants are directly responsible for biodiversity loss, water consumption, congestion, and waste generation in the places where they settle (Population–Environment Balance 1992; Abernethy 2000; Kuper 2005; Chapman 2006). Under the neo-Malthusian perspective, current immigration levels must be reduced to preserve local environments (Parsons 2000; Meyerson 2004).

To the extent that migration flows occur between developing and developed countries, immigration results in moving people from places where they have a small *ecological footprint* to places where that footprint is much larger (Hunter 2000a, 2000b). An ecological footprint is a measure of the impact of humans on the planet (Rees 1992). A person living in rural Bangladesh, for example, has a smaller ecological footprint than a Bangladeshi immigrant living in the United States. This is due in no small part to the fact that the Bangladeshi immigrant living in the United States is much more likely to drive a car than the person who remains in Bangladesh. On average, a car driven in the United States emits about 5.1 metric tons of carbon dioxide into the atmosphere every year. The

Immigration, nativism, and "greenwashing"

Some environmentalists oppose immigration on the grounds that population growth – especially growth in the developed world – is harmful to the environment. Muradian (2006) separates these environmentalists, whom he labels "Malthusians," from those he calls "environmental nativists" (209), anti-immigrant forces that have adopted an environmental stance to make a stronger case against immigration. *Nativist groups* are organizations with anti-immigration agendas motivated by racial concerns that immigration fundamentally alters the ethnic and racial composition of a nation and destroys "Western" values. As overtly racist logic is no longer tolerated in popular Western discourse, nativist groups have sought more rational grounds for asserting their argument. *Environmental nativists* are nativist groups that push environmental concern as a socially palatable reason for advocating reduced immigration flows into their country; unlike Malthusian groups, environmental nativist groups do not have an overarching environmental agenda.

Essays on the environmental harm attributed to immigrants are appearing more frequently in nativist publications. The *Social Contract* is a magazine for "the preservation and promotion of a shared American language and culture" (http://thesocialcontract.com), and their website links to openly racist groups such as American Patrol and Predatory Aliens. *Occidental Quarterly* is an overtly white supremacist publication. Both magazines have published many articles on the dangers that immigrants pose to the environment. In the United States, the Carrying Capacity Network, the Center for Immigration Studies, the Federation for American Immigration Reform, and Numbers USA are groups that advocate for reducing immigration; in recent years, they have been stressing how harmful immigrants are to the environment (Muradian 2006; Røpke 2006; Price and Feldmeyer 2012).

The Southern Poverty Law Center has documented attempts by nativist groups to infiltrate environmental organizations (Beirich 2010). The *New York Times* and other outlets have reported attempts in the 1990s to take control of the board of the Sierra Club in order to push an agenda that would make anti-immigration an official stance (Mock 2013). Nativist efforts to create opposition to immigration through stressing the environmental harm caused by immigrants are a form of *greenwashing* and are often referred to as *the greening of hate* (see Aufrecht 2012).

same car will also emit other dangerous greenhouse gases such as methane, nitrous oxide, and hydrofluorocarbons (Environmental Protection Agency 2011). Thus, immigration can be harmful to the environment if it means that immigrants will adapt to a more environmentally damaging lifestyle.

The settlement patterns of immigrants may also be linked to ecological damage. About 95 percent of all US immigrants live in urban areas (Singer 2013) and thus contribute to the growth of cities. In fact, nearly half of all immigrants to the United States live in just five metropolitan areas, called *gateways* (ibid.). By settling predominantly in a few concentrated areas, immigrants contribute to urbanization and sprawl, which are associated with environmental degradation (Bartlett and Lytwak 1995; Cole and Neumayer 2004; Ewing 2008). It is hardly surprising that the factors that attract in-migrants to some cities, such as job growth, also attract immigrants. Many of the United States' fastest-growing cities in the 1990s and the first decade of the twenty-first century are *new destinations* for immigrants, and many of these new destinations have high levels of urban sprawl (Lopez 2014). For example, nearly 2 million people settled in and around the Atlanta metropolitan areas in the 1990s, and about a quarter of these people were immigrants (Atiles and Bohon 2003).

Demographers measure *urbanization* as the percentage of an area's total population living in urban areas (i.e., how many people are densely settled around a central city) or by the average rate of change in the size of the urban population over time. Urbanization and sprawl are associated with *population density* (Fulton et al. 2001; Ewing 2008; Orenstein and Hamburg 2010), which is measured as the number of people per area, usually a square mile or a square kilometer. For example, Washington, DC's density is more than 10,000 people per square mile. Regardless of how urbanization is measured, it is associated with environmental damage – especially air pollution – because of the concentration of emissions-producing activities (e.g., manufacturing and automobile use) in a relatively small area (Cole and Neumayer 2004).

Immigrant settlement patterns can increase the environmental stress on already burdened urban areas. As of the 2010 Census, about a fifth of all US immigrants resided in Los Angeles (Grieco et al. 2012), one of the largest immigrant receiving destinations in the United States. Public officials in this desert area have long struggled to find ways to supply fresh water to Los Angeles' large population (Glennon 2009), and the area currently imports 87 percent of its fresh water. Certainly, access to water would still be a problem in Los Angeles in the absence of immigrants, but the increased population due to immigrant settlement adds additional stress to this ecosystem.

Like urbanization, *sprawl* is one of the biggest environmental concerns related to the population growth of cities. Sprawl happens with or without immigration. In recent years, however, some have argued that immigration is a major cause of sprawl (see Muradian 2006). In the 1920s, demographers assumed that all immigrants initially settled in inner cities and moved very slowly, over generations, to inner and then outer suburbs in *concentric zones* (Park, Burgess, and McKenzie 1925). In the 1980s, Ward (1982: 57-8) argued that sprawl occurred as the result of immigration because the "tidal wave" of immigrants was too great for cities to "metabolize." Since the 1990s, considerable evidence suggests that more immigrants are choosing suburbs as their first destination rather than collectively settling in the inner city (Alba et al. 1999; Puentes and Warren 2006; Singer, Hardwick, and Brettell 2008). This information has led neo-Malthusians to press

Urban sprawl

Although there are no widely agreed-upon measures of sprawl (Fulton et al. 2001), conceptually, sprawl refers to the relationship between population growth and land consumption. As the population of a metropolitan area grows, land surrounding the area is increasingly consumed by roads, businesses, or residences. Sprawl occurs because a population is growing, and population pressures force urbanized areas to spread. However, sprawl can also occur in the absence of population growth, if the residents of an urban area simply spread out. Ecologists generally consider the latter to be the most harmful (Orenstein and Hamburg 2010). In the most general sense, sprawl refers to the continuing spread of a city across previously rural land, and it generally encapsulates the idea that the spread is wider than strictly necessary. Thus, sprawl occurs when a metropolitan area becomes less dense, not as a result of population decline, but because of the movement of city dwellers to the increasingly distant suburbs.

Sprawl implies the overtaking of the natural environment by the built environment, which can have widespread and harmful ecological consequences. When people live further apart, public transportation is unviable, and people have to drive farther than if they lived close together (Kahn 2000). Additionally, more roads, power lines, and other materials are needed to connect houses and businesses in sprawling areas like suburbs than are required in densely populated areas like inner cities. Nearly 60 years ago, Landsberg (1955) scrupulously examined findings from the existing scientific literature to demonstrate that the spread of urban areas alters the surface of the earth, generates pollution, and increases local temperatures, which, in turn, affects the climate. Some 40 years later, Jäger and Barry (1990) found little evidence to refute Landsberg's earlier findings. The horizontal spread of cities can have disastrous climatic effects. For example, demographers have documented that spreading asphalt where vegetation once thrived raises the surface temperature of the earth, which, in turn, increases the likelihood of experiencing a destructive tornado at that location (Aguirre et al. 1993).

harder for severe restrictions on US immigration (see, for example, Beck, Kolankiewicz, and Camarota 2003).

Is immigration really harmful to the environment?

Despite the fact that demographers have assumed for more than two centuries that population growth – including growth attributable to immigration – is harmful to the natural environment, there is surprisingly little research on the direct environmental impacts of immigration (Pfeffer and Stycos 2002; Price and Feldmeyer 2012). Few researchers have examined whether pollution increases in the places where immigrants settle or whether environmental problems are greater in countries that receive more immigrants. Even when research is abundant, the outcome is contested. One often-cited "problem" of immigration is that immigrants have high levels of fertility, and children raised in developed countries have a greater impact on the environment than children raised in developing countries (Ehrlich and Ehrlich 2004). Of course, most international migration occurs *between* developed countries, so this fear is overstated. However, this fear is exaggerated even when considering immigration between developing countries. Macunovich (2000), for example, argues that immigrants have fewer children in their country of destination than if they had stayed in their country of origin, even if they have more children than native women in the country of destination, which may not be the case (see chapter 5). From this perspective, immigration may actually reduce global economic pressures resulting from overpopulation, but it may also contribute to greater resource use.

The absence of research directly linking immigration to the environment is problematic. Just as there is speculation that immigrants harm the environment, there is also speculation that some kinds of immigration may be helpful to local ecosystems. For example, the practice of population relocation may remove important stressors from the environment in immigrant sending countries. Certainly, highly damaging environmental behaviors in developing countries, such as deforestation and slash-and-burn agriculture, are related to population pressures (Abel et al. 2013; Caviglia-Harris, Sills, and Mullan 2013), and these pressures can be reduced through fertility decline and immigration.

Immigrants might also benefit local ecosystems if they are sufficiently organized to combat environmental degradation in their neighborhoods; however, scholars disagree as to whether or not immigrant communities are sufficiently resourced to provide this protective function. For example, *social disorganization theory* (see Bursik 2006) suggests that immigrants may throw neighborhoods into disarray because they bring greater poverty and different languages to the area, thereby reducing resources and making it more difficult for people to communicate with their neighbors. As a consequence, residents may be unable to combat social problems that occur at the local level, including locally sourced pollution (Martinez and Valenzuela 2006; Stowell 2007; Price and Feldmeyer 2012).

On the other hand, studies have documented that the growth of the immigrant population in residential neighborhoods has actually reduced crime and improved health, leading researchers to consider the effects of immigration from a *community resource perspective* (Sampson 2008; Desmond and Kubrin 2009; Feldmeyer 2009). In contrast to social disorganization theory, the community resource perspective views immigrant presence as a stabilizing force. The stability of immigrant communities can be explained, in part, through how these communities are formed. As a result of *network migration*, recent immigrants tend to settle in destination areas that have a large and well-defined co-ethnic population (Massey 1987; Portes and Rumbaut 2006). By settling among an established group of co-ethnic neighbors, immigrants benefit from the support of an extended network of friends and family members, including access to the accumulated knowledge

(Hernández-León and Zúñiga 2003), capital (Portes and Rumbaut 2006), and social support (Hagan 1998; Conley and Bohon 2010) of immigrants who came before them, and their offspring. As a result, immigrants might be better able to mobilize their neighbors to fight potentially polluting incursions into their community, thus improving local environmental conditions (Price and Feldmeyer 2012).

Of course, acting to improve the environment requires that immigrants have orientations toward environmentalism. Although not everyone concerned about the environment behaves in environmentally friendly ways, social scientists believe that pro-environmental behaviors are generally predicated on concerns about environmental harm (Dietz, Fitzgerald, and Shwom 2005). Research conducted in the 1990s examining differences in environmental attitudes and behaviors shows little difference between the environmental attitudes of all immigrants and US natives; however, immigrants who entered the United States as adults (i.e., at age 16 or older) expressed greater concern about pesticides, chemicals, pollution, and greenhouse effects than other immigrants or the US-born. Immigrants who arrived in the United States as adults were also more likely than US natives to engage in behaviors that benefit the environment, such as recycling (Hunter 2000b).

With regard to environmental behaviors and concerns, recent research confirms that immigrants are not much different from natives. However, when behaviors differ, immigrants are often more likely than natives to engage in conservation behavior, like saving water (Pfeffer and Stycos 2002). These behavioral differences may stem from the fact that immigrants may come from countries where they have faced severe drought or famine, or they may be more conscious of using resources like gasoline, electricity, or water, because these resources were relatively expensive in their home countries (Hunter 2000b). Immigrants also drive less, live in more densely populated households, and eat fewer processed foods (Neumayer 2006; White 2007; Bohon, Stamps, and Atiles 2008), and these environmentally friendly behaviors can influence non-immigrant residents in their communities to engage in similar behaviors (Feldmeyer 2009).

One of the reasons that there is little evidence that immigrants harm, improve, or have no effect on the environment – despite much speculation in all directions – is that it is very difficult to empirically establish exactly how harmful people are to the environment, regardless of whether or not they are immigrants (Lee 2011). Most ecologists have long considered environmental degradation, especially pollution, to be primarily caused by population growth, increases in population consumption, and the development of modern technology (Commoner, Corr, and Stamler 1971; Chertow 2001). Discussions of the interrelationship between these factors (cf. Ehrlich and Holdren 1971) assume – rather than establish – that population has an environmental impact (Dietz and Rosa 1994, 1997; Fischer-Kowalski and Amann 2001). This assumption is largely untested because environmental impact and technology are difficult to measure. For example, should environmental impact be determined by the level of a pollutant, or can it be better measured as resource use? Additionally, scientists have never resolved the debate regarding whether population pressures force technology improvements or whether technology improvements – like the creation of desalination plants – increase the carrying capacity of a place so that more human life can be sustained (Boserup 1981; Kates 1997).

Despite these difficulties, some researchers (e.g., Fischer-Kowalski and Amann 2001) have explicitly accounted for immigration in modeling human impact on the environment. They find little direct evidence of environmental harm. Still, many questions about the link between immigration and the environment remain unanswered.

Immigrants, in-migrants, and children

To determine whether immigrants have harmful impacts on the environment, demographers have suggested that it is necessary to separate the impact of immigrants from that of other people living in the areas where immigrants settle (Kraly 1998; Squalli 2009). Immigration is only one way in which an area's population can increase; local populations can also grow due to *in-migration* or increased fertility. In an area facing environmental problems like acid rain and air pollution, we must question the extent to which immigrants have contributed to these problems. Would environmental problems be lessened in the absence of immigrants?

To answer this question, Squalli (2010) examined air pollution levels in US states to see whether immigration was associated more strongly than in-migration with various types of air pollution. His results showed that the levels of nitrous oxide and sulfur dioxide in the air – which usually result from burning coal and can lead to acid rain and water contamination – are lower in states with a greater share of immigrants. Similar analysis at the county level (Squalli 2009) showed that levels of nitrous oxide and sulfur dioxide are higher in counties with relatively higher proportions of US-born residents. Furthermore, sulfur dioxide levels were lower in counties with a larger proportion of foreign-born residents.

Price and Feldmeyer (2012) extended Squalli's work to look at six measures of pollution in US metropolitan areas (the places where immigrants are concentrated) in an attempt to understand which type of growth – immigration, fertility, or internal migration – was most harmful to air quality. They found that immigration could not be linked directly or indirectly to air pollution levels even when air quality was measured in several different ways. In fact, a concentration of immigrants was associated with lower levels of nitrogen dioxide in the air, which suggests that immigration may stabilize local places and thereby encourage environmentally protective behaviors. At the same time, domestic migration (i.e., the redistribution of people within a country) was associated with higher concentrations of carbon monoxide, ground-level ozone, and overall air pollution. Population growth due to fertility was also associated with higher levels of nitrogen dioxide, ground-level ozone, and overall air pollution. From these findings, Price and Feldmeyer (2012: 137) conclude, "policies calling for reduced immigration on the grounds that it harms the environment may not be in line with social realities."

Part of the reason that immigrants do not contribute appreciably to air pollution and may actually reduce it is that their mode of travel is different. In the United States, more than three-quarters of American workers travel to work by driving alone each day, but immigrants are less likely to drive alone (Bohon, Stamps, and Atiles 2008). Examining workers in California, Blumenberg and Shiki (2008) discovered that immigrants are much more likely than the US-born to carpool to and from work. Furthermore, immigrants are still more likely than the US-born to carpool many years after immigrating, even though the likelihood that an immigrant drives alone to work increases with more time spent in the United States.

Of course, generating pollution is just one way that people can harm the environment. Examining the issue of sprawl, Fulton and his colleagues (2001) analyzed land use and population growth in every metropolitan area in the United States over a 15-year period. Defining sprawl as the increase in urban land use relative to the increase in population size, they found that metropolitan areas with high levels of immigration actually experienced less sprawl than places with fewer immigrants. Furthermore, the single greatest predictor of low levels of sprawl was the percentage of foreign-born residents. From these findings, the researchers concluded that "efforts by anti-immigration groups to link sprawl with immigration are misguided. Instead, immigration seems to be good for density and to mitigate other factors that lead to sprawl" (ibid.: 11). In fact, Los Angeles, the largest immigrant destination in the United States, is one of the few US metropolitan areas that is actually becoming denser (i.e., sprawling less) over time. This may be because most immigrants to the United States still settle in inner cities (Marcelli 2001) and because those who settle first in suburbs tend to choose older suburbs that are much closer to the inner city (Puentes and Warren 2006).

Immigration in global perspective

The interrelationship between immigration and the environment is complicated. Most demographers agree that the world is over-populated, and there is no possibility of an immediate end to population growth (cf. Røpke 2006). Thus, we tend to examine the effect of immigration on the environment from the perspective of receiving countries. But should we? The small body of work on immigrants and the environment demonstrates that immigrants who live in developed countries are at least less harmful to the environment than natives in the country of destination, especially if that destination is in the United States (Hunter 2000b; Neumayer 2006; White 2007; Bohon, Stamps, and Atiles 2008; Price and Feldmeyer 2012). At the same time, there is no arguing that rampant population growth can cause environmental harm. However, the focus on population size, distribution, and density in a single immigrant receiving area overlooks the global complexity of immigration and environmental degradation.

From an environmental perspective, the number of people on the planet is far less important than the impact of each person on the environment (see Pfeffer and Stycos 2002). In fact, people in developing countries have less impact per capita than those in developed nations (Ehrlich and Ehrlich 2004). Thus, some demographers worry that the migration of people from developing countries to developed countries increases the ecological footprint of the person who migrates (Kraly 1998). The United States – the world's leading immigrant receiver (Alonso 2011) – is populated by *superconsumers* (Daily, Ehrlich, and Ehrlich 1995). Writing for the Carrying Capacity Network, DinAlt (1997) notes, "The last thing the world needs is more Americans. The world just cannot afford what Americans do to the earth, air, and water." Although this may be true, we should consider the ethical ramifications of keeping people in one part of the world in extreme poverty so that those in another part of the world can continue to over-consume. Røpke (2006) argues:

> Usually these people [those who emigrate from developing countries and settle in developed countries] are among those whose conditions ought to be improved, so this should rather be seen as an advantage. If migration simultaneously implies an increase in total consumption (a question which is not directly addressed), the challenge is to decrease consumption levels of the already affluent rather than to avoid poor people improving their living conditions. Otherwise, the reasoning

tends to become ethically problematic – implying that the already established citizens of the affluent countries have more right to maintain high consumption levels than newcomers have to approach a high standard. (193)

The flow of immigrants from developing nations to developed nations is often attributable to environmental destruction and economic havoc created by corporations headquartered in the global North (Gustin and Ziebarth 2010). For this reason, environmental demographers (cf. Kraly 1998; Neumayer 2006) have argued that the best way to control population growth due to immigration is to remove the underlying causes that force migration in the first place. This can be done by improving education and the conditions of women in developing countries and creating more equitable income distributions worldwide (Pinstrup-Andersen and Pandya-Lorch 2001; United Nations 2001; Røpke 2006). The best method for reducing the impact of population on the environment is not to end immigration from the developing world, but for superconsumers in the developed world to consume much less (Ehrlich and Ehrlich 2004; Røpke 2006).

5

The Fertility of Immigrants

In 2006, the US *total fertility rate* – an estimate of the average number of children that women are likely to have – reached 2.1 children, its highest point in 35 years. The 2006 rate was especially notable because 2.1 is considered *replacement fertility* – the level at which women are replacing themselves and their partners. In the absence of immigration, numbers below the replacement rate eventually lead to population decline, and numbers above the replacement rate lead to population growth.

The announcement of the 2006 fertility rates received mixed responses. Many economists greeted the news with enthusiasm (Huang 2008), since population at replacement levels is assumed to stabilize the tax base and the future work force. However, some Americans were alarmed that the small rise in US fertility was largely attributable to the fertility of immigrants, many of whom are people of color. Research centers espousing the restriction of immigration, such as the Center for Immigration Studies (CIS), distributed policy briefings stressing that immigrants from countries that send the most immigrants to the United States were having more children than women who remained in their home countries (Camarota 2005). Nativist organizations such as the Federation for American Immigration Reform (FAIR) pressed legislators to enact policies aimed at reducing the impact of immigrant fertility by limiting government assistance and denying citizenship to the children of immigrants. In 2007, 97 legislators co-sponsored the Birthright Citizenship Act (Huang 2008), which sought to deny

---

The Fourteenth Amendment

The Fourteenth Amendment to the US Constitution, which was enacted in 1868, guarantees that "All persons born or naturalized in the United States, and subject to the jurisdiction thereof, are citizens of the United States and of the state wherein they reside." This means that any child born in the United States is a US citizen by birth, regardless of the immigration and citizenship status of his or her parent. Although several politicians have suggested changing this, amending the US Constitution is notoriously difficult – the most recently enacted Twenty-Seventh Amendment was proposed in 1789 and took 203 years to be ratified – and only one amendment has ever been repealed. Thus, it is unlikely that the United States will make a radical change to their citizenship requirements for some time.

---

citizenship to US-born children of immigrants. Although the 2007 bill ultimately failed, it has since reappeared numerous times. In 2013, 13 members of Congress introduced a bill in the House of Representatives to repeal the birthright citizenship provision of the Fourteenth Amendment to the US Constitution. These recent actions reflect alarm about immigrant fertility and popular concerns about "anchor babies."

"Anchor baby" is a pejorative term used to describe a child born in the United States to non-citizen immigrant parents. Under the principle of *jus soli* (right of soil), children born in the United States are US citizens, regardless of the immigration status of their parents. Since family reunification is one pathway by which immigrants may become lawful permanent residents (LPRs) of the United States, nativist groups have argued that some unauthorized immigrants enter the United States for the sole purpose of giving birth to children whose *birthright citizenship* can pave the way for the authorized entry of other family members

(Jacobson 2006). In reality, US-born children of immigrant parents must be 21 before they can petition for LPR status for their parents. At that time, their parents – if they are unauthorized immigrants – must usually return to their country of origin for at least ten years before they are eligible to re-enter the United States in authorized status. Thus, having a baby for the purpose of obtaining LPR status results in a process too lengthy to be practical. Nonetheless, an article in the ultra-conservative *Journal of American Physicians and Surgeons* argues that the children of immigrants are a criminal class and refers to the births of children to unauthorized immigrants as "illegal aliens' stealthy assaults on medicine" (Cosman 2005:6).

In retrospect, the 2006 rise in fertility represented a short-lived phenomenon. By 2010 – a year when the immigrant population of the United States had reached a record high – the US birth rate had actually dropped to its lowest recorded levels, with fertility declining 8 percent since 2007. Most of the decline was attributable to the decrease in childbearing among immigrant women. While US-born women's fertility dropped 6 percent in three years, fertility among foreign-born women dropped by 14 percent. For women born in Mexico – the country that sends the most immigrant women to the United States – the decline was 23 percent (Livingston and Cohn 2012).

Despite this decline, immigrant fertility represents a disproportionate share of all fertility. About 4 million babies are born annually in the United States, and about a quarter of those births are to immigrant women, even though immigrants comprise only 13 percent of the US population (ibid.). This is likely due to the fact that a large proportion of immigrants are of childbearing age (Parrado 2011). The immigrant population in every country is largely comprised of young people, while the native populations of most destination countries tend to be older. Consequently, a sizeable portion of current fertility and the projections for future growth depend upon the childbearing patterns of immigrants.

Fertility norms

Fertility is a biological (or *natural*) process. However, *fertility norms* and *fertility intentions* are socially determined. Fertility norms vary from country to country and shape women's fertility intentions, including the age at which women typically have children, how many children they have, and how closely they space their births (Bongaarts and Potter 1983). For example, women in Singapore and South Korea usually give birth at a much later age than women in the United States, and they tend to have fewer children. In the United States, women typically have two children. American women are expected to have, and expect to have, at least one child, but having an only child is somewhat stigmatized (Hagewen and Morgan 2005). At the same time, having four or five children is also an oddity. In countries such as Germany and Italy, it is common to have no children, and most women who have children have only one. In contrast, it is not unusual for women in developing countries to have four or five children, since children are considered an economic boon to parents and often the only means of a parents' social and economic support in old age.

Immigration results in changing social environments. This, in turn, may result in changing family formation patterns (Carlson 1985a). Thus, how fertility norms are altered through international migration is of great interest to demographers.

Many international migration flows originate in developing countries and terminate in developed countries (Okun and Kagya 2012). Since developing countries are marked by high fertility, and developed countries are marked by low fertility, scholars have often wondered how the interplay of developed and developing country fertility norms will play out in the short and long run. Overall, it is clear that immigrants have different fertility patterns from natives in the countries where they settle. The fertility patterns of immigrant women also differ from those of women in their country of origin. Explaining these differences has been difficult for demographers, and few demographers who study fertility agree on a single best explanation.

Currently, demographers offer several different theories to explain how the immigration process impacts the fertility of immigrant women and their children. These theories include the *disruption hypothesis, selection* (or *social characteristics*) *hypothesis, interrelation of events* (or *life course*) *hypothesis, adaptation hypothesis, assimilation hypothesis, socialization hypothesis*, and *legitimacy hypothesis* (see Kulu 2005; Milewski 2007, 2010; Okun and Kagya 2012). These theories are designed to explain differences in a variety of fertility measures between foreign-born and native-born women and sometimes between women who choose to immigrate and those who do not (Chattopadhyay, White, and Debpuur 2006). These fertility measures include *total fertility* (sometimes just called *fertility*), which is the average number of children women can expect to have if they do not die during their childbearing years and fertility patterns do not change. Other measures are *timing*, which refers to the age of the mother when she has a child or the length of time before a woman has a child after an important event (like marriage or the birth of an earlier child), and *lifetime* (or *completed*) *fertility*, which measures how many children women actually have.

The disruption hypothesis

The *disruption hypothesis* focuses on differences in birth timing between immigrant women and women who remain in their country of origin. This theory suggests that the process of migration temporarily disrupts the fertility of immigrant women; thus, women's fertility will decline immediately after immigration and later increase as immigrants spend more time in their host country (Mayer and Riphahn 2000).

Scholars who argue for the disruption hypothesis (Goldstein 1973; Carlson 1985b; Stephen and Bean 1992; Ng and Nault 1997; Abbasi-Shavazi and McDonald 2000; Roig Vila and Castro Martín 2007) point out that all moves are stressful. Immigrants must find jobs and homes in their new country and otherwise adjust to life in a new environment (Okun and Kagya 2012). The period of time immediately before, during, and after immigration is hectic and worrying, entailing great economic and psychological costs. These stressors preclude having children (Kulu 2005; Milewski 2007; Okun and Kagya 2012). Few women, given the choice, would choose to undertake an international move while pregnant, especially if those women already have small children to care for, and the adjustment period after immigration may be too stressful to consider adding an infant to the family (Milewski 2010). Additionally, migration may entail a periodic separation of spouses, which makes pregnancy unlikely (Chattopadhyay, White, and Debpuur 2006).

Finally, adjusting to a new country usually means adjusting to a vastly different way of life. When international migration involves movement from a developing country to a developed country, immigrants may experience on a personal level the changes that countries undergo during development, but at an accelerated pace (Coleman 1994; Milewski 2007). Among those who migrate from one developed country to another, their occupational status may be downgraded because credentials and job experience from their home country may not be valued equally in their new setting (Stier and Levanon 2003; Okun and Kagya 2012). This effect is seen among Russian immigrants in Israel (Gorodzeisky and Semyonov 2011). The drastic changes in day-to-day life in a new country may be so overwhelming that couples may postpone childbearing in order to minimize the number of simultaneous adjustments that they must make (Milewski 2007).

Upon adjusting to life in their new country, women may increase their fertility in order to achieve their fertility intentions; thus, fertility rates among immigrant women may spike a few years after migration (Mayer and Riphahn 2000; Milewski 2010; Lichter et al. 2012). In fact, many demographers assume that the higher fertility rates of immigrants represent the resumption of childbearing that was delayed due to migration (Goldstein and Goldstein 1981; Ford 1990; Toulemon and Mazuy 2004; Milewski 2007). Thus, immigrant fertility rates may be higher or lower than those of natives depending on which cohort of immigrant women is examined and the period of time since migration (Mayer and Riphahn 2000). If the fertility rates of the most recent immigrants are compared to natives, immigrant fertility will look especially low. Conversely if longer-term immigrant fertility is compared to the fertility of natives, then immigrant fertility will usually appear to be high (Kulu 2005; Milewski 2010).

There is mixed evidence for the disruption hypothesis. Early work by Goldstein in Thailand (1973) showed that the *lifetime fertility* of immigrant women – the total fertility of women who have completed their childbearing – was equal to that of natives, while the fertility of recent immigrants was much lower. Studies in the 1980s and 1990s supplied evidence of a disruption effect in Brazil (Hervitz 1985), Peru (White, Moreno, and Guo 1995), Australia (Carlson 1985b; Abbasi-Shavizi and McDonald 2000, 2002), Canada (Ram and George 1990; Ng and Nault 1997), and several African countries (Brockerhoff 1995). Mexican women who migrate to the United States also experience a disruption effect (Bean and Swicegood 1985; Stephen and Bean 1992), although the disruption seems to be short-lived (Ng and Nault 1997).

More recent research tends to refute the disruption hypothesis. Compellingly, Singley and Landale (1998) compared first-birth risks among women born in Puerto Rico living in the US mainland, women born in Puerto Rico living in Puerto Rico, and women of Puerto Rican descent born in and living in the US mainland. Although Puerto Rican women living in the United States are not immigrants, per se, their demographic characteristics more closely resemble those of immigrants than of mainland-born Americans (Spickard 2007). Overall, Puerto Rican women who moved to the US mainland had a higher risk of conception than the other two groups, which Singley and Landale attribute to the use of migration as a part of – rather than a delay of – the family building process. Milewski (2007: 884) speculates that having a child actually "marks the end of a couple's migration process. A child may also strengthen the position of an immigrant wife who 'completes' the union of the partners by becoming a mother, and this adds to the union the status of family." Findings similar to Singley and Landale's have also been seen in work on immigrants to Sweden (Andersson 2004), western Germany (Milewski 2007), and the Netherlands (Mulder and Wagner 2001).

Although recent studies offer little support for the disruption hypothesis, some researchers continue to find evidence suggesting that the uncertainty and hardship of international migration disrupts fertility for some groups. For example, the very low fertility of immigrants from former Soviet countries who live in Israel has been attributed to disruption, since fertility among these women appears to decline substantially in the years just before and after immigration and increases after two or more years in Israel (Okun and Kagya 2012). Recent work in the United States comparing Mexican immigrants in new destinations (who show a disruption effect) to those in established destinations (who do not) also demonstrates that some destinations are more disruptive of fertility than others (Lichter et al. 2012). Overall, there is evidence for a disruption hypothesis with some groups in some places.

The selection hypothesis

The *selection hypothesis* (sometimes called the *social characteristics hypothesis*) attempts to explain why the fertility of immigrant women often differs from the fertility of women in their country of origin (Milewski 2010; Lichter et al. 2012; Okun and Kagya 2012). For example, Mexican women living in the United States have more children, on average, than those who continue to reside in Mexico (Parrado and Morgan 2008), possibly because those who migrate tend to be from rural areas and are less well educated than those who remain in Mexico (Frank and Heuveline 2005). Proponents of the selection hypothesis (e.g., Chattopadhyay, White, and Debpuur 2006) stress that those who choose to immigrate are different from those who stay, and that these differences can have a marked effect on fertility. In general, immigrants are younger and more highly educated than the people they leave behind; there may also be a difference in marriage rates between movers and stayers (Macisco, Bouvier, and Renzi 1969; Goldstein, White, and Goldstein 1997; Hwang and Saenz 1997; Frank and Heuveline 2005). Highly educated couples are more likely to carefully plan their pregnancies; as a result, the more educated tend to have fewer children (Coleman 1994; Ng and Nault 1997; Okun and Kagya 2012). At the same time, most people have children when they are young adults, so immigrants – who tend to be younger – often appear to have high fertility because they are arriving in a new country at a time when they are beginning to have children. Despite this appearance of high fertility, their completed fertility often ends up being low (Toulemon 2004; Parrado 2011).

Immigrants may also vary from non-immigrants in ways that are more difficult to observe and measure. Those who immigrate may be more ambitious, more upwardly mobile, or have higher educational aspirations for their children than those who do not immigrate. These immigrants are likely to want fewer children (and to have them at later ages) than those who remain in their country of origin (Lindstrom and Saucedo 2007; Milewski 2007). Difficult to measure differences such as intentions and ambitions are referred to as *unobserved selectivity*. Unobserved selectivity likely accounts for many of the fertility differences between movers and stayers (Kulu 2005).

People who immigrate voluntarily are also free (within limits) to select their destination (Kulu 2005). In doing so, immigrants may select countries where women's fertility is closer to their own intended family size (Mussino and Strozza 2012; Okun and Kagya 2012). Among those who choose to migrate, those who desire large families may select one destination, while those who desire small families may choose another (Lindstrom and Saucedo 2002; Chattopadhyay, White, and Debpuur 2006; Lichter et al. 2012). In this situation, the completed fertility of immigrant women will be roughly the same as the completed fertility of women in the country of destination but different from women in their country of origin and different from women of the same national origin living in a different country (Macisco, Bouvier, and Renzi 1969; Hwang and Saenz 1997; Kreyenfeld 2002; Milewski 2007).

A substantial body of research spanning nearly half a century comparing rural–urban, urban–urban, and rural–rural moves *within* countries such as Ghana (Chattopadhyay, White, and Debpuur 2006), Peru (White, Moreno, and Guo 1995), Thailand

(Goldstein and Goldstein 1981), and the Philippines (Hendershot 1971), provides consistent evidence that some destinations attract one type of migrant while other destinations attract another. Fewer studies establish a selection effect among international migrants; however, some recent research (e.g., Milewski 2007) suggests that selection affects fertility. Okun and Kagya's (2012) study of immigrants from the former Soviet Union to Israel demonstrates that these immigrants tend to be highly selective from among those with very high occupational and income aspirations. As such, immigrant women in Israel tend to postpone childbearing and have fewer children.

The selection process can also be quite complicated. Milewski's (2007, 2010) work on migration to western Germany illustrates that some immigration is motivated by childbearing, while other immigration *to and from the same country* is not. Milewski shows that Turkish, Greek, Slavic, Italian, and Spanish women who migrate to Germany to be reunited with a spouse or to get married generally have a first child soon after migration. In contrast, women who are single when they immigrate have delayed childbearing patterns, possibly because of the added difficulty of finding a partner in a new environment. Additionally, it is harder for women with children to immigrate than those without; as a consequence, immigrant women may delay childbearing until after their move, aligning both the selection and the disruption hypotheses (Toulemon 2004).

Overall, when we compare fertility rates between immigrants and non-immigrants of the same age, education, and marital status, we usually observe few differences (Bean and Tienda 1990; Schoorl 1990; Frank and Heuveline 2005; Poston, Chang, and Dan 2006; Milewski 2007). This provides considerable support for the idea of immigrant selection.

The interrelation of events hypothesis

Demographers have long speculated on the potential impact of immigrant fertility on the future of developed countries (see, for example, Sevak and Schmidt 2008; Ceobanu and Koropeckyj-Cox 2013). On the one hand, high fertility among immigrant women could offset the problems of population aging in low-fertility nations by providing a pool of younger workers who contribute to national retirement and health care systems (Jonsson and Rendall 2004; Sevak and Schmidt 2008), although there are strict conditions under which this can happen (see chapter 6). On the other hand, high fertility among immigrant women will substantially alter the ethnic (and, in some cases, racial) composition of countries, leading some social commentators to argue that these demographic changes may result in ethnic strife and social fragmentation (Huntington 2004a).

Scholars such as Parrado (2011) suggest that both the optimistic and pessimistic visions of the demographic future are distorted because the total fertility rates for immigrant women are often inaccurate representations of the true fertility patterns of these women. Thus, although the Census Bureau estimates that Latinos will become the majority of the US population by 2042 (US Census Bureau 2008), Parrado (2011) argues that this prediction is over-blown, as estimates of the fertility of immigrant women from Latin America are inflated by the failure to account for, among other things, the *interrelation of events* around immigration.

The interrelation of events hypothesis (also sometimes called the *family formation* or *life course hypothesis*) is based on the idea that migration and union formation are often interrelated events (Okun and Kagya 2012). When couples form a household, at least one, and usually both, of the partners relocate. Although this family-motivated relocation usually occurs within countries, some of it occurs across national boundaries. Since childbearing generally occurs soon after marriage, childbearing will often soon follow immigration if immigration occurs because of marriage (Milewski 2007, 2010). Thus, the fertility rate of recent immigrants may be high because immigration also coincides with marriage, cohabitation, or partner reunification.

In fact, immigrant fertility may have no important impact on the future of developed countries; if there is an impact, it is impossible to predict. To understand this, it is important to note that the *total fertility rate* (TFR) is calculated by estimating the number of children a woman will have, on average, if she survives her childbearing years (usually assumed to be ages 15 to 44) and she gives birth at the same age-specific fertility rates as other women. Because the fertility rate calculation is premised on certain assumptions, the TFR is a hypothetical rate, rather than a measure of the true fertility experience of women. In contrast, the *completed fertility rate* (CFR) provides the average number of children born to women who are now beyond their childbearing years (usually 50 or older). Although the CFR is more accurate than the TFR, the TFR is usually used in projecting the size and composition of future populations, since the CFR often changes from generation to generation. In any given year, the TFR will underestimate the CFR if women delay childbearing. In other words, when used in population projections, the TFR will underestimate future population size. Conversely, if women accelerate childbearing, the TFR will overestimate the CFR, and population projections will overestimate future population size. If the interrelation of events hypothesis holds, then US population projections overestimate the future size of the Latino population.

The interrelation of events hypothesis contrasts sharply with the disruption hypothesis; whereas the former theory assumes that fertility will spike soon after immigration, the latter assumes that fertility will fall during the same period. Yet, the two theories are not entirely at odds. In general, immigrants experience disruption; however, immigrants whose motivation for moving is linked specifically to union formation demonstrate higher rates of fertility immediately after the move (Andersson 2004; Lindstrom and Saucedo 2007), but we should not assume that the completed fertility rates of these immigrants will be high in the long run. For example, Toulemon (2004) found that women who immigrated to France between the ages of 25 and 30 had a higher fertility rate than French-born women; however, completed fertility for immigrant women was ultimately lower. He attributes the difference to union- and reunion-associated migration behavior. Milewski (2007) finds a similar pattern among immigrants to Germany; Milewski also points out that some women immigrate to join their husbands because they are pregnant. The interrelation of events hypothesis is also supported by research in the Netherlands (Schoorl 1990; Alders 2000), Canada (Ram and George 1990; Ng and Nault 1997), Sweden (Andersson 2004), and the United States (Singley and Landale 1998; Parrado 2011).

The adaptation and assimilation hypotheses

The disruption and interrelation of events theories attempt to explain immigrant fertility in the short run. In contrast, the adaptation hypothesis provides a mid-range perspective, and the assimilation hypothesis provides a long-term perspective. Although theoretically distinct (Okun and Kagya 2012), both the adaptation and the assimilation hypotheses assume that the fertility intentions and behaviors of immigrants will become indistinguishable from the fertility behaviors of women in the host society as immigrants adapt to their new environment (Kulu 2005; Chattopadhyay, White, and Debpuur 2006; Milewski 2007; Okun and Kagya 2012). Assuming the new country has lower fertility norms, immigrant women will bear fewer children the more time they spend in a new country. Thus, when immigrants from high-fertility countries move to low-fertility countries, the completed fertility of immigrant women or their children will be very similar to that of women in the host society (Kahn 1988; Chattopadhyay, White and Debpuur 2006). The adaptation hypothesis predicts that immigrant fertility will decline so that immigrant women will have fewer children than women in their native country. According to the assimilation hypothesis, over time and generations, the fertility of the descendants of immigrants will become indistinguishable from the fertility of women in their host country.

Demographers have posited two explanations for why immigrants adapt their fertility behaviors (Kulu 2005; Chattopadhyay, White and Debpuur 2006). The first explanation is based in economic change. Sometimes people migrate from places that put a high economic value on children to places where children are an economic burden. In agrarian societies with low levels of economic development, children are an economic boon to their parents, providing household labor when they are young and economic support to their parents when they are adults. In developed societies, children are more costly – primarily due to education – so children represent a substantial opportunity cost in terms of earnings and education potentially forgone by their parents (Becker and Tomes 1976). Assuming that people make a trade-off between the "quality" and quantity of children (Angrist, Lavy, and Schlosser 2005), people in developed countries often forgo large families in order to seek greater earning potential and more education, and they desire the same for their children.

Socioeconomic conditions in developed countries are also less conducive to large families. Researchers examining rural–urban migration within countries, for example, note that single-family dwellings in rural locations provide more space for children than multi-family units in cities, and this explains the decline in fertility among rural-to-urban migrants (Michielin 2002; Kulu 2005). On an international scale, higher costs of living, more expensive trans-portation systems, and more costly social demands also depress fertility in developed countries (Kohler, Billari, and Ortega 2002; Adserà 2004; Perelli-Harris 2008), and immigrants from develop-ing countries experience these factors immediately when they enter a developed country. Additional economic hardships associated with immigration also depress fertility (Okun and Kagya 2012). As Milewski (2007: 886) notes, "Immigrants react to similar cir-cumstances in a similar manner to people of the host society. This applies to the impact of educational attainment, employment, and union formation on fertility and confirms the hypothesis of adap-tation." For all of these reasons, women who enter a low-fertility society from a high-fertility society tend to have fewer children than women who remain in their country of origin.

Although socioeconomic conditions in developed countries explain fertility adaptation (i.e., the lower fertility of immigrant women from developing countries), a second explanation for fertil-ity decline – the explanation that supports assimilation theory – is that of sociocultural change. Developed countries operate under *modern fertility regimes* where a high value is placed on small families. Although some of the low fertility rates in developed nations can be attributed to the economic trade-off between the "quality" and quantity of children, Morgan (1996) argues that economic justifications do not fully account for differences in fertility patterns *between* countries. Although it is unusual to have four or more children in all developed country contexts, childlessness is uncommon in the United States and fairly common in Germany and Italy. The United States also has a high level of teen childbearing, while teen childbearing is virtually unheard of in Japan. These differences are attributable to cultural norms and values related to childbearing (Hartnett 2012). As immigrants from developing countries spend more time in a developed country, they gradually adopt these cultural norms and values through interactions with new friends and peers (Caldwell 1982; Kohler 2000; Okun and Kagya 2012). Additionally, the children of immigrants are likely to be even more immersed in a new culture in which they will be socialized with low-fertility norms and values.

Considerable evidence supports both the adaptation and assimilation hypotheses, although the processes are difficult to distinguish empirically. For many years, researchers have shown that fertility differences between immigrants and natives converge over time (Nauck 1987; Ford 1990; Mayer and Riphahn 2000). In fact, the fertility-depressing effect can occur rapidly, and this has led many demographers to conclude that socioeconomic conditions may play a larger role in suppressing fertility than cultural conditions (Friedlander, Eisenbach, and Goldscheider 1980; Gjerde and McCants 1995; Andersson and Scott 2005). For example, Andersson (2004) finds that the fertility patterns of most immigrants in Sweden are indistinguishable from those of native-born Swedes after only five years, which he attributes to economic conditions. Roig Vila and Castro Martín (2007) find a similar five-year convergence between immigrants to Spain and Spanish-born women. In fact, a review of the immigrant fertility literature shows that, across Europe, most immigrant fertility patterns converge with native fertility patterns within ten years (Sobotka 2008), which probably is not enough time for immigrants to be resocialized with new norms and values.

Convergence does not always happen quickly, however (Lindstrom and Saucedo 2007; Lichter et al. 2012). It may take a generation or more for immigrant fertility to parallel the fertility of natives. In Germany and the United States, the fertility patterns of the children of immigrants are often indistinguishable from those of natives (Mayer and Riphahn 2000; Milewski 2007; Parrado and Morgan 2008; Fischer and Mattson 2009). Moreover, immigrants who enter their host country at an early age tend to adopt the fertility patterns of their host country (Toulemon 2004; Parrado 2011), a finding that supports the importance of culture.

The socialization hypothesis

The socialization hypothesis does not predict a distinct outcome for immigrant fertility; instead, the socialization hypothesis argues that women's fertility behavior is influenced most by the dominant values, norms, and behaviors in the society where they spent their childhood (Goldberg 1959; Kulu 2005; Milewski 2007). Thus, if a woman immigrates as an adult, she is likely to conform to the fertility behaviors common to women in her country of origin. If a woman immigrated as a child, she is more likely to adapt to the fertility patterns of the host society.

Understanding the effect of socialization on fertility is complicated by the fact that it is difficult to determine the extent to which immigrants and their descendants are immersed in the meaning-system of their new country (Milewski 2010). Early researchers assumed a linear process of fertility assimilation, such that each subsequent generation of immigrants would have fewer children than their parents (Gordon 1964; Kahn 1988; Stephen and Bean 1992). More recently, however, demographers acknowledge that poor reception contexts and racial and ethnic discrimination often force immigrants to insulate themselves from broader society by creating strong co-ethnic communities (Portes and Zhou 1993; Kahn 1994; Milewski 2007, 2010). The distinctive cultural traits of some co-ethnic communities, such as pronatalist values, early marriage norms, and traditional gender roles, may slow fertility assimilation (Hartnett 2012; Lichter et al. 2012; Okun and Kagya 2012). This phenomenon of segmented assimilation calls into question the socialization hypothesis' simple assumption that women's fertility norms will be most influenced by the country in which they spent their childhood.

Much of the evidence for the socialization hypothesis is indirect. Milewski (2010) finds that the decline in fertility of women from Turkey, the former Yugoslavia, Greece, Italy, and Spain after immigrating to Germany depends somewhat on the fertility levels of their home countries, but their children tend to exhibit fertility patterns similar to women from western Germany. Other European countries experience similar patterns (Schoorl 1990; Alders 2000; Andersson and Scott 2005; Sobotka 2008). Hartnett (2012) argues that socialization also explains why Latina immigrants in the United States are happier about unintended pregnancies than US-born Latinas.

Sometimes the effect on fertility is different from what is expected, and researchers have to rethink the mechanisms by which socialization may be operating. Lichter and his colleagues (Lichter et al. 2012) assumed that Latino immigrants in established destinations in the United States would have higher fertility than those in new destinations, because it would be easier for indigenous Latino fertility norms to operate in established destinations where the Latino immigrant population is larger. Instead, they found that fertility rates were higher among immigrants in new destinations – a result they call "surprising" (ibid.: 788).

The legitimacy hypothesis

A very recent theory of immigrant fertility that has not been widely explored by demographers is the legitimacy hypothesis. This theory concentrates less on the number of children that immigrant women have and focuses instead on the motivation for having children. According to this theory, immigrant women may be motivated to have children not because of socialization or assimilation factors, but because having a child in a host country may strengthen family efforts to gain rights in their new society (Bledsoe 2004). The focus for these immigrants is on family security and the way that the right to remain in their host country and to gain resources can be secured through a child (Toulemon and Mazuy 2004; Bledsoe, Houle, and Sow 2007; Milewski 2007). According to the legitimacy hypothesis, women are motivated to have a child soon after immigration to ensure the family's security in their new setting.

The legitimacy hypothesis can only be applied to immigrants in countries where the sociopolitical conditions are such that childbearing is beneficial. Even so, demographers have not found much empirical support for the hypothesis in such countries, although it has not been tested extensively (Milewski 2007). However, there are important reasons to consider how political contexts might affect fertility. In the United States, the Fourteenth Amendment guarantees citizenship to children of immigrants, and immigration policy prioritizes family reunification. In Germany, women receive a two-year child-care benefit. At the same time, women who immigrate to Germany for the purposes of family reunification are prohibited from obtaining work permits during the first few years after immigrating. These policies, in tandem, may motivate women to have a child soon after immigrating (ibid.).

Immigration and fertility

Table 5.1 summarizes the various theories used by demographers to explain the interrelationship between immigration and fertility.

These theories are not necessarily mutually exclusive. For example, the disruption hypothesis assumes that fertility initially declines after immigration and then increases, but this theory is not intended to predict lifetime fertility for individual women or to suggest whether total fertility rates for immigrant women will be lower or higher than those of native women in the long run (Mayer and Riphahn 2000). Instead, disruption affects only fertility timing, not overall fertility (Lindstrom and Saucedo 2002;

Table 5.1 Immigrant fertility theories

Theory	Impact on fertility
Disruption	Fertility will decline in the period immediately prior to and following immigration but will increase with time in the destination country.
Selection	Immigrant fertility will differ from the fertility of women from the same origin country who do not immigrate.
Interrelation of events	Immigrant fertility will increase immediately after immigration, but completed fertility may ultimately be higher than, lower than, or the same as women in the destination country.
Adaptation	Immigrant fertility will be lower than that of women from their sending countries if women move from a high-fertility regime to a low-fertility regime.
Assimilation	Over time and generations, immigrant fertility will become indistinguishable from the fertility of women in the host country.
Socialization	Fertility change among immigrants will depend on the values, norms, and behaviors that were dominant in the environment in which they spent their childhood.
Legitimacy	Immigrant women will have at least one child as soon as possible after immigrating.

Chattopadhyay, White, and Debpuur 2006). The assimilation hypothesis predicts changes in fertility over generations that can occur in the presence or absence of disruption. Moreover, these hypotheses do not necessarily compete in their explanatory power. Thus, researchers found strongest support for the adaptation hypothesis in a study of fertility among migrants and non-migrants in Estonia (Kulu 2005), but they also found evidence for the inter-relation of events hypothesis and the selection hypothesis. In a study of immigrants from the former Soviet Union to Israel (Okun and Kagya 2012), the authors found evidence of both disruption and socialization.

At the same time, some theories point to similar outcomes, so it is difficult to establish which mechanism best explains fertility patterns. For example, if women reduce their fertility immediately after immigrating, is it because of disruption or because of adaptation (see Ben-Porath 1973)? In other words, are falling fertility rates due to short-term disruptions or are they explained by an early move to convergence with native fertility levels? A similar issue arises when women have children immediately after immigrating. Is such a pattern due to the reception context as the legitimacy hypothesis might suggest, or do such patterns result from the selection of younger women as immigrants or the interrelationship of immigration, marriage, and childbearing?

6

Replacement Migration to Offset
Population Aging

One of the most pressing demographic issues faced by developed
nations is *population aging* (Schafer 1998; Bonin, Raffelhüschen,
and Walliser 2000; Herrmann 2012). Population aging occurs
when the proportion of older people grows faster than the
working-age and child populations, because *vital rates* – the rates
at which people die and give birth – are low (Preston, Himes and
Eggers 1989). In countries like Italy, women, on average, have
only one child, which means that the number of people in the
younger generations is much smaller than that in the older generations for whom fertility rates were higher (Bouvier 2001).

The age at which someone is "old" is both personal and cultural (Martin 1991). However, most demographers mark old age
at 65, since this is the age at which people in developed societies
usually begin to disengage from work and other social responsibilities (Uhlenberg 1992). Demographers also designate a subset
of the old as the *oldest old*, usually people who are 85 and older
(Jacobsen et al. 2011). In most of Europe, Japan, Korea, and the
United States, the number of people in the oldest old age group
has remained fairly stable for some time, but the number of people
between 65 and 85 is growing rapidly and will continue to grow
(United Nations 2001).

There is no single way to measure population aging, nor is
there a consensus regarding at what point a society is considered
old. Simpler methods of measuring the age of society include
calculating the *mean* (or average) *age* of the people living in a

country, estimating the *median age* (the age point at which half of the population is older and half of the population is younger), or examining the percentage of people 65 and older. Somewhat more complex measurements include the *old-age dependency ratio* which is calculated by dividing the total number of people aged 65 and older by the total number of working-age people (usually considered ages 15–64) and multiplying the quotient by 100. The product represents the total number of elderly persons for every 100 working-age persons in the population (Northcott 1994).

Each method of measuring population age shows that most populations are aging. The mean age is getting older and the proportion of the aged is increasing everywhere in the world except Africa. This trend has been occurring for some time (cf. Preston, Himes, and Eggers 1989; Jacobsen et al. 2011). Population aging is most evident in Japan, where 25 percent of the population is 65 or older; Italy and Germany are close behind. In the United States, 10 percent of the population was 65 or older in 1970; by 2050, it is projected that the proportion of the elderly will double (Jacobsen et al. 2011).

As the proportion of older people grows and the number of working-age people declines, societies struggle to maintain a strong tax base and economic productivity while providing adequate health care and public pensions for the aged. Policies to offset the problems of population aging through demographic change are limited (Espenshade 1994; Herrmann 2012; Ceobanu and Koropeckyj-Cox 2013), and it is generally expected that life expectancy everywhere will continue to increase at least modestly (Bouvier 2001; United Nations 2001). Several countries have tried to encourage women to have more children, but such policies have proven largely ineffective (Martin 1991; Hoem 2008). Thus, many societies have considered encouraging immigration from developing nations to increase the stock of working-age people (Lutz and Prinz 1992; Ceobanu and Koropeckyj-Cox 2013). This type of population movement is referred to as *replacement migration* (United Nations 2001).

To some extent, population aging is an inevitable outcome of economic development (Espenshade 1994). This is illustrated

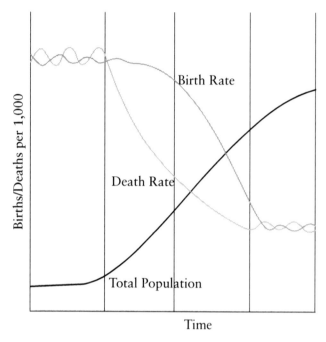

Figure 6.1 Demographic transition model

Source: Wikimedia Commons (NikNaks)

in the *demographic transition theory*. Initially articulated by Thompson (1929), the theory suggests that modernization occurs in four stages. Each of these stages is related to dramatic population change. In the first, or pre-modern, stage of the demographic transition, levels of economic development are low, and fertility and mortality levels are high. Since pre-modern societies are largely agrarian, there is little motivation to limit fertility and few means to do so. Because of widespread disease and hunger, few children survive into adulthood, and those who do are unlikely to survive to old ages. As societies begin to urbanize and industrialize – the second stage of the demographic transition – they develop more complex sanitation systems and invent more efficient methods of producing food. As a consequence, mortality declines dramatically. Still, the second stage is marked with high population growth, and fertility remains high as people continue to anticipate the death of many children. As modernizing societies become more confident that their children will live, they begin to have fewer children, thus putting the society into the third stage. In this stage, population growth slows as fertility declines. In the fourth – or post-modern – stage of the demographic transition, both fertility and mortality rates are low. In this final stage, populations grow slowly, stagnate, or even decline. Most importantly, populations age (Kirk 1996).

The demographic transition theory offers substantial insight into the link between economic development and population aging (Caldwell 2006), and it provides theoretical support for the idea of replacement migration: every society should benefit if "excess" people from countries in the second or even third stage of the demographic transition relocate to countries in the fourth stage with aging populations (cf. Bouvier 2001).

Social problems associated with population aging

Population aging is associated with many social problems. First, as the working-age population shrinks, productivity potentially declines, thereby reducing economic growth (Bluestone, Montgomery, and Owen 1990; Bijak, Kupiszewska, and Kupiszewski 2008; Herrmann 2012). Second, aging populations are likely to experience economic recession, since the elderly tend to buy less than younger people (Dohm 2000). Third, aging societies face greater demands for health care, including mental health care and longer-term care (Espenshade 1994; Herrmann 2012). Fourth, population aging is associated with increased economic insecurity for some groups. This is because fertility among racial minorities tends to be somewhat higher than fertility among whites, and racial minorities disproportionately live in poverty. Moreover, the elderly who are racial minorities often have smaller pensions and savings, and those who are immigrants may have less access to social security programs (Preston et al. 2013).

Fifth, and perhaps most importantly, aging populations face

the task of maintaining adequate public pension systems as an increasing number of people reach retirement age (Herrmann 2012). In the United States, some worry that the retirement of the baby boom generation will bankrupt the Social Security system (Knickman and Snell 2002), a pay-as-you-go program whereby the working-age population provides income for the aged through payroll taxes. A similar system operates in Japan, where the proportion of elderly is much larger (Martin 1991; Jacobsen et al. 2011). Both countries must maintain enough working-age people to fund an income stream for a growing elderly population. Other countries like Singapore have a fully funded provident system, in which money contributed during the working ages is saved and invested to fund those same workers when they reach retirement age. However, as the elderly population grows, Singapore, too, must contend with the potential for insufficient public pension funds, especially in the face of economic shocks that have decimated investments (Martin 1991; Beng 2012). Regardless of the system, the elderly in all developed countries are primarily dependent upon public pension systems for support in their old age, and the collapse of these systems would have a disastrous effect on the economic security of the aged (Uhlenberg 1992).

The United States is currently debating a wide-scale reform of its immigration system. A primary target of reform is to reduce the number of unauthorized immigrants residing in the United States by providing better pathways to legal residency (Capps and Fix 2013; Sommers 2013). Such reforms would improve the lives of millions currently living in the shadows, but the United States' Social Security system is heavily supplemented by unauthorized immigrants who currently deposit billions of dollars into Social Security coffers by working with falsified documents, including fake Social Security Numbers. In 2007, 10.8 million workers deposited more than US$90 million into the Social Security system with Social Security Numbers that could not be matched to individuals (Goss et al. 2013). Because unauthorized immigrants cannot draw Social Security in their old age, and because their contributions are usually entered with false identification numbers, their contributions effectively act as free money to the federal system.

A loss of this income stream will eventually have a negative effect on the US Social Security system, and opponents of immigration reform have used this argument as grounds for halting humanitarian reforms (Biggs 2013). Few demographers would support the continued exploitation of unauthorized workers simply to protect the public pension system, but loss of Social Security revenue is a real problem that must be managed if immigration reform takes place.

Most people support societal goals of maintaining an economically secure elderly population (Herrmann 2012). Economic security means that people have enough money to provide for their needs and that people can be generally assured of an adequate flow of income (Preston et al. 2013). However, economic well-being is not enough. Policies to support the aged are also aimed at ensuring physical, social, and emotional well-being. Ensuring these types of well-being means maintaining a level of health sufficient to live independently, interact with others, and perform daily activities (Kaneda, Lee, and Pollard 2011).

Maintaining the health of the elderly is increasingly expensive because the number of elderly people is growing, people are living longer, and health care costs are escalating. The majority of health issues occur in old age, and the diseases of old age (e.g., cancer, heart disease, and stroke) are expensive to treat. Every developed country provides publicly funded health care for the elderly, and, each year, the cost of providing this care has increased. As with concerns about pension programs, most countries worry that they will not be able to sustain the quality of life of the elderly of future generations.

Policymakers in developed countries have framed the social problems associated with population aging in terms of an abundance of elderly people, rather than as the mismanagement of social security funds, a problem of stagnating economic growth, or an attachment to excessively lavish lifestyles that makes maintaining an aging population difficult (Abernethy 2001; Grant 2001; Meyerson 2001; Coleman 2002; Saczuk 2003; Herrmann 2012). Because of this frame, policymakers are limited in their ability to offer good solutions to offset the immense costs of maintaining an aging population with an acceptable level of well-being. For example, a focus on aging instead of unemployment ignores the fact that countries can maintain high levels of productivity even if the working-age population shrinks (Herrmann 2012).

Because the aging population is framed as a problem, and old people are seen as the source of the problem, commonly proposed solutions to population aging are to increase the tax burden on the working-age population, increase the retirement age, encourage more working-age people – especially women – to participate in the labor force, and reduce social benefits to the elderly or limit benefits only to the neediest of the old (United Nations 2001; Herrmann 2012). The US government has done all four. In 1983, the Congress amended the Social Security Act by increasing the retirement age from 65 to 67, increasing the percentage salary contribution of working-age people to the Social Security system, and reducing social security benefits (Espenshade 1994).

The extent to which people will tolerate policy changes of this type varies from country to country. Canadians, for example, have expressed a strong reluctance to tolerate reduced benefits (Northcott 1994). This makes replacement migration an attractive political solution (Ceobanu and Koropeckyj-Cox 2013) in many European countries and Australia, and there has been much discussion about this approach in the United Nations (Dini 2000; Annan 2004 in Ceobanu and Koropeckyj-Cox 2013), in Australia and Canada, and in the European Parliament (Ceobanu and Koropeckyj-Cox 2013). As Herrmann (2012: 24) notes:

> It sometimes appears as though countries are caught between a rock and a hard place, and have at best limited policy leverage to escape this situation. Either they increase taxes on the active labor force and effectively decrease the living standards of the labor force, or they decrease benefits to dependents and thereby decrease the living standards of dependents, or they run up public debt and thereby decrease living standards of future generations. Any possible action by countries, it seems, will lead to the impoverishment of somebody.

Can immigration offset population aging?

In 2001, the United Nations Population Division released a report on the future of Europe, Japan, Korea, and the United States. The report concluded that most of these countries will experience a shrinking and aging population in the twenty-first century due to low levels of fertility. The report implies that every country except the United States needs to increase international migration from its current levels "as the only option in the short to medium term to reduce decline" (United Nations 2001: 4).

Overall, demographers have been less enthusiastic than politicians about the concept of replacement migration. In response to the United Nations report, several demographers (Bouvier 2001; Espenshade 2001; Keely 2001; Coleman 2002; Saczuk 2003) criticized its tone and conclusions. Beyond the concern that the report seemed to focus exclusively on replacement migration as the only solution to population aging, demographers also noted that the United Nations' projections of the size of the future elderly population may be overstated. Determining the size and composition of future populations – using a variety of methods called *population forecasting formulas* – is an inexact science. Forecasting is based on current or expected fertility and mortality trends, and unanticipated changes can yield forecasts that are scientifically sound but nevertheless incorrect (Lutz and Prinz 1992; Uhlenberg 1992). Additionally, accurate population forecasting requires accurate estimates of future changes to the immigrant population, and those numbers are the most difficult to estimate (Young 1994).

Most population projections – including those generated by the United Nations – suggest that immigration can offset population aging in the short run because most immigrants are of working age, so their presence immediately increases the size of the working population relative to other age groups (Lutz and Prinz 1992). Additionally, immigrants tend to migrate in their childbearing years, so it is reasonable to assume that they will have children, which will in turn lower the median age of the population (Espenshade 2001). There is also a widespread assumption that women who immigrate to developing countries have higher fertility than native women. However, as we discussed in chapter 5, this assumption is called into question, at least in the US context, in recent work by Parrado (2011).

There is a general consensus among demographers that increasing immigration will be ineffective at reducing the pressures of population aging in the long run (Bouvier 2001; Espenshade 2001; Keely 2001; Coleman 2002; Bijak et al. 2008; Coleman 2008). The simplest reason is that immigrants – like all other humans – age. Unless immigrants return to their country of origin when they reach old age, immigration only provides a temporary solution. Replacement migration is only effective at lowering the age structure in the short run. Thus, Coleman refers to the political promotion of replacement migration as a demographic "Ponzi scheme" (2008: 467).

For replacement migration to be effective over the long run, the stream of immigrants would need to be very large and immediate, and the high level of immigration would need to be sustained indefinitely (Bouvier 2001; Coleman 2008). To illustrate this, demographers rely on the *stationary population* concept. A stationary population is a hypothetical population in which there is no immigration and the birth and death rates are constant. Although the population can increase or decrease in size, the percentage of the population in each age group remains constant over time. That is, the population does not age. In the absence of immigration, most developed countries would approximate stationary populations, since both fertility and mortality decline more slowly as they reach their limits. Opening a stationary population to immigration would increase the proportionate size of the working- and young age groups for a short time and would decrease the proportionate size of the aging population – not because there are fewer old people, but because the percentage of elderly would go down. However, if immigration continued at a constant rate, the population would again become stationary (Martin 1991) unless immigrants and their descendants had fertility rates higher than replacement fertility, which is rarely the case (see chapter 5).

Most population projections suggest that increasing fertility would be far more effective than encouraging replacement migration to reduce the problems of population aging (Lutz, O'Neill, and Scherbov 2003; Bijak et al. 2007). Although pronatalist policies have never been seriously considered in the United States (Martin 1991), several countries in Europe, East Asia, and Oceania offer tax rebates and other financial incentives to encourage women to have children (Guest 2007; Bongaarts 2008). Overall, these "baby bonus" policies have had little effect on increasing fertility (McDonald 2006; Hoem 2008). Additionally, policies that ban contraception or abortion raise ethical issues, even though they would likely increase fertility (Teitelbaum and Winter 1985). Thus, replacement immigration remains a politically viable (although ultimately ineffective) alternative.

As previously noted, replacement migration may reduce population aging if the migration were large-scale and if immigrants did not ultimately contribute to the old-age cohorts. However, the experience with guest workers in Germany and unauthorized immigrants in the United States shows how such schemes can be doomed to failure. West Germany instituted a formal guest worker program in the late 1950s and 1960s with Italy, Greece, Turkey, Morocco, Portugal, Tunisia, and Yugoslavia, to alleviate labor shortages resulting from rapid economic growth and the construction of the Berlin Wall which halted immigration from East Germany. By 1978, guest workers comprised nearly 13 percent of West Germany's work force and about 8 percent of the population; about a third of these immigrants were Turks (Rist 1978). In the case of the agreement between West Germany and Turkey, the intent of the guest worker program was to provide short-term employment for foreign workers in order to shore up West Germany's flagging labor supply by providing work visas for one or two years. When the agreement ended in 1973, however, few Turks returned home. Many were unwilling to trade employment in West Germany (and later Germany) for unemployment in their home country. By 1985, it was obvious that many of the "temporary guest workers," who brought their families to West Germany, had settled to stay (Castles 1985). Today, there are more than 4 million people of Turkish descent living – and aging – in Germany (Ewing 2003; Mandel 2008).

A similar story unfolds in the United States. In the 1940s, the United States initiated the *bracero program* with Mexico to ensure an adequate supply of temporary farm workers. The program formally ended in 1964, but when legal pathways to entry from Mexico to the United States were exhausted, many immigrants began to enter the United States without visas. This unauthorized migration stream effectively created its own "guest worker" program (Castles, Miller, and Ammendola 2003). Until the mid-1990s, the flow of unauthorized immigrants to the United States remained fairly steady, contributing to a stock of about 3 to 5 million. Many of these immigrants worked seasonally or temporarily in the United States and returned to Mexico when their economic goals had been met (Passel, Cohn, and Gonzalez-Barrera 2012). These immigrants also contributed to the Social Security coffers by contributing payroll taxes through falsified Social Security Numbers. In the mid-1990s, however, the United States created several policies to tighten control of the border. Rather than reducing the flow of unauthorized immigration, these policies effectively increased the resident unauthorized population. Once in the United States, few unauthorized immigrants were willing to risk returning to Mexico. Many demographers believe that these changes are responsible for the increase of the unauthorized immigrant population to nearly 12 million in 2012. Ultimately, these immigrants, who are unlikely to return to their home countries, will contribute to US population aging (Massey 2005; Passel, Cohn, and Gonzalez-Barrera 2012).

The German experience with guest workers and the American experience with unauthorized immigrants underscore the difficulty of maintaining an effective flow of replacement migration. However, even if immigration could effectively offset population aging, three additional issues suggest that replacement immigration is an ineffective solution to population aging. First, most developed countries desire highly skilled immigrants, but most developing countries want to retain these same workers. Thus, there may be a considerable mismatch between the international supply and demand for workers (OECD 2010). Second, increasing the flow of immigrants means increasing population size, and a growing number of people oppose increased immigration for environmental reasons (cf. Squalli 2009, 2010) – a point we discussed in chapter 4. Although immigrants tend to engage in more environmentally friendly behaviors than natives and have a lower impact on the environment (Price and Feldmeyer 2012), any increase in the population size of a developed nation is likely to contribute to environmental impacts that result from crowding.

Third, the volume of immigrants required is unlikely to be tolerated by the native populations (Ceobanu and Koropeckyj-Cox 2013). Residents of the United States and Europe have expressed strong opposition to increased immigration, and many people believe the present level of immigration in their country is too high (Espenshade 1994; Saczuk 2003; Coleman 2004a, 2004b; Ceobanu and Escandell 2011). Those who express resistance to immigration generally fear ethno-racial change, job loss, or welfare abuse (Luedtke 2005; Mayda 2006; Sides and Citrin 2007; Ceobanu and Escandell 2008), even when data indicate that immigrants have a net positive impact on society.

Population aging cannot be effectively reduced by an increase in immigration. At the same time, scholars warn that a rapid reduction in immigration in countries with high levels of immigration could cause rapid population aging (cf. Preston, Himes, and Eggers 1989; United Nations 2001). Thus, it is important for policymakers to consider the negative repercussions on the age structure of the population if they intend to pursue aggressive policies to limit current levels of immigration.

Although replacement migration likely offers an ineffective means of offsetting population aging, policymakers could consider other solutions proffered by demographers. These solutions include increasing labor productivity (Tarmann 2000; Coleman and Rowthorn 2011; Herrmann 2012), modifying retirement policies and eliminating mandatory retirement in some countries (Grant 2001; Meyerson 2001), and making other social and economic adjustments (Abernethy 2001; Coleman and Rowthorn 2011).

7

Immigrant Health

When people in the developed world are asked to express their view on the impact of immigration, many voice concerns about how much of their taxes is being spent on immigrants enrolled in medical assistance programs (see Mohanty et al. 2005). Some people fear that their country's health care system is over-burdened by immigrants who consume large quantities of the nation's limited health resources. In the United States, some worry that immigrants enter the country primarily for the purpose of obtaining health care. Many Americans express concern that unauthorized immigrants, in particular, receive all of their health services at the expense of US taxpayers (Berk et al. 2000). Across the developed world, many worry that immigrants – many of whom come from developing countries – may spread infectious diseases and bring with them new chronic diseases and behavioral problems (Gushulak 2007). All of these fears are unfounded, but given the importance of health care and the costs of maintaining it, it is easy to see how the impact of immigrants on the health care system would be a vital concern.

People living in developed countries live considerably longer and have better general health than people in developing countries. Much of that longevity is attributable to higher-quality medical care and better access to such care. However, good medical care comes at a cost. Developed countries spend, on average, about $2,000 per person annually on health care. In the United States, health care spending is considerably higher, at nearly $8,000 per person and more than 17 percent of gross domestic product (OECD 2011). Health care costs in the United States are also rising faster than national income, and employer-paid premiums for workers' health insurance policies increased 97 percent between 2002 and 2008 (Goodell and Ginsburg 2008). Given the high and rising cost of health care, it is understandable that many US-born residents worry about the impact of immigration on the escalation of these costs.

To the extent that the public funds the health care system, the health of immigrants directly affects the cost to taxpayers (Dunn and Dyck 2000). In nearly all developed countries, health care is administered through a national health care system, and all residents have access to catastrophic care at the very minimum (Fuchs 2013). In the United States, which does not have a national health care system, health care is privatized, and most people are individually responsible for their own health care costs; however, health care is provided by the government to the very poorest through programs such as Medicaid and to the elderly through Medicare. Most authorized immigrants who have been in the United States for five years or less are prohibited from applying for Medicaid, and access is severely restricted for all unauthorized immigrants; however, these facts are not widely known.

Immigrant use of health care

Immigrants in the United States use far less health care than natives, and their health care costs are disproportionately lower than those of the overall population (Goldman, Smith, and Sood 2006; Gushulak 2007). Immigrants – especially unauthorized immigrants – are less likely to visit a physician. Nationwide, about 75 percent of US residents visit a physician at least once a year, while as few as 27 percent of unauthorized immigrants do so. Rates of hospitalization – except for hospital visits for childbirth – are the same as for the general population (Berk et al. 2000).

In the United States, many poor people – especially those

without access to government-provided health assistance programs – cannot afford or gain access to primary care through a physician's office. As a consequence, they often seek care in emergency rooms where non-profit hospitals are required to provide medical attention, even if the patient cannot pay. It is a general misconception that unauthorized immigrants in the United States abuse this system for care. In fact, researchers have demonstrated that unauthorized immigrants are less likely to use emergency room care than the country as a whole (Berk et al. 2000). The children of immigrants – many of whom are US-born citizens – also tend to make fewer visits to the emergency room (National Center for Health Statistics 2004; Howell and Hughes 2006). It is also worth noting that non-profit hospitals do not provide emergency care to the poor for free. With the exception of some emergency procedures, like childbirth, that are covered by Medicaid, services are billed to the patient. Those who cannot pay are referred to collection agencies, and many end up filing for bankruptcy (Hollingworth et al. 2007).

In some European countries, such as the Netherlands, elderly immigrants have more chronic conditions than natives, so they make more visits to the doctor (Denktaş 2011; Solé-Auró, Guillén, and Crimmins 2012). However, in many countries, including the United States, immigrants use fewer health care resources than natives. One primary explanation for this fact is that immigrants in these countries tend to be healthier than natives, and they therefore need less care (Bostean 2013). Also, research in some developed countries suggests that recent immigrants, on average, perceive that they have better health than natives of the same age and race, which may keep them from seeking or needing care. For example, immigrants to Israel from former Soviet countries perceive themselves to be healthier than natives (Baron-Epel and Kaplan 2001); this pattern does not necessarily hold in the United States, where Spanish-speaking immigrants are more likely to rate their health as "fair" or "poor" rather than "good" or "excellent." However, most epidemiologists believe this finding is an artifact of how these terms are translated from English to Spanish in surveys (Bostean 2013).

Universal health care

Of the 34 most developed countries in the world, the United States alone lacks a universal health care system. These systems include single-payer systems, two-tier systems, and universal insurance mandates. A single-payer system is one in which the government provides insurance for all residents or citizens and pays health care expenses. A two-tier system is one in which the government provides a minimum level of insurance coverage that can be supplemented with additional insurance. An insurance mandate is one in which all residents are required to purchase insurance. With the passage of the Affordable Care Act (ACA; also known as Obamacare), the United States has a universal insurance mandate as of 2014, although there continue to be political efforts to repeal the legislation.

Successful implementation of the ACA would extend health insurance to many currently uninsured Americans. In 2009, the US Census Bureau reported that 49 million people in the United States lacked health insurance. More than half of these people are working adults, many of whom do not make enough to afford private insurance and are not provided private insurance by their employers. At the same time, their income is too high to be eligible for Medicaid or similar programs. Some of the uninsured are "uninsurable" because of pre-existing conditions (DeNavas-Walt, Proctor, and Smith 2010). The ACA prohibits insurance companies from denying coverage due to pre-existing conditions and supplements the cost of private insurance for those who cannot otherwise afford it.

Another reason that immigrants in many countries use fewer health care resources is that immigrants are also far more likely than natives to be uninsured, and thus they are more likely to lack access to affordable health care (DeNavas-Walt, Proctor, and

Smith 2010). In the United States, federal mandates restrict immigrant health care coverage, causing authorized immigrants to fear that health care seeking will adversely affect their legal status (Fix and Passel 1999; Cacari-Stone and Avila 2012; Viladrich 2012). For unauthorized immigrants, the fear that health care seeking will lead to deportation prevents many from seeking any medical attention (Berk et al. 2000).

The immigrant health paradox

The relationship between poverty, development, and health (see Jones 2001) suggests that people who migrate from less developed countries should be less healthy than the native population of the developed nations to which they relocate. Despite the fact that immigrants benefit from access to modern health care and sanitation in the places where they settle, and their chances of contracting an infectious disease decline because of better sanitation conditions and less exposure to people with tuberculosis, polio, measles, and other diseases (Powles 1990; Abraído-Lanza et al. 1999; Khlat and Darmon 2003; Bostean 2013), recent immigrants are often poor (Dunn and Dyck 2000), and poverty is highly correlated with lower life expectancy and poorer health (Adler et al. 1994; Rogers, Hummer, and Nam 2000). In the United States, the working poor often cannot afford health insurance, and a disproportionate number of immigrants are without insurance (Solis et al. 1990; DeNavas-Walt, Proctor, and Smith 2010).

Early childhood exposure to infectious diseases and poor nutrition should also lend themselves to chronic conditions in later life (Barker 1990; Frank 2001). We would expect immigrant health to decline precipitously with age as pre- and neo-natal health care deficiencies, poor childhood nutrition, and exposure to diseases in early ages show their effects at older ages. For example, childhood deprivation is linked to stomach cancer and stroke, but these effects are generally seen in older adulthood – that is, usually a long time after immigration (Kennedy, McDonald, and Biddle

2006). Indeed, this seems to be the case for elderly immigrants living in some European countries (Solé-Auró et al. 2012).

Conditions during and after immigration also point to poorer health outcomes (Florez et al. 2012). First, the immigration process itself is often stressful, especially for unauthorized immigrants (Beiser and Hyman 1994; Dunn and Dyck 2000; Bacio, Mays, and Lau 2013). Second, migrants tend to be segregated in impoverished neighborhoods where they are more exposed to violence and pollution (Karoly and Gonzalez 2011; Fu and VanLandingham 2012; Bacio, Mays, and Lau 2013), and where they tend to live in poor-quality homes that increase risk for diseases such as asthma (Atiles and Bohon 2003; Rosenbaum and Friedman 2007). Third, language and other structural barriers impede access to health care (Guarnaccia and Lopez 1998; Pumariega, Rothe, and Pumariega 2005; Bostean 2013). Fourth, immigrants from developing countries are often ethnic and racial minorities, and these factors are also associated with poorer health and greater mortality risk in the countries to which they migrate (Frank 2001), probably due to different experiences over the life course (Hayward et al. 2000). For example, in the United States, blacks and Latinos have a greater risk of cancer, poorer access to high-quality cancer care, and lower odds of surviving after cancer treatment (Clegg et al. 2007).

Finally, immigrants are often employed in *3-D jobs* – those that are dangerous, dirty, and demeaning (Rosenfeld and Tienda 1999; Richardson, Ruser, and Suarez 2003; Passel 2006) – which puts them at a disproportionate risk for work-related injury and illness (see Kandel 2008; Kandel and Donato 2009). For example, Latinos working in construction (many of whom are immigrants) are much more likely than non-Latino white or black construction workers to die from a fall from a roof, and Latino immigrants are most likely to experience fatal falls (Dong et al. 2013). In fact, Latino construction workers are twice as likely to die from all occupational injuries as non-Latino construction workers (Dong and Platner 2004). Unauthorized immigrants in 3-D jobs – especially those in the United States – have fewer opportunities to obtain work with better employment conditions (Rothenberg 1998; Hotchkiss and Quispe-Agnoli 2008) or better pay (Kossoudji and Cobb-Clark 1996; Donato et al. 2008), forcing them to continue in risky jobs.

Despite the multiple barriers to good health, immigrants from developing countries (and sometimes their offspring) are often healthier than natives in the developed countries to which they migrate (Abraído-Lanza et al. 1999; Kennedy, McDonald, and Biddle 2006; Chiswick, Lee, and Miller 2008; Mehta and Elo 2010; Florez et al. 2012). For example, immigrants from the Mediterranean countries of Southern Europe and North Africa have lower mortality rates than natives in France and Germany (Khlat and Darmon 2003), and Turkish immigrants and their children have lower mortality rates than native Germans (Razum et al. 1998). Mortality rates are also usually lower for immigrants than for compatriots who remain in the home country (Marmot, Adelstein, and Bulusu 1984; Boulogne et al. 2012). For example, Finns who reside in Sweden are healthier than those who reside in Finland (Westman et al. 2008).

The anomalous finding that immigrants face conditions that should make them unhealthy, and yet they are often quite healthy, is referred to as the *immigrant health paradox* (Markides and Coreil 1986; Abraído-Lanza et al. 1999; Vega and Sribney 2011; Bacio, Mays, and Lau 2013; Bostean 2013). In the United States, the immigrant health paradox is seen most strongly among Mexican immigrants (Flores and Brotanek 2005) and is often referred to as the *Hispanic paradox* (Frank 2001; Flores and Brotanek 2005; Kennedy, McDonald, and Biddle 2006; Bostean 2013). Despite their generally low socioeconomic status, Mexican immigrants in the United States have lower mortality rates and fewer chronic conditions than US-born Latinos and native whites (Abraído-Lanza et al. 1999; Bostean 2013). For example, even though Latino immigrants, on average, have reduced access to cancer care and receive poorer-quality cancer treatment (Clegg et al. 2007), they have lower income-adjusted mortality rates for most cancers than US-born whites (Abraído-Lanza et al. 1999). Additionally, while about 14 percent of poor, US-born Mexican American women give birth to underweight babies, only 3 percent of Mexican immigrants do (Flores and Brotanek 2005).

Salmon bias

Demographers have struggled to explain the immigrant health paradox, although it is still not completely understood (Bacio, Mays, and Lau 2013). One widely tested hypothesis to explain the generally better health of immigrants is *salmon bias*. Drawing on the analogy of salmon swimming upstream to spawn – and ultimately die – in their place of birth, the salmon bias hypothesis suggests that sick immigrants may return to their country of origin in order to be surrounded by family and friends (Shai and Rosenwaike 1987; Pablos-Méndez 1994). Through emigration, the least healthy immigrants are removed from the population of the destination country and become "statistically immortal" (Pablos-Méndez 1994: 1237), which inflates the average health profile of the immigrant population and artificially reduces the immigrant mortality rate (Abraído-Lanza et al. 1999).

Since immigrants in many countries engage in *return migration* – the practice of entering and later leaving a country – the idea of salmon bias seems reasonable. A study conducted of authorized immigrants who entered the United States in 1971 (Jasso and Rosenzweig 1982) estimated that as many as 56 percent of Mexicans, 72 percent of South Americans, and 69 percent of Central Americans and Caribbeans returned to their country of origin within ten years of migrating. Another study from that era (Reichert and Massey 1979) showed that 75 percent of households in one Mexican border town contained return migrants. Although return migration from the United States slowed considerably as the result of stricter border controls initiated in the mid-1990s (Durand and Massey 2002), the most recent evidence suggests that, between 2005 and 2010, as many Mexicans returned to Mexico as entered the United States (Passel, Cohn, and Gonzalez-Barrera 2012).

Despite the regularity of return migration, the direct evidence for salmon bias is weak. When Abraído-Lanza and her colleagues (1999) compared the mortality rates of US-born whites to those of immigrants from Cuba, they found that rates were lower for Cubans than for native non-Latino whites. This difference cannot be explained by salmon bias, since political conditions in Cuba make return migration unlikely. A more recent study comparing Mexican immigrants living in the United States with those who returned to Mexico found that return migrants were less likely to report having poor health than immigrants living in the United States, and the prevalence of diabetes, high blood pressure, heart disease, and cancer was the same in both groups (Bostean 2013).

The healthy migrant hypothesis

Although some researchers argue a salmon bias in mortality and morbidity statistics, others maintain that lower mortality and greater health among immigrants is real (Markides and Coreil 1986; Scribner 1996). One widely touted explanation is the *healthy migrant hypothesis* (Shai and Rosenwaike 1987; Sorlie et al. 1993). Drawing on theories of *selective migration* – the idea that those who migrate are different from those in their country who do not migrate – the healthy migrant hypothesis suggests that only those in excellent health will be willing to make a stressful journey and undergo the long and difficult process of adjusting to a new culture (Bostean 2013). Moreover, unhealthy people may begin the immigration process but may not be successful in completing it (Crimmins et al. 2005). In general, immigrants are younger and more highly educated than those who do not migrate (Jasso et al. 2004; Feliciano 2005), and younger and more highly educated people are generally healthier than those who are older and less well educated (Rogers, Hummer, and Nam 2000).

The healthy migrant hypothesis also suggests that immigrants from developing countries engage in cultural practices that protect them from *degenerative diseases* (Williams and Collins 1995; Scribner 1996; Bostean 2013). Degenerative diseases, which include cancer, heart disease, and stroke, are those illnesses caused by multiple experiences over the life course. Because degenerative diseases usually manifest themselves in old age, these diseases are most prevalent in developed countries where people live longer. In developing countries, *infectious diseases* – those caused by a single agent such as a bacteria or virus – are more prevalent (Omran 2005).

Many immigrants' everyday behaviors protect them from degenerative conditions such as heart disease (Abraído-Lanza et al. 1999; Razum and Twardella 2002). They walk and regularly engage in other physical activities that lead to lower rates of obesity (Himmelgreen et al. 2004; Flores and Brotanek 2005). Many immigrant groups are also less likely to smoke (Pérez-Stable, Marín, and Marín 1994; Blue and Fenelon 2011) and less likely to drink alcohol (see Bacio, Mays, and Lau 2013) than many native populations. Immigrants also tend to eat healthier diets that are low in fat, saturated fat, calories, and sodium (Mazur, Marquis, and Jensen 2003) and high in fiber, vitamins, and other nutrients (Dixon, Sundquist, and Winkleby 2000; Neuhouser et al. 2004; Flores and Brotanek 2005). Immigrants also often have strong social support networks and greater family cohesion which reduces stress and leads to better health (Bostean 2013).

In many countries, the healthy immigrant effect may also be a byproduct of a health screening process upon entry. In Canada, for example, immigrants who cannot pass screenings for chronic diseases or existing infectious diseases are denied entry. Additionally, in countries like the United States, entry policies preference the admission of well-educated, younger immigrants, which increases the likelihood that immigrants will be healthy (Gushulak 2007).

Despite the common finding of a healthy immigrant effect, exactly how healthy immigrants are is subject to debate. US data from the mid-1990s showed that most immigrant groups reported better self-rated health, fewer activity limitations, and fewer days in bed due to illness than the US-born (Stephen et al. 1994); however, more recent data and analyses provide weaker support for the healthy immigrant hypothesis. For example, Bostean (2013) tested the healthy migrant hypothesis by comparing Mexican immigrants in the United States, US-born Mexican Americans, those living in Mexico who never migrated, and former Mexican immigrants who had returned to Mexico after living for some time in the United States. The healthy migrant effect suggests that Mexican immigrants should be healthier than non-migrants and return migrants in Mexico and US-born Mexican Americans. However, she found that immigrants living in the United States actually reported having poorer health than non-migrant Mexicans or those who returned to Mexico. Rubalcava and his colleagues (2008) also found that rural Mexican men and women with poor self-rated health were more likely to migrate to the United States than those reporting better health.

Furthermore, despite the better health of immigrants overall, the health of immigrants varies widely depending on where immigrants are from and the countries to which they migrate, which suggests that the relationship between immigration and health is quite complicated. For example, in Canada, immigrants are more likely than natives to self-report poor health; however, immigrants from Europe are more likely to report poor health than immigrants from Latin America or Asia (Dunn and Dyck 2000). Immigrants from China living in the United Kingdom have better health than immigrants from Bangladesh, Pakistan, and India (Smith, Kelly, and Nazroo 2009). Immigrants from Southern European countries like Italy and Greece who are currently living in Sweden have higher levels of heart disease than immigrants from other countries (Pudaric, Sundquist, and Johansson 2003). Finally, in the United States, immigrants from former Soviet states have higher average education than US-born whites, but their levels of disability are considerably higher (Mehta and Elo 2010). This suggests that at least some higher socioeconomic status immigrants do not share in the healthy immigrant effect.

The finding that immigrants are healthier than the native-born is also contingent upon the type of health being measured and the immigrant group being considered (Cunningham, Ruben, and Narayan 2008). For example, although immigrants in general are less likely to suffer from heart disease and are less likely to die from cardiovascular disease compared to the native-born population (Singh and Siahpush 2001; Jasso et al. 2004), South Asian immigrants in the United States are more likely to die from coronary artery disease compared to the US-born and other Asian immigrants (Klatsky et al. 1994). Another study found that foreign-born women in the United States are more likely to die from coronary artery disease, hypertension, and hypertensive heart disease compared to US-born women (Rubia, Marcos, and Muennig 2002). In contrast, the mortality rates of foreign-born men for coronary artery disease are significantly lower than for US-born men, while there are no significant differences in mortality rates for hypertension and hypertensive heart disease between foreign-born and US-born men (ibid.). This evidence suggests that immigrant health outcomes are complex and that immigrants do not always fare better than the native-born.

Health transitions

A difficulty in testing the healthy immigrant hypothesis is that the health of immigrants declines over time (Gushulak 2007; Bostean 2013). That is, immigrants may start out healthy, but it is clear that they become less healthy with more years in their destination country; thus, the longer an immigrant spends in a developed country, the less healthy they become (Boulogne et al. 2012). For example, recent immigrants in Canada are healthier than natives, but that effect does not persist over time (De Maio and Kemp 2010). Thus, statistics on immigrant health are likely skewed by the existence of healthier recent immigrants or less healthy earlier entrants. In sum, when researchers study whether immigrants are healthier than those in their country of origin, their findings are often distorted by a *health transition* that occurs as the result of migration.

Understanding why immigrants' health declines over time is an important step toward improving the health of immigrants and natives. Although immigrants tend to be healthier and use less health care than natives in many countries, improvements or declines in immigrant health as immigrants adjust to life in their country of destination can provide valuable information about how the health of the destination country can be improved (Read, Amick, and Donato 2005; Kennedy, McDonald, and Biddle 2006). Immigration thus provides a natural experiment with regard to the general health behaviors of a population (Huijts and Kraaykamp 2012).

Demographers have attempted to explain the immigrant health transition by testing a variety of theories including acculturation stress theory, assimilation theory, erosion of cultural values, and increased exposure to risky environments (Flores and Brotanek 2005; Kennedy, McDonald, and Biddle 2006; Bacio, Mays, and Lau 2013). *Acculturation stress theory* suggests that the process of immigration can produce harmful health effects (Abraído-Lanza et al. 1999). This stress is exacerbated by experiences after immigration such as discrimination and language barriers (Bacio, Mays, and Lau 2013). Adolescent children of immigrants, in particular, may engage in stress management responses that are maladaptive, such as drinking, using illegal drugs, and affiliating with street gangs (Gil, Wagner, and Vega 2000). Thus, over time, immigrant health will decline.

Assimilation theory suggests that, over time and generations, immigrants will replace the behaviors and attitudes learned in their country of origin with those of their country of destination, and that this may have detrimental health effects (Flores and Brotanek 2005; Boulogne et al. 2012; Cacari-Stone and Avila 2012). As immigrants from developing countries become more exposed to the diets of developed countries, their body mass indices and glucose rates increase, putting them at greater risk for obesity, heart disease, stroke, and diabetes (Gushulak 2007). Behaviors also change. For example, Caetano and Clark (2003) show that immigrants often take on the drinking patterns of their host society. In the United States, more acculturated adolescents are more likely to engage in binge drinking (Crimmins et al. 2005; Fu and VanLandingham 2012), marijuana smoking (Epstein, Botvin, and Diaz 2001; Read, Amick, and Donato 2005; Fu and VanLandingham 2012), and other illegal drug use (Velez and Ungemack 1989; Siddharthan and Ahern 1996; Fu and VanLandingham 2012). Rates of tobacco use, especially among women, also increase as immigrants become more acculturated (Gfroerer and Tan 2003). It is also possible that traditional healing practices that may be beneficial in protecting health are replaced with modern medical procedures that may be less effective in some cases (Mertz and Finocchio 2010). Ultimately, such changes in attitudes and behaviors can negatively affect health.

In 1976, Marmot and Syme first provided evidence for the assimilation theory of immigrant health by studying Japanese men living in Japan, Hawaii, and California. The three study sites were considered gradations of cultural experiences with Japan seen as "most Japanese," California seen as "most American," and Hawaii – a state with a large Japanese immigrant population – seen as a point in between. Marmot and Syme found that levels of heart disease were lowest in Japan, higher in Hawaii, and highest in California. They attributed their findings to different social and cultural conditions which included (but were not limited to) differences in diet and smoking. Their findings prompted demographers and epidemiologists to consider more carefully the role that assimilation to a Western lifestyle plays in creating health risks.

Modern researchers studying assimilation theory as it relates to immigrant health transitions are quick to point out that it is the process of absorbing a new culture (*acculturation*) and divesting old cultural habits (*assimilation*), rather than simply being in a new country, that matters most (Flores and Brotanek 2005). In a study of Arab immigrants to the United States, Read and her colleagues (Read, Amick, and Donato 2005) determined that Arab immigrants who naturalized were less healthy than their non-citizen counterparts, regardless of how long they had lived in the United States. In Germany, children of less acculturated Turkish immigrants had a lower prevalence of asthma, contact dermatitis, and allergies (Gruber et al. 2002). Less "Americanized" Latino adolescents are more likely to delay sexual initiation than their more assimilated counterparts (Adam et al. 2005). Latina immigrant women are also less likely to adequately immunize their children as these women become more acculturated (Anderson, Wood, and Sherbourne 1997; Prislin et al. 1998), and less-acculturated youth are also more likely to regularly use seat belts and eat breakfast (Ebin et al. 2001).

Immigrants may also experience an *erosion of cultural values* over time and generations that results in worsening health

(Barrera et al. 2004; Mogro-Wilson 2008). A key cultural value is orientation toward traditional family values and practices (cf. Gil, Wagner, and Vega 2000; Gonzales et al. 2008; Castro, Stein, and Bentler 2009; Germán, Gonzales, and Dumka 2009). In work on Latino immigrants, traditional family functioning is often referred to as *familismo*. Research on Latino families in the United States shows that more acculturated parents are less likely to monitor their adolescent children (Driscoll, Russell, and Crockett 2008; Mogro-Wilson 2008) and are less likely to maintain a close relationship with them (Bacio, Mays, and Lau 2013). After immigrating, both parents may have to work outside of the home, sometimes in multiple jobs. These practices make it difficult to closely supervise their children. Changes such as these may explain why later-generation immigrant youth are more likely than first-generation youth to engage in risky health behaviors such as excessive alcohol consumption (Bacio, Mays, and Lau 2013).

A final theory regarding immigrant health transitions is *exposure to risky environments*. The children and grandchildren of immigrants are more likely than children who are immigrants to associate with peers who use alcohol and drugs (Gil, Wagner, and Vega 2000; Lopez et al. 2009; Prado et al. 2009), and teen alcohol abuse increases with each immigrant generation (Bacio, Mays, and Lau 2012). This provides some evidence that health deterioration may also be due to environmental risks. Additional evidence for this position is seen in work by Rosenbaum and Friedman (2007), who document the poor housing conditions of immigrants in New York City that put newcomers at risk for crime, teen pregnancy, respiratory illness, and other health factors. As bad as these conditions are, they are worse for their children and grandchildren.

Ultimately, acculturation stress, assimilation, erosion of cultural values, and environmental risk are all at work to reduce immigrant health. One point worth noting is that the decline in immigrant health after immigration has undermined the assertion by some epidemiologists that immigrants from some racial and ethnic groups may have a genetic advantage over natives (see Scribner 1996; Frank 2001). This clearly is not true.

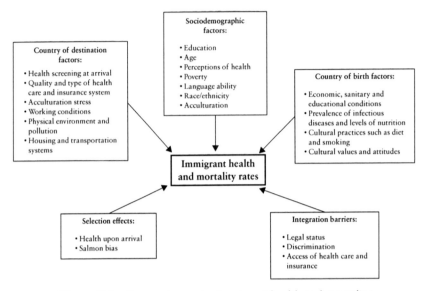

Figure 7.1 Factors impacting immigrant health and mortality

Figure 7.1 shows how country-of-origin effects, country-of-destination effects, immigrant selection, integration, and sociodemographic factors work in concert to impact immigrant health and, ultimately, mortality rates. A greater understanding of the inter-relationship of all of these processes will help health researchers achieve a better understanding of the immigrant health transition (Trovato 2003; Schenk 2007; Kohls 2008; Boulogne et al. 2012).

Immigrant diversity and health

In summary, immigrant health and health transitions are complex. The health of immigrants depends greatly on who they are, where they are from, where they settle, and the conditions that led to the immigration decision. No single factor can explain why immigrants are healthy or not, which means that simply extending universal health care, for example, will not guarantee that immigrants will be as healthy as natives (see Lorant, Van Oyen, and Thomas

2008). Despite how complicated the processes are, understanding immigrant health is important. Many people have speculated that pre-immigration experiences – especially those in childhood – can have a lasting effect throughout life (Burvill 1998; Dunn and Dyck 2000; Kennedy, McDonald, and Biddle 2006). These experiences include how immigrants are socialized about health behaviors, the levels of nutrition and disease in the country of origin (Ho, Bos, and Kunst 2007; Gagnon and Mazan 2009), and experiences with war or political conflicts (Huijts and Kraaykamp 2012). Others have suggested that genetic conditions may also be passed from country to country through immigration, although genetic explanations are undermined by the fact that immigrant health tends to decline precipitously after immigration (see Frank 2001). Thus, it would seem reasonable that immigrants from countries where the health of the population is poor will also tend to have poorer health, even if their health is better in their country of destination than in their country of origin (Huijts and Kraaykamp 2012). However, most current research provides only mixed support for the idea that immigrants from countries with low levels of health will produce unhealthy immigrants. Early experiences with illness and deprivation do not necessarily account for health outcomes after migrating. At the same time, complicated conditions such as early experiences with political violence and an immigrant's religious background have lasting effects on health, even into the second and third generation (ibid.). Understanding these complex processes will take more work.

Examining the health of different immigrant groups living in a variety of settings gives researchers a better understanding of how early life (pre-immigration) conditions affect health as well as how immigrants' current social environment impacts their health (cf. Kasl and Berkman 1983; Vega and Rumbaut 1991; Carballo, Divino, and Zeric 1998). If we can understand more clearly the exact components of some traditional cultures that lend themselves to better health, we can begin to adopt those behaviors. At the same time, examining how acculturation and assimilation reduce health outcomes may allow us to tackle some of our most pressing public health concerns.

8

Educating Children in Immigrant Families

In 2001, the US Congress passed the No Child Left Behind Act (NCLB). The new law required every US state to create and implement measurable standards of achievement for schools in order to continue to receive federal funding for education. The basic idea was simple: schools should find ways of ensuring that all children completing a grade level can read and solve math equations at that same grade level. Schools failing to meet performance targets could be subject to a range of sanctions, including allowing parents to withdraw their children from the school, requiring that schools offer after-school and other supplementary education programs, school restructuring, or even closure (US Department of Education 2002).

Early proponents of the legislation noted that NCLB had great potential to improve the educational outcomes for *English language learners* (ELL; Capps et al. 2005). ELL students are usually children who are immigrants, although they are sometimes the US-born children of immigrant parents who grow up in neighborhoods with few English speakers. Title I of the bill requires that schools assess the reading and math proficiency of ELL and racial minority students and demonstrate progress in improving these students' outcomes. Title II of the bill requires that schools also demonstrate annual improvements in English proficiency among ELL children (US Department of Education 2002). The law also requires that English as a Second Language (ESL) classrooms be staffed by credentialed teachers with a degree in the subject that they are teaching (US Department of Education 2004a), although these teachers do not necessarily have to be certified to teach ESL (Harper, de Jong, and Platt 2008). Schools are also required to communicate with non-English-speaking parents in their own language "to the extent practicable," although the text of the legislation stresses written communication (US Department of Education 2004b: 5), ignoring the fact that some immigrants are unable to read even in their native language (Bohon, Macpherson, and Atiles 2005).

Within a few years of implementation, NCLB was widely criticized by parents, teachers, and researchers for removing teachers' agency to adapt to their classrooms (Cochran-Smith and Lytle 2006); setting math and reading outcomes over art, history, science, citizenship, critical thinking, conflict resolution, and other important goals (Rothstein 2008); effectively eliminating bilingual education programs that improved learning outcomes (Harper, de Jong, and Platt 2008); and virtually guaranteeing that schools serving immigrant, low-income, and/or minority children would fail (Rothstein 2008).

One of the biggest concerns stressed by critics is the NCLB emphasis on passing standardized tests. Because schools place a premium on the percentage of students passing, teachers tend to pay a lot of attention to "bubble kids," those children who have great potential either for passing or for failing. Students who are most likely to pass the exams, and students who do not have a hope of passing, are virtually ignored (Hursh 2007). This has serious implications for immigrant children who fall into the latter category. Years after implementation, ELL students continued to lag far behind other students, with nearly half falling below grade level in math, and almost three-quarters falling behind grade level in reading (Fry 2007). It is no wonder that one critic referred to NCLB as "incoherent, unworkable, and doomed" (Rothstein 2008: 50).

The debate over No Child Left Behind underscores that, although there is considerable agreement on the importance of education to future success and the problems that can occur when some groups in society are denied access to the same quality and amount of education as others, there is little agreement on how education goals can be met. In the landmark *Brown* v. *Board of Education* (1954: 347) Supreme Court case, the Justices wrote:

> education is perhaps the most important function of state and local governments. Compulsory school attendance laws and the great expenditures for education both demonstrate our recognition of the importance of education to our democratic society. It is required in the performance of our most basic public responsibilities, even service in the armed forces. It is the very foundation of good citizenship . . . In these days, it is doubtful that any child may reasonably be expected to succeed in life if he is denied the opportunity of an education. Such an opportunity, where the state has undertaken to provide it, is a right which must be made available to all on equal terms.

Today, most Americans continue to endorse the values of this statement in principle (Salerno 2006), yet there is considerable evidence that some children – including many children from immigrant families – fair far worse in the US education system than others (Kao, Vaquera, and Goyette 2013). Given that at least one in four school-age children in the United States has at least one immigrant parent (O'Hare 2004), it will be a struggle for the United States to ameliorate these differences.

Education and later-life outcomes

Education provides undeniable benefits. People with more education have greater earnings and higher social status. In the United States, the difference in median income between those with advanced degrees, such as a Master's or law degree, and those who dropped out of high school was about $44,000 in 2009 (Ryan and Siebens 2012). However, the benefits of education extend far beyond earnings. The well-educated are less likely to be unemployed or in poverty (cf. Behrman and Stacey 1997; Stevens, Armstrong, and Arum 2008). They are more likely to be married, they tend to enjoy better physical and mental health, and they are happier (Hao and Johnson 2000; Schnittker 2004;

Franzini and Fernandez-Esquer 2006; Zhang and Ta 2009). They also live longer (Lleras-Muney 2005). Perhaps most importantly, well-educated people can pass their class advantages on to their children, so that subsequent generations are able to fare as well as, or better than, their parents (cf. Sewell, Hauser, and Featherman 1976; Jencks, Crouse, and Mueser 1983; Bohon, Kirkpatrick Johnson, and Gorman 2006). Well-educated parents can provide their children with good information about the best high school classes to take to prepare for college and can often afford to pay for college preparatory classes and college tuition (Kao, Vaquera, and Goyette 2013).

Education is also an important predictor of self-employment (Neupert and Baughn 2013), and self-employment is an important means by which many immigrants achieve socioeconomic success in their host country (Raijman and Tienda 2000; van Tubergen 2005; Valdez 2006; Bohon, Massengale, and Jordan 2009). In many countries, but especially in the United States and Canada, immigrants are far more likely than the native born to be self-employed, and a recent study of 21 developed countries linked education to immigrant entrepreneurship (Neupert and Baughn 2013).

Unfortunately, how well an immigrant fares in life depends only partially on their education (Mattoo, Neagu, and Özden 2005), and an ample body of research suggests that some immigrants get different returns on their education than others (Kao and Tienda 1995; Portes and Rumbaut 2006; Keller and Tillman 2008; Gibson and Carrasco 2009). Some of these differences derive from differential values placed on education or other skills acquired in some places rather than others (Ferrer and Riddell 2008). For example, in the United States, a medical degree from Harvard or Johns Hopkins University is considered more prestigious, and hence "better," than the same degree from a school in the Caribbean. Other differences arise from cultural factors such as language skills (Schwartz and Soifer 2012). A highly trained, highly skilled immigrant who does not speak the language of his or her host country fluently may find it difficult to get good work, despite having a high level of human capital. Race also matters (Jencks and Phillips 1998; Carter 2003; White and Glick 2009). Racial minorities, especially blacks and Latinos, earn less than whites in the US labor market, even when they have the same amount of education (Arrow, Bowles, and Durlauf 2000). Despite these issues, education remains one of the most important pathways to future economic success for all people; however, it is important to note that it benefits some more than others, and that immigrants face considerable barriers in obtaining an education in their host countries.

Educational attainment

Although education is highly valued and produces great benefits, *educational attainment* – the number of years of education or the total degrees that a person completes – varies markedly across different immigrant groups, underscoring the sizable educational barriers that some immigrant groups face (Kao, Vaquera, and Goyette 2013). Figure 8.1 shows the differences in the percentage of adults (age 25 and older) with a bachelor's degree or better for immigrants from the five largest Asian and Latin American sending countries, as well as the educational attainment of US-born residents of Asian and Latino origin. Notice that immigrant groups from the five largest Asian sending countries have considerably larger percentages of college graduates than immigrants from the five largest Latin American sending countries. The most educated Latino group (Cubans) has about the same proportion of college graduates as the least educated Asian group shown (Vietnamese).

Differences in educational attainment linked to country of origin can be explained by factors such as how many monetary assets immigrants can bring with them, the characteristics of the countries from which immigrants arrive (particularly that country's educational structure), the neighborhoods in which immigrants settle, ability to speak the language of the host country and the ease with which it can be learned, and the racio-ethnic characteristics of the immigrant groups that lend themselves to discrimination. Consider two immigrant children – one Canadian

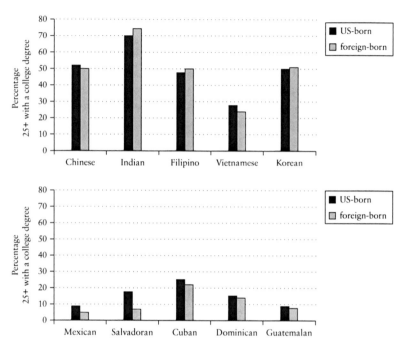

Figure 8.1   Percentage of US-born and foreign-born college graduates among the five largest Asian and Latino ethnic groups, 2008

Note: Chinese also includes those from Taiwan and Hong Kong

Source: adapted from the American Community Survey, 2008

and one Vietnamese – who enter the United States at age 14. The Canadian immigrant has an immediate advantage over the Vietnamese immigrant in terms of both language and culture, and these advantages can be more easily parlayed into high school and college success for the Canadian immigrant. If the Canadian immigrant is white, and if his or her family settles in a middle-class neighborhood, they will not be stigmatized in the classroom in the way that children of color and poor children often are (Kao 1995; Milner 2013).

Parents play a vital role in the educational success of their children, and this is true for immigrants as much as (or more than) for natives. Parents with high levels of education have children who typically also have high levels of education, and the children of poorly educated parents often discontinue high school or college before completion (Black, Devereux, and Salvanes 2003; Currie and Moretti 2003; Bauer and Riphahn 2006). This is seen among the US-born Asians in figure 8.1, many of whom are the children of foreign-born parents. Note that educational attainment for the US-born is very similar to that of the foreign-born.

Note also that in figure 8.1, US-born Latinos are more likely to graduate college than foreign-born Latinos. This shows an advantage seen in immigrant families when immigrant parents are poorly educated. Immigrants with low levels of education often stress to their children that their migration to a new country was a sacrifice in order to improve their children's later-life conditions, and they have high expectations for their children's success (Zhou 1997b). For this reason, many US-born children from immigrant families are better educated than US-born children with similar race and poverty characteristics who have native-born parents (Kao and Tienda 1995; Vernez and Abrahamse 1996; Farley and Alba 2002). This is not the case in Europe, where children from immigrant families continue to lag behind their native peers in educational attainment in countries such as Italy (Di Bartolomeo 2009), Spain (Vaquera and Kao 2012), the Netherlands (Van Ours and Veenman 2003), and Germany (Riphahn 2003); however, the children of immigrants in Europe – as among many immigrant groups in the United States – demonstrate higher educational attainment than their parents.

Parental involvement in the school system is important to educational outcomes (Comer and Haynes 1991; Lee and Bowen 2006), and it is here that children from immigrant families may be disadvantaged, because immigrant parents may be less involved in the schools than native parents (Gonzalez et al. 2013). Immigrant parents from some sending countries are less likely to meet with their children's teachers, attend school functions, or participate in classroom activities. Some educators interpret such inactivity as a sign that some immigrant groups value education less than other immigrant groups or natives. This is a particularly common stereotype of Mexican immigrants to the United States (Valencia and Black 2002). In reality, lack of school participation is usually the result of structural barriers, including lack of transportation or inability to speak the language of the host country (Bohon, Macpherson, and Atiles 2005). However, despite there being good reasons for limited involvement, the fact remains that children of uninvolved parents usually have lower educational attainment in the long run (Berger and Riojas-Cortez 2011).

The context of reception (i.e., the degree to which immigrants are welcomed; Portes and Böröcz 1989; McHugh, Miyares, and Skop 1997; Portes and Rumbaut 2006; Borch and Corra 2010) also affects educational attainment, as does *social capital.* Social capital refers to the network of connections people have with other people that can be parlayed into advantages (Bourdieu 1980; Coleman 1988). One example of social capital is knowing people who can help you get a job (Granovetter 1974). Elements of social capital include obligations between people, shared information, and the transmission of class-related norms (Coleman 1988; Kao 2004). Bankston (2004) and Portes (1998) have both demonstrated that social capital is crucial for the educational attainment of immigrants and their children and for the ability to translate that education into earnings. Kao and her colleagues (Kao, Vaquera, and Goyette 2013) stress that immigrants' connections to other people are important to educational attainment if social networks are with people who "hold the right types of information" (85). Thus, friends and relatives can help in encouraging an immigrant to finish college if those friends and relatives are themselves college-educated and can provide good information about how to succeed.

Immigration status also matters. In the United States, children who are unauthorized immigrants cannot be barred from primary and secondary education (*Plyler v. Doe* 1982), and all children age 16 and under must attend school. However, many states have erected barriers to keep unauthorized immigrants from attending college, such as requiring them to pay higher tuition and barring them from receiving financial aid. These barriers often discourage unauthorized immigrant children – the majority of whom are

Mexican – from completing high school, since they see no reason to earn a high school diploma if they cannot use it as a stepping-stone to higher education (Bohon, Macpherson, and Atiles 2005). This has been used to push for legislation like the DREAM (Development, Relief, and Education for Alien Minors) Act, which would provide a path to authorized residency and eventual citizenship for unauthorized immigrant youth who grow up in the United States, provided that they complete either two years of service in the military or two years of attendance at an institution of higher education. The DREAM Act has been broadly considered to be the most accessible and bipartisan first step to comprehensive immigration reform in the United States. However, it failed in Congress when it was put for a vote in 2010.

The social class standing of an immigrant also affects their educational attainment. For example, Stanton-Salazar (2001) demonstrates that differences in educational attainment between non-Latino and Mexican American youth in the United States are partially attributable to differences in average social class standing and the networks that result from these class distinctions. Bohon and her colleagues (Bohon, Kirkpatrick Johnson, and Gorman 2006) also demonstrate that family income explains much of the difference across Latino groups in both the desire to attend college and the belief that earning a college diploma is possible. This is true for both immigrant children and the US-born children of immigrants. Social class also links to social capital. Middle-class immigrants often have middle-class friends and family members, and these connections can provide the type of information necessary for success.

Race and the achievement gap

While educational attainment refers to the amount of education completed, *educational achievement* refers to how well a student performs in school. Achievement is usually measured by grades and test scores. In the United States, grade point average is one of the most commonly used measures of achievement, although college entrance exam scores, such as the SAT, and scores on other standardized tests are also widely used. A few studies look at outcomes such as the frequency with which students do homework, grades in particular subjects such as reading and math, or rank in class. These indicators are all designed to measure variations in the level of student knowledge (Hanushek and Woessman 2008).

Decades of research (starting with Blau and Duncan 1967) have documented the important link between educational achievement and future socioeconomic success. Educational achievement (apart from educational attainment) matters because most measures of achievement are actually measures of *cognitive skills*, or the brain's ability to process thoughts (Anderson 1982). Cognitive skills are learned behaviors, and these skills are a strong predictor of future earnings (Hanushek and Woessman 2008).

Because we tend to focus on test scores and grades when measuring achievement, it is easy to associate learning and the development of cognitive skills with schooling; however, schools are just one place where a student develops cognitive skills. These skills are also learned or reinforced at home and in the child's neighborhood (Alexander, Entwisle, and Dauber 2002; Turney and Kao 2009), so it is important to consider how all of these factors come into play when examining the educational achievement of immigrants. For example, Cardak and McDonald (2001) show that Asian immigrants to Australia are more likely to do better in school and graduate high school if they live in neighborhoods dominated by highly educated, high-skilled immigrants and their descendants from the same country of origin.

Educational achievement is strongly linked to racio-ethnic status, with non-Latino white and Asian students consistently outscoring non-Latino black and Latino students, on average (Lee 2002; Hartney and Flavin 2014). Education researchers label these systematic differences in school performance by race the *achievement gap*. In the United States, the achievement gap narrowed substantially after the civil rights era, but the gap widened again in the 1990s, partially due to a decline in socioeconomic conditions among racial minorities relative to non-Latino whites during that decade (Lee 2002).

The consistent presence of an achievement gap has led some scholars to speculate that there are real racial differences in cognitive ability among racial groups, and that cognitive functioning is genetic (Herrnstein and Murray 1994). This perspective has been widely discredited by education researchers, demographers, sociologists, and cognitive psychologists (Fischer et al. 1996; Delvin 1997; Montague 1999) in favor of an empirically supported perspective that suggests that structures in society create larger barriers to achievement for some groups than others (Hartney and Flavin 2014). Systematic racial differences in socioeconomic status, family size, and family composition are important factors in explaining racial difference in academic achievement. Orr (2003) shows that differences in wealth explain much of the difference in achievement by race in the United States. This is important because middle-class African Americans have only a fraction of the wealth of same-education, same-income non-Latino whites (Merida 1995). One reason for this is that the legacy of slavery has provided African Americans with substantially fewer opportunities to acquire wealth over generations in the same way as non-Latino whites – through inheritance (Oliver and Shapiro 1995).

Although there is considerable ethnic variation among people who constitute a race (for example, Chinese-origin students have higher educational achievement than Vietnamese-origin students; see figure 8.1), racial labels still matter. That is, an immigrant to the United States from Spain may feel they have very little in common with an immigrant from Mexico, but many Americans will lump the two together into a larger Hispanic/Latino classification. Because people perceive that racial differences signify real difference, and because these real differences play out in everyday interactions (Omi and Winant 1994), an immigrant's racial group influences his/her access to power and resources. Ultimately, these racial categories have real meaning for the educational attainment of children of immigrant (and native) families. (See chapter 2 for a discussion of Latinos and race.)

Immigrants, teachers, and schools

Children of highly educated parents generally have a high socio-economic status as adults, primarily because their parents are able to provide many advantages to their children, such as sending them to elite colleges and universities. However, in the United States, many children in immigrant families have parents with low educational attainment. For these children, the quality of the schools that they attend will have a great influence on their later-life *mobility*. Mobility refers to movement up or down the socioeconomic status ladder. Not only will a good school produce educated children, it will also socialize children to be productive and well-adjusted adults. For children in immigrant families, school may be the primary place where they acquire most of the tools they need to be successfully integrated into the host country.

Katz (1987) argues that the successful integration of Irish immigrants into the United States was a function of universal education. Other historians (e.g., Bryk, Lee, and Holland 1993) attribute universal education with the successful integration of Eastern and Southern European immigrants who entered the United States in the early twentieth century. In the early 1900s, more than half of the children in the publicly funded schools in New York, Chicago, Boston, and San Francisco had immigrant parents, so local governments used schools to distribute health and other social services to immigrants at that time (Ravitch 2000). A recent fact sheet issued by the White House argues that guaranteeing access to college education for US children who are unauthorized immigrants would improve the nation's economy. The Congressional Budget Office (2010) estimates that passage of the DREAM Act would increase government revenues by $2.3 billion in ten years and reduce the federal deficit by $1.4 billion. The link between education and federal revenue was made in a recent speech by US Secretary of Education Arne Duncan who argues that extending college access would allow "these young people to live up to their fullest potential and contribute to the economic growth of our country."

No Child Left Behind places considerable pressure on schools to raise the achievement of all students, including students from immigrant families. However, much is unknown about how changes in the characteristics of a school or its teachers will affect student outcomes. Studies that have tried to link measurable characteristics of teachers (such as experience and training) to student achievement have generally failed to show that the two factors are linked. However, Rivkin, Hanushek, and Kain (2005) have examined more extensive teacher and school quality characteristics to understand how they might impact student achievement. Their study shows that the quality of instruction, especially in elementary school, has a sizable impact on students' achievements both in the primary school and in later grades. However, what predicts quality of instruction is not easy to measure. Teachers with more training and more experience are not necessarily better-quality teachers. The research by Rivkin and his colleagues (ibid.) also demonstrates that school characteristics such as classroom size matter to student achievement, but not as much as the quality of instruction.

It is difficult to quantify what makes a teacher a high-quality instructor. Since involved parents often put pressure on schools to place their children with certain teachers, this suggests that parents and students can identify the best instructors. Whether or not children from immigrant families are disadvantaged in instruction quality because their parents may not be included in information networks about quality teachers is a question yet to be fully answered.

A school's ability to improve immigrant student outcomes also depends on factors that are external to the school. For example, parental involvement in schools has a profound impact on children's education (Domina 2005; Jeynes 2007). Certainly, children from immigrant families benefit from parental involvement in the schools (Kim 2002; Kao 2004); this involvement can take the form of parental attendance at parent–teacher conferences and PTA meetings, volunteering at the school, and parental intervention in educational activities (Lareau 2000). Unfortunately, immigrant parents have more limited participation in schools, on average, than native parents (Bohon, Macpherson, and Atiles 2005; Turney and Kao 2009; Carreón, Drake, and Calabrese Barton 2005). In the United States, limited participation stems from real and perceived barriers that are experienced more acutely by parents who are immigrants, especially Asian immigrants (see Turner and Kao 2009), than by US-born white parents. These barriers include limited English fluency, limited knowledge of the education system, and lack of transportation to the schools. With regard to intervention in educational activities, Bohon, Macpherson, and Atiles (2005) document that Latino parents who have recently immigrated to the United States hold teachers in greater esteem than do US-born parents and are less likely to challenge teachers if they are unhappy about their children's learning outcomes. Turney and Kao (2009) find that school involvement among immigrant parents increases with length of time spent in the United States and the acquisition of better English skills. In fact, when English fluency and time in the United States are accounted for, Latino parents may be more involved in their children's schooling than non-Latino whites.

Of course, just as schools and teachers can improve students' outcomes, they can also have a detrimental effect on immigrant children. Valenzuela (1999) documents what she calls *subtractive education* – a process whereby some immigrant children begin to feel devalued because of their racio-ethnic identity. Overall, researchers have found that some minority groups in the United States have lower levels of academic achievement than other groups, on average. Since many immigrants are racio-ethnic minorities, they may be subject to the same racial processes that limit the achievement of minority natives. One explanation for the race gap in achievement is that teachers and other members of society hold negative-ability stereotypes regarding certain racial groups (particularly blacks and Latinos). As students experience these stereotypes in action, they reduce their academic performance. This theory of differential academic achievement across racial groups is called *stereotype threat*.

There are two paths through which stereotyping leads to poor performance. One path is through *stereotype externalization*: (1) minority students recognize that the group with which they are associated is stereotyped as being less intelligent (Steele and Aronson 1995); (2) minority students feel considerable pressure to perform well in order to overcome the stereotype; and (3) this *performance burden* places significant psychological stress on the student, leading them to perform more poorly than they otherwise would (Massey and Fischer 2005). Another path that explains the racial achievement gap is through *stereotype internalization*. Over time, minority students may come to believe the negative stereotypes of their group and may not try as hard to perform well. This type of academic disengagement is called *disidentification* (Steele and Aronson 1995) when the internalization of negative racial stereotypes leads students to uncouple their feelings of self-worth from their academic performance. Disidentified students often become disengaged from school, skip classes, and fail to complete homework.

Demographers Owens and Lynch (2012) question whether race-centered paths to lowered academic achievement operate in the same way for immigrants as they do for natives. Immigrants tend to be determined and hopeful (Conzen et al. 1992; Gans 1992b), viewing their new country as a place with plentiful opportunities (Bean and Stevens 2003). Immigrants may also live in neighborhoods dominated by co-ethnic neighbors (Grasmuck and Pessar 1991), and they are often able to maintain strong ties to friends and family in their native countries (Menjívar 2000). These factors buffer immigrants from self-identifying with the negative stereotype of the racio-ethnic groups to which they belong. In their research on college freshman, Owens and Lynch (2012) demonstrate that immigrant students are resistant to both the externalizing and internalizing processes of negative stereotyping, but that second-generation immigrants (i.e., the children of immigrants) are susceptible to internalization of negative racial stereotypes, but not externalization.

Just as children in immigrant families may learn to internalize negative racial stereotypes through their experiences at school, they may also learn other behaviors and attitudes that are undesirable. Many researchers have documented strained relationships between immigrant parents and their children as these children

Immigrant generations

Demographers usually refer to immigrants by generation. *First-generation immigrants* are those who live in a host country but were born in another country. *Second-generation immigrants* are those born in the host country with at least one immigrant parent. The *third and later generations* are those born in the host country to parents also born in the host country (i.e., the grandchildren and great-grandchildren of immigrants). This group is often referred to as natives (the second generation is sometimes referred to as natives, too). Demographers almost never distinguish the third generation from later generations because they assume that differences between them are insignificant for outcomes like educational attainment and because there are few data to capture differences between third, fourth, fifth, and later generations (Kao, Vaquera, and Goyette 2013).

Differences between the first, second, and third generations matter a great deal in terms of the educational success of immigrants, and differences *within* the first generation are important, too (Orellana 2008; Suárez-Orozco, Suárez-Orozco, and Todorova 2008). One group of education scholars notes, "A child who arrives at age 2, when he or she is just starting to learn and develop language skills, will have a very different experience from a 12-year-old who has completed a number of years of education in his or her country of origin, has time to develop friendships in that country and has a mastery of their non-English mother tongue" (Kao, Vaquera, and Goyette 2013: 9). Because of these differences, Rumbaut (2004) proposes a more refined sectioning of the first generation into 1, 1.25, 1.5, and 1.75.

The 1 generation are those who arrived in their host country as adults and whose educational attainment is largely dependent on conditions in their host country. Immigrants entering the United States since 1965 have higher educational attainment, on average, than immigrants who entered in the first half of the twentieth century. However, the average obscures the hourglass shape of the educational distribution for the first generation: many current immigrants are either very well educated or very poorly educated (Fix and Passel 1994). This stands in sharp contrast to the US-born population that tends to be neither very poorly nor very well educated (Kao, Vaquera and Goyette 2013).

The 1.25 generation are those immigrants who arrived in their host country as adolescents and spent most of their formative years in another country. The 1.5 generation refers to those who arrived during their school years but prior to adolescence. These children will have been educated in both their sending and their receiving country. The 1.75 generation refers to children who arrived in their host country prior to entering the first grade. These children will have experience only with the host-country school system, and they will generally have the same educational experiences as natives. As such, we should not expect the outcomes for the 1.75 generation to be much different from those of the second generation.

learn behaviors from their peers at school that conflict with the culture of their parents' homeland (Waters 1990; Zhou 1997b; Lee 2005). Examining Chinese immigrants to the United States and their children, Fung and Lau (2010) found that parents who experienced more stress from attempting to acculturate to their new society also reported having more disagreements with their children.

An irony of the work on parent–child conflict in immigrant families is that this research documents that family strain may be the result of how effective schools are in teaching cultural adjustment to immigrant children. Through schools, children acquire the language of their host country much more quickly than their parents (Tyyskä 2008), thus creating intergenerational power and language conflicts (Ochocka and Janzen 2008). Family roles become reversed as immigrant parents have to rely on their children to mediate dealings with service providers. In school, adolescents also meet and form friendships (including romantic relationships) with other adolescents from different ethnic or caste backgrounds, which can be troubling for parents attempting to preserve their traditional values (Tyyskä 2008). In sum, the studies of intergenerational conflict between immigrant parents and their children also provide extensive support for the idea that schools are considerable sites for immigrant adaptation, adjustment, and acculturation. This process can be beneficial to children from immigrant families as it lends itself to educational attainment and later-life success, but it can also lead to deleterious outcomes as negative racial stereotypes are reinforced and poverty-related barriers to success are more acutely encountered.

9

Conclusions

Policymakers face constant pressures to make decisions that benefit the general welfare while keeping their constituents happy. In the case of immigration policy, it is especially difficult to enact immigration laws that will stimulate the economy, reunite families, protect refugees, and maintain national security when many people are either uninformed or misinformed about immigration and the role of immigrants in society. In this book, we have sought to summarize and clarify the demographic perspective on immigration as well as some of the major issues and debates within the field in order to distinguish between what is assumed about immigration and what has been discovered through systematic inquiry. The topics covered within this text – assimilation and ethnic change, immigrant labor, immigrants in the environment, fertility, aging, health, and immigrant education – have explored the role of immigration in shaping the population processes in sending and receiving countries as well as the impact of immigration on the migrants themselves.

Demographers broadly agree that immigrants have a net positive impact on their host country. Immigrants are, on the whole, an economic boon, providing labor, paying taxes, creating jobs, and stimulating local economies. Immigrants often fill jobs that native-born workers are either untrained or unwilling to do (Linton 2002), and they provide an expanded labor force for developed countries with an otherwise aging and low-fertility population. Immigrants also pay taxes as both workers and consumers, and their tax contributions far outweigh what they consume in public services at the national level (Lofstrom and Bean 2002; Greenstone and Looney 2010). Thus, the tax revenue generated by immigrants helps to offset the substantial costs associated with an aging native-born population. Immigrants also create jobs: for one, they are more likely than the native-born to start their own businesses; additionally, their presence as consumers creates demand for goods and services, which in turn encourages business expansion and job creation. In parts of the United States confronting economic stagnation and the outmigration of the young native-born population, immigrant settlement has expanded the tax base, stabilized population loss, and helped to revitalize the local economy (Johnson et al. 2005; Johnson and Lichter 2008; McDaniel 2014). Beyond these economic impacts, immigrants provide less tangible benefits to their host countries, including benefits associated with cultural diversity such as access to different types of foods, styles of clothing and music, and other cultural benefits (Shutika 2008).

Despite these benefits, native-born populations around the world often view immigrant newcomers with ambivalence, suspicion, or even hostility. In the United States, the native-born population evinces a deep ambivalence toward immigrants and immigration, simultaneously embracing the nation's immigrant origins while remaining wary of successive waves of immigrant newcomers. Much of this ambivalence is fueled by the economy, as periods of economic insecurity correspond to higher levels of xenophobia and anti-immigrant sentiment (Higham 1955; Olzak 1992). Although immigrants are a net benefit to the host society, the native-born fear the labor market impacts of immigrants, particularly their impacts on wages and employment opportunities (Espenshade and Hempstead 1996; Espenshade and Belanger 1998). The native-born also worry that immigrants abuse public resources, including health care services (Berk et al. 2000), even though immigrants in the United States use far fewer health care services than the native-born (Goldman, Smith, and Sood 2006; Gushulak 2007). Finally, the native-born worry that immigrants threaten the very identity and cohesion of the host society (cf. Huntington 2004a, 2004b), and immigrants are often portrayed and perceived as a criminal and destructive element, even though immigrant presence has been shown to reduce crime (Feldmeyer 2009) and successive generations of immigrants have integrated into their host societies over time (Alba and Nee 1997; Waters and Jiménez 2005; Citrin et al. 2007).

Economic and cultural fears such as these have resulted in restrictionist legislation and immigrant scapegoating across the United States and Europe, as politicians scramble to prove themselves tough on immigration. In the United States, immigrant scapegoating has recently emerged through state-level restrictionist policies that seek to make life exceedingly difficult for unauthorized immigrants. For example, in 2010, the state of Arizona passed sweeping legislation which, among other provisions, required law enforcement officers to make a "reasonable attempt" to determine the citizenship or immigration status of anyone who was stopped during the course of an officer's regular duties – such as during traffic stops or arrests – or whenever the officer had a "reasonable suspicion" that the individual was unlawfully present in the United States. Shortly after Arizona SB 1070 was passed into law, representatives in more than half of the state legislatures in the nation introduced similar bills. By the following year, Utah, Indiana, Georgia, South Carolina, and Alabama had passed Arizona copycat legislation. Similarly, the real or perceived influx of immigrants in places like France, Germany, and Greece has been accompanied by an anti-immigrant backlash that has manifested itself through racially charged attacks on immigrants and immigrant-owned businesses (Koopmans et al. 2005; Haddad and Balz 2006; Givens 2007; Faiola 2012).

Current controversies and directions for future research

Although many of the concerns expressed by native-born populations have been firmly contradicted by empirical data, there remain several controversies and directions for future research with regard to the impacts of immigrants and immigration on

Conclusions

host societies. Here, we enumerate many of the disagreements and unanswered questions that emerge from the preceding chapters.

As discussed in chapter 2, scholars continue to debate the processes by which immigrants adapt to and integrate into their host countries. Some researchers (Gans 1992a; Portes and Zhou 1993; Portes, Fernández-Kelly, and Haller 2005) have argued that many immigrant goups confront structural barriers to integration, resulting in a segmented assimilation that produces differential outcomes for different immigrant groups. Others (Alba and Nee 1997) suggest that past generations of immigrants have integrated into their host country over a period of generations, and therefore we should not be surprised when the children of immigrants are not immediately assimilated. In sum, we do not yet have enough evidence to determine whether the theory of segmented assimilation adequately predicts the future failure of integration of some immigrant groups, and it may be that we can only verify the claims of this theory through hindsight, as groups integrate or fail to integrate into mainstream society over time.

Similarly, there is some controversy around the degree to which assimilation is desirable and beneficial for immigrants. In the United States, immigrant assimilation has been linked to a number of detrimental consequences, especially in relation to health outcomes (Flores and Brotanek 2005; Boulogne et al. 2012; Cacari-Stone and Avila 2012). As immigrants adopt the unhealthy lifestyles of their host country, they are more likely to suffer from diabetes, heart disease, obesity, and other negative health effects (Gushulak 2007). Some have even argued that assimilation may cause immigrants to fare worse on educational outcomes and other measures of success, especially when they abandon cultural values related to educational attainment and sacrifice (Chua and Rubenfeld 2014). Finally, immigrant assimilation may not be entirely desirable for the host country, either. For example, some researchers have suggested that immigrants to the United States may contribute to environmental harm if they adapt to the nation's superconsumer lifestyle (Daily, Ehrlich, and Ehrlich 1995; Kraly 1998).

On the other hand, some posit that immigrants who do not

fully assimilate into their host country may face negative consequences related to their limited integration. For example, Dewind and Kasinitz (1997: 1101) wonder whether strong co-ethnic ties, which are embedded in networks of community obligation, might "outlive their protective usefulness and result in economic, cultural and psychic disadvantages as well as advantages." At the same time, immigrants are chastised for perceived inadequacies in their assimilation into the host country, and some argue that immigrants who do not fully integrate contribute to ethno-racial tensions and threaten national identity and cohesion (Huntington 2004a, 2004b). Accepting the possibility of adaptation without assimilation will also force countries like France to rethink citizenship policies that are predicated on assimilation into the dominant culture. In summary, there continues to be disagreement about the processes by which, and extent to which, immigrants assimilate, and whether assimilation is always advantageous for all immigrant groups and host countries; future research should continue to examine and test these hotly contested issues.

With regard to the impact of immigrants on the economy, empirical data regularly demonstrate that immigrants are a boon. However, some evidence indicates that immigrant workers may have a negative impact on the wages and employment opportunities of native-born workers of lower socioeconomic status or on immigrants who arrived earlier (Card and DiNardo 2000; Card 2001; Lewis 2005), which raises concerns about the impact of "low skill" immigration on the economic opportunities of the most vulnerable native-born populations and other immigrants. Additionally, although there is general consensus that immigrants in the United States contribute more in taxes than they receive in benefits (American Immigration Council 2013), the tax contributions of immigrants accrue differently over time at different levels of government and in different states. For example, the federal government benefits directly from taxes collected on immigrants' paychecks, and many immigrants pay taxes into social security, even though those who are unauthorized will never be able to access those funds when they retire (Gross et al. 2013). At the same time, the costs associated with providing services to immigrants –

such as education and health care – often fall to states, and these costs are not shared equally across all states. Border states like Arizona, New Mexico, and Texas are disproportionately burdened by these costs, and they will only recoup these expenses from immigrant taxpayers over a number of years (Greenstone and Looney 2010). Thus, the fiscal benefits of immigrants are not equitably shared with those who take on the costs.

As detailed in chapter 4, scholars have only just begun to empirically study the relationship between immigrants and the environment. Consequently, we do not yet fully understand the environmental impacts of immigrants on their host country, nor do we understand immigrants' attitudes toward the environment. Although scholars have assumed that population growth – including growth due to immigration – inevitably contributes to environmental degradation, research has not conclusively shown that immigrants harm the environment, for example, through their contributions to pollution, urban sprawl, and consumption (Bartlett and Lytwak 1995; Cole and Neumayer 2004; Ewing 2008). On the contrary, some research indicates that immigration may actually slow environmental degradation, as outmigration decreases resource pressure on under-resourced sending countries (Abel et al. 2013; Caviglia-Harris, Sills and Mullan 2013). Likewise, some evidence suggests that immigrants may exhibit more environmentally friendly behaviors than the native-born, such as resource conservation and carpooling (Pfeffer and Stycos 2002; Blumenberg and Shiki 2008; Bohon, Stamps, and Atiles 2008). More research is needed to better understand the impact of immigrants on the environments of both sending and receiving nations.

Scholars continue to debate the fertility rates of immigrants, as described in chapter 5. Different theories and models of immigrant fertility suggest that immigrants have fewer children, more children, or the same number of children as the native-born or as non-immigrant women from the same sending countries. Some of the discrepancies in fertility outcomes between immigrants and the native-born result from differences in how researchers measure fertility – for example, whether they compare current or lifetime fertility rates between groups. Still, we do not yet have sufficient evidence to explain why the fertility rates of immigrants may differ from that of the native-born. Several theories – the disruption hypothesis, selection hypothesis, interrelation of events hypothesis, adaptation hypothesis, assimilation hypothesis, socialization hypothesis, and legitimacy hypothesis – attempt to explain potential differences in fertility. However, it is difficult to determine the explanatory power of these hypotheses because they do not necessarily offer exclusive explanations; at the same time, fertility patterns may be different for different groups in different places. More research is needed to resolve current debates over the fertility norms of immigrants in terms of whether, how, and why they differ from the norms of native-born women.

Understanding immigrant fertility is especially important in gauging the effectiveness of replacement migration to offset aging in developed countries, as we discuss in chapter 6. Many policymakers see the migration of younger workers who are likely to have children as the key to replacing an aging work force that must be supported in their older ages. However, since immigrants age, too, and because immigrants may have completed fertility that is no different from that of natives, replacement migration may be ineffective to offset population aging in the long run. More research is needed to understand the consequences of these processes.

As detailed in chapter 7, immigrants tend to be healthier than the native-born of receiving developed countries in the aggregate, but we do not conclusively understand why this difference occurs. The healthy migrant hypothesis suggests that the healthiest people in a sending country are more likely to migrate successfully (Crimmins et al. 2005; Bostean 2013) and that immigrants tend to engage in more protective health behaviors than the native-born, such as eating healthier diets and exercising regularly (Abraído-Lanza et al. 1999; Razum and Twardella 2002; Mazur, Marquis, and Jensen 2003; Himmelgreen et al. 2004; Flores and Brotanek 2005). On the other hand, salmon bias suggests that unhealthy immigrants may return to their country of origin to convalesce or die (Shai and Rosenwaike 1987; Pablos-Méndez 1994), so that immigrants who remain in the host country are mostly healthy. Increasingly, studies of immigrant health find that differences in health outcomes between immigrants and the native-born are largely dependent on measures of health as well as the demographic characteristics of the immigrant group being studied (Cunningham, Ruben, and Narayan 2008). Thus, future research should carefully examine differences in health outcomes within and between different immigrant groups, the native-born of receiving countries, and those who remain in their country of origin, as well as differences based on gender and other characteristics.

Finally, as we discuss in chapter 8, countries that receive immigrants face the challenge of educating children who may not speak the national language, who may have little or no prior education, and who come from families where parents are unfamiliar with the education system. Moreover, since the implementation of No Child Left Behind in the United States, the presence of English language learners makes teachers and administrators anxious about the impact of these children on the test scores to which school performance is benchmarked. Although it is often costly and challenging to educate immigrant children, empirical evidence suggests that an educated populace is ultimately beneficial to the national economy. It is too early to tell whether or not US policymakers will pass the DREAM Act or similar educational measures that increase economic opportunities for future generations, or whether they will bow to public pressures to persist in denying resources to the foreign-born. Future research should continue to examine the impact of structural barriers on the educational attainment of immigrants and their children.

The robust debates within the field of demography and the abundance of opportunities for future research indicate the complexity of immigration as a demographic process. Yet, the topic of immigration is not confined to the realm of academia; today, media, politicians, and everyday people use the catchphrase "demographic change" to describe the world around us, and many wonder how immigration and immigrants will impact our society. Although the field of demography cannot provide us with definitive answers to our political and ethical questions about immigration, it can help us better understand larger trends among immigrant groups and host societies, as well as how immigrants and receiving populations are affected by immigration; it can also dispel unproven allegations about the negative impacts of immigrants and immigration so that our decisions are guided not by assumptions, but rather by empirical data. To know how best to respond to our changing society, we must first examine and understand the processes underlying this change.

References

Abbasi-Shavazi, Mohammad Jalal, and Peter McDonald. 2000. "Fertility and Multiculturalism: Immigrant Fertility in Australia, 1977–1991." *International Migration Review* 34(1): 215–42.

Abbasi-Shavazi, Mohammad Jalal, and Peter McDonald. 2002. "A Comparison of Fertility Patterns of European Immigrants in Australia with Those in the Countries of Origin." *Genus* 58: 53–76.

Abel, Guy, Jakub Bijak, Allan Findlay, David McCollum, and Arkadiusz Wiśniowski. 2013. "Forecasting Environmental Migration to the United Kingdom: An Exploration Using Bayesian Models." *Population and Environment*. Available online at http://link.springer.com/article/10.1007%2 Fs11111-013-0186-8.

Abernethy, Virginia Deane. 2000. "Comments on Diane Macunovich." *Population and Environment* 21(3): 339–41.

Abernethy, Virginia Deane. 2001. "Comment on Bermingham's Summary of the UN's Year 2000 *Replacement Migration: Is it a Solution to Declining Population and Aging?*" *Population and Environment* 22(4): 65–375.

Abraído-Lanza, Ana F., Bruce P. Dohrenwend, Daisy S. Ng-Mak, and J. Blake Turner. 1999. "The Latino Mortality Paradox: A Test of the 'Salmon Bias' and Healthy Migrant Hypotheses." *American Journal of Public Health* 89(10): 1543–8.

Adam, Mary B., Jenifer K. McGuire, Michele Walsh, Joanne Basta, and Craig LeCroy. 2005. "Acculturation as a Predictor of the Onset of Sexual Intercourse among Hispanic and White Teens." *Archives of Pediatrics and Adolescent Medicine* 159(3): 261–5.

Adler, Nancy E., Thomas Boyce, Margaret A. Chesney, et al. 1994. "Socioeconomic Status and Health: The Challenge to the Gradient." *The American Psychologist* 49(1): 15–24.

Adserà, Alícia. 2004. "Changing Fertility Rates in Developed Countries: The

References

Impact of Labor Market Institutions." *Journal of Population Economics* 17(1): 17–43.

Aguirre, B. E., Rogelio Saenz, John Edmiston, Nan Yang, Elsa Agramonte, and Dietra L. Stuart. 1993. "The Human Ecology of Tornadoes." *Demography* 30(4): 623–33.

Ainsworth-Darnell, James W., and Douglas B. Downey. 1998. "Assessing the Oppositional Culture Explanation for Racial/Ethnic Differences in School Performance." *American Sociological Review* 63(4): 536–53.

Akee, Randall Kekoa Quinones, David A. Jaeger, and Konstantinos Tatsiramos. 2007. "The Persistence of Self-Employment across Borders: New Evidence on Legal Immigrants to the United States." Department of Economics Working Paper 69. Williamsburg, VA: College of William and Mary.

Alba, Richard. 1990. *Ethnic Identity: The Transformation of White America*. New Haven, CT: Yale University Press.

Alba, Richard, and Victor Nee. 1997. "Rethinking Assimilation Theory for a New Era of Immigration." *International Migration Review* 31(4): 826–74.

Alba, Richard, Rubén G. Rumbaut, and Karen Marotz. 2005. "A Distorted Nation: Perceptions of Racial/Ethnic Group Sizes and Attitudes toward Immigrants and Other Minorities." *Social Forces* 84(2): 901–19.

Alba, Richard D., John R. Logan, Brian J. Stults, Gilbert Marzan, and Wenguan Zhang. 1999. "Immigrant Groups in the Suburbs: A Reexamination of Suburbanization and Spatial Assimilation." *American Sociological Review* 64(3): 446–60.

Alders, Maarten. 2000. "Cohort Fertility of Migrant Women in the Netherlands: Developments in Fertility of Women Born in Turkey, Morocco, Suriname, and the Netherlands Antilles and Aruba." Research Report. Voorburg, the Netherlands: Statistics Netherlands.

Aldrich, Howard A., and Roger Waldinger. 1990. "Ethnicity and Entrepreneurship." *Annual Review of Sociology* 16: 111–35.

Alexander, Karl L., Doris R. Entwisle, and Susan L. Dauber. 2002. *On the Success of Failure: A Reassessment of the Effects of Retention on the Primary Grades*. Second edition. New York: Cambridge University Press.

Alonso, José Antonio. 2011. "International Migration and Development: A Review in Light of the Crisis." CDP Background Paper 11(E). New York: United Nations.

American Immigration Council. 2013. "Tackling the Toughest Questions on Immigration Reform: Short Answers to the Most Common Questions." Special report. Washington, DC: Immigration Policy Center.

Anderson, John R. 1982. "Acquisition of Cognitive Skills." *Psychological Review* 89(4): 369–406.

Anderson, Laurie M., David L. Wood, and Cathy Donald Sherbourne. 1997. "Maternal Acculturation and Childhood Immunization Levels among Children

References

in Latino Families in Los Angeles." *American Journal of Public Health* 87(12): 2018–21.

Andersson, Gunnar. 2004. "Childbearing after Migration: Fertility Patterns of Foreign-Born Women in Sweden." *International Migration Review* 38(2): 747–75.

Andersson, Gunnar, and Kirk Scott. 2005. "Labour-market Status and First-time Parenthood: The Experience of Immigrant Women in Sweden, 1981–97." *Population Studies* 59(1): 21–38.

Angrist, Joshua D., Victor Lavy, and Analia Schlosser. 2005. "New Evidence on the Causal Link between the Quantity and Quality of Children." NBER Working Paper 11835. Cambridge, MA: National Bureau of Economic Research.

Anrig, Greg, and Tova Andrea Wang (eds.) 2007. *Immigration's New Frontiers: Experiences from the Emerging Gateway States.* Washington, DC: The Brookings Institution Press.

Antecol, Heather, Peter Kuhn, and Stephen J. Trejo. 2006. "Assimilation via Prices or Quantiles? Sources of Immigrant Earnings Growth in Australia, Canada, and the United States." *The Journal of Human Resources* 41(4): 821–840.

Appadurai, Arjun. 1996. *Modernity at Large: Cultural Dimensions of Globalization.* Minneapolis: University of Minnesota Press.

Appave, Gervais, and Frank Laczko (eds.) 2011. *World Migration Report 2011: Communicating Effectively about Migration.* Geneva: International Organization for Migration.

Arrow, K. J., H. B. Chenery, B. S. Minhas, and R. M. Solow. 1961. "Capital-labor Substitution and Economic Efficiency." *The Review of Economics and Statistics* 43(3): 225–50.

Arrow, Kenneth Joseph, Samuel Bowles, and Steven N. Durlauf (eds.) 2000. *Meritocracy and Economic Inequality.* Princeton, NJ: Princeton University Press.

Atiles, Jorge H., and Stephanie A. Bohon. 2002. *The Needs of Georgia's New Latinos: A Policy Agenda for the Decade Ahead.* Atlanta: Carl Vinson Institute of Government, University of Georgia.

Atiles, Jorge H. and Stephanie A. Bohon. 2003. "*Camas Calientes*: Housing Adjustments and Barriers to Adaptation among the South's Rural Latinos." *Southern Rural Sociology* 19(1): 97–122.

Aufrecht, Monica. 2012. "Rethinking 'Greening of Hate': Climate Emissions, Immigration, and the Last Frontier." *Ethics and the Environment* 17(2): 51–74.

Bacio, Guadelupe A., Vickie M. Mays, and Anna S. Lau. 2013. "Drinking Initiation and Problematic Drinking among Latino Adolescents: Explanations of the Immigrant Paradox." *Psychology of Addictive Behaviors* 27(1): 14–22.

Bankston, Carl L., III. 2004. "Social Capital, Cultural Values, Immigration, and Academic Achievement: The Host Country Context and Contradictory Consequences." *Sociology of Education* 77(2): 176–9.

161

References

Barker, D. J. P. 1990. "Fetal and Infant Origins of Adult Disease: The Womb May be More Important than the Home." *The British Medical Journal* 301(6761): 1111.

Baron-Epel, Orna, and G. Kaplan. 2001. "Self-reported Health Status of Immigrants from the Former Soviet Union in Israel." *The Israel Medical Association Journal* 3(12): 940–6.

Barrera, Manuel, Nancy A. Gonzales, Vera Lopez, and A. Cristina Fernandez. 2004. "Problem Behaviors of Chicana/o and Latina/o Adolescents: An Analysis of Prevalence, Risk, and Protective Factors." Pp. 83–109 in *The Handbook of Chicana/o Psychology and Mental Health*, edited by R. J. Velásquez, L. M. Arellano, and B. McNeill. Mahwah, NJ: Lawrence Erlbaum.

Bartlett, Albert A., and Edward P. Lytwak. 1995. "Zero Growth of the Population of the United States." *Population and Environment* 16(5): 415–28.

Bauer, Philipp, and Regina T. Riphahn. 2006. "Timing of School Tracking as a Determinant of Intergenerational Transmission of Education." *Economics Letters* 91(1): 90–7.

Bauer, Thomas K., Magnus Lofstrom, and Klaus F. Zimmermann. 2000. "Immigration Policy, Assimilation of Immigrants and Natives' Sentiments toward Immigrants: Evidence from 12 OECD-Countries." IZA discussion paper 187. Bonn: The Institute for the Study of Labor.

Bean, Frank D., and Gillian Stevens. 2003. *America's Newcomers: Immigrant Incorporation and the Dynamics of Diversity*. New York: Russell Sage Foundation.

Bean, Frank D., and Gray Swicegood. 1985. *Mexican American Fertility Patterns*. Austin: University of Texas Press.

Bean, Frank D., and Marta Tienda. 1990. "The Hispanic Population in the United States." In *The Population of the United States in the 1980s*. (National Committee for Research on the 1980 Census.) New York: Russell Sage Foundation.

Bebout, Lee. 2012. "The Nativist Aztlán: Fantasies and Anxieties of Whiteness on the Border." *Latino Studies* 10(3): 290–313.

Beck, Roy, Leon Kolankiewicz, and Steven A. Camarota. 2003. "Outsmarting Smart Growth: Population Growth, Immigration, and the Problem of Sprawl." Report. Washington, DC: Center for Immigration Studies.

Becker, Gary S., and Nigel Tomes. 1976. "Child Endowments and the Quantity and Quality of Children." NBER Working Paper 123. Stanford, CA: National Bureau of Economic Research.

Behrman, Jere R., and Nevzer Stacey (eds.) 1997. *Social Benefits of Education*. Ann Arbor: University of Michigan Press.

Beirich, Heidi. 2010. "Greenwash: Nativists, Environmentalism and the Hypocrisy of Hate." A special report of the Southern Poverty Law Center. Montgomery, AL: Southern Poverty Law Center.

Beirich, Heidi. 2011. "The Year in Nativism, 2010." *Intelligence Report*.

References

Available online at www.splcenter.org/get-informed/intelligence-report/browse-all-issues/2011/spring/the-year-in-nativism.

Beiser, Morton, and Ilene Hyman. 1994. "Mental Health of Immigrants and Refugees." Pp. 73–86 in *Mental Health Care in Canada: New Directions for Mental Health Services*, edited by Leona L. Bachrach, Paula Goering, and Donald Alexander Wasylenki. San Francisco: Jossey-Bass.

Belot, Michéle V. K., and Timothy J. Hatton. 2012. "Immigrant Selection in the OECD." *The Scandinavian Journal of Economics* 114(4): 1105–28.

Beng, Chew Soon. 2012. "Employment-based Social Protection in Singapore: Issues and Prospects." *ASEAN Economic Bulletin* 29(3): 218–29.

Ben-Porath, Yoram. 1973. "Economic Analysis of Fertility in Israel: Point and Counterpoint." *Journal of Political Economy* 81(2): 208–33.

Berger, Eugenia Hepworth, and Mari Riojas-Cortez. 2011. *Parents as Partners in Education: Families and Schools Working Together*. Eighth edition. New York: Maxwell Macmillan.

Bergeron, Claire. 2013. "Going to the Back of the Line: A Primer on Lines, Visa Categories, and Wait Times." Report. Washington, DC: Migration Policy Institute.

Berk, Marc L., Claudia L. Schur, Leo R. Chavez, and Martin Frankel. 2000. "Health Care Use among Undocumented Latino Immigrants." *Health Affairs* 19(4): 51–64.

Betts, Katharine. 2004. "Demographic and Social Research on the Population and Environment Nexus in Australia: Explaining the Gap." *Population and Environment* 26(2): 157–72.

Bieter, Johng and Mark Bieter. 2004. *An Enduring Legacy: The Story of Basques in Idaho*. Reno: University of Nevada Press.

Biggs, Andrew G. 2013. "Immigration Reform and Social Security." *National Review Online*. Available online at www.nationalreview.com/article/352298/immigration-reform-and-social-security-andrew-g-biggs.

Bijak, Jakub, Dorota Kupiszewska, and Marek Kupiszewski. 2008. "Replacement Migration Revisited: Simulations of the Effect of Selected Population and Labor Market Strategies for the Aging Europe, 2002–2052." *Population Research and Policy Review* 27(3): 321–42.

Bijak, Jakub, Dorota Kupiszewska, Marek Kupiszewski, Katarzyna Saczuk, and Anna Kicinger. 2007. "Population and Labour Force Projections for 27 European Countries, 2002–2052: Impact of International Migration on Population Ageing." *European Journal of Population* 23(1): 1–31.

Black, Sandra E., Paul J. Devereux, and Kjell G. Salvanes. 2003. "Why the Apple Doesn't Fall Far: Understanding Intergenerational Transmission of Human Capital." *American Economic Review* 95(1): 437–49.

Blalock, Hubert. 1967. *Toward a Theory of Minority-Group Relations*. New York and London: John Wiley and Sons.

Blanchflower, David G. 2004. "Self-employment: More May Not Be Better."

References

NBER Working Paper 10286. Cambridge, MA: National Bureau of Economic Research.

Blau, Peter M., and Otis Dudley Duncan. 1967. *The American Occupational Structure*. New York: Wiley.

Bledsoe, Caroline H. 2004. "Reproduction at the Margins: Migration and Legitimacy in the New Europe." *Demographic Research* 3(4): 87–116.

Bledsoe, Caroline H., René Houle, and Papa Sow. 2007. "High Fertility Gambians in Low Fertility Spain: The Dynamics of Child Accumulation across Transnational Space." *Demographic Research* 16(12): 375–412.

Blue, Laura, and Andrew Fenelon. 2011. "Explaining Low Mortality among US Immigrants Relative to Native-born Americans: The Role of Smoking." *International Journal of Epidemiology* 40(3): 786–93.

Bluestone, Irving, Rhonda J. V. Montgomery, and John D. Owen. 1990. *The Aging of the American Work Force: Problems, Programs, Policies*. Detroit: Wayne State University Press.

Blumenberg, Evelyn, and Kimiko Shiki. 2008. "Immigrants and Resource Sharing: The Case of Carpooling." Paper presented at the 87th annual meeting of the Transportation Research Board, January 13–17, 2008, Washington, DC.

Blumer, Herbert. 1958. "Race Prejudice as a Sense of Group Position." *Pacific Sociological Review* 1(1): 3–7.

Bohon, Stephanie. 2001. *Latinos in Ethnic Enclaves: Immigrant Workers and the Competition for Jobs*. New York: Routledge.

Bohon, Stephanie A., Monica Kirkpatrick Johnson, and Bridget K. Gorman. 2006. "College Aspirations and Expectations among Latino Adolescents in the United States." *Social Problems* 53(2): 207–25.

Bohon, Stephanie A., Heather Macpherson, and Jorge H. Atiles. 2005. "Educational Barriers for New Latinos in Georgia." *Journal of Latinos and Education* 4(1): 43–58.

Bohon, Stephanie A., Laura Gerard Massengale, and Audrey Jordan. 2009. "Mexican Self-Employment in Old and New Latino Places." Pp. 197–222 in *Global Connections and Local Receptions: New Latino Immigration to the Southeastern United States*, edited by F. Ansley and J. Shefner. Knoxville: The University of Tennessee Press.

Bohon, Stephanie A., Katherine Stamps, and Jorge H. Atiles. 2008. "Transportation and Migrant Adjustment in Georgia." *Population Research and Policy Review* 27(3): 273–91.

Bongaarts, John. 2008. "What Can Fertility Indicators Tell Us about Pronatalist Policy Options?" Pp. 39–55 in *Vienna Yearbook of Population Research*, Volume VI. Vienna: Austrian Academy of Sciences Vienna Institue of Demography.

Bongaarts, John, and Robert G. Potter. 1983. *Fertility, Biology, and Behavior: An Analysis of the Proximate Determinants*. New York: Academic Press.

References

Bonin, Holger, Bernd Raffelhüschen, and Jan Walliser. 2000. "Can Immigration Alleviate the Demographic Burden?" *FinanzArchiv / Public Finance Analysis* 57(1): 1–21.

Borch, Casey, and Mamadi K. Corra. 2010. "Differences in Earnings among Black and Non-black African Immigrants in the United States, 1980–2000: A Cross-sectional and Temporal Analysis." *Sociological Perspectives* 53(4): 573–92.

Borjas, George J. 1985. "Assimilation, Changes in Cohort Quality, and the Earnings of Immigrants." *Journal of Labor Economics* 3: 463–89.

Borjas, George J. 1995. "Assimilation and Changes in Cohort Quality Revisited: What Happened to Immigrant Earnings in the 1980s?" *Journal of Labor Economics* 13: 201–45.

Borjas, George J. 2003. "The Labor Demand Curve is Downward Sloping: Reexamining the Impact of Immigration on the Labor Market." *The Quarterly Journal of Economics* 118(4): 1135–374.

Borjas, George J. 2006. "Native Internal Migration and the Labor Market Impact of Immigration." *The Journal of Human Resources* 41(2): 221–58.

Borjas, George J., Jeffrey Grogger, and Gordon Hanson. 2008. "Imperfect Substitution between Immigrants and Natives: A Reappraisal." NBER Working Paper 13887. Cambridge, MA: National Bureau of Economic Research.

Borjas, George J., and Lawrence F. Katz. 2007. "The Evolution of the Mexican-born Workforce in the United States." Chapter 1 in *Mexican Immigration to the United States*, edited by George J. Borjas. Chicago: University of Chicago Press.

Boserup, Ester. 1981. *Population and Technological Change*. Chicago: University of Chicago Press.

Bostean, Georgiana. 2013. "Does Selective Migration Explain the Hispanic Paradox? A Comparative Analysis of Mexicans in the US and Mexico." *Journal of Immigrant and Minority Health* 15(3): 624–35.

Boulogne, Roxanne, Eric Jougla, Yves Breen, Anton E. Kunst, and Gregoire Rey. 2012. "Mortality Differences between the Foreign-born and Locally-born Population in France (2004–2007)." *Social Science and Medicine* 74(8): 1213–23.

Bourdieu, Pierre. 1980. "Le capital social." *Actes de la Recherche en Sciences Sociales* 31: 2–3.

Bouvier, Leon F. 2001. "Replacement Migration: Is it a Solution to Declining and Aging Populations?" *Population and Environment* 22(4): 377–81.

Bratsberg, Bernt, Erling Barth, and Raaum Oddbjørn. 2006. "Local Unemployment and the Relative Wages of Immigrants: Evidence from the Current Population Surveys." *The Review of Economics and Statistics* 88(2): 243–63.

Brimelow, Peter. 1996. *Alien Nation: Common Sense about America's Immigration Disaster*. New York: Harper Perennial.

References

Brockerhoff, Martin. 1995. "Fertility and Family-Planning in African Cities: The Impact of Female Migration." *Journal of Biosocial Science* 27(3): 347–58.

Brown, Susan K., and Frank D. Bean. 2006. "Assimilation Models, Old and New: Explaining a Long-term Process." *Migration Information Source*. Washington, DC: Migration Policy Institute. Available online at www.migrationinformation.org/feature/display.cfm?id=442. *Brown v. Board of Education*. 1954. 347 US 383.

Brücker, Herbert, and Elke J. Jahn. 2011. "Migration and Wage-setting: Reassessing the Labor Market Effects of Migration." *The Scandinavian Journal of Economics* 113(2): 286–317.

Bryk, Anthony S., Valerie E. Lee, and Peter B. Holland. 1993. *Catholic Schools and the Common Good*. Cambridge, MA: Harvard University Press.

Buchanan, Patrick. 2006. *State of Emergency: The Third World Invasion and Conquest of America*. New York: St. Martin's Press.

Budig, Michelle J. 2006. "Intersections on the Road to Self-Employment: Gender, Family and Occupational Class." *Social Forces* 84(4): 2223–39.

Bullard, Robert Doyle, Reuben C. Warren, and Glenn S. Johnson. 2005. *The Quest for Environmental Justice*. San Francisco: Sierra Club Books.

Bursik, Robert J., Jr. 2006. "Social Disorganization and Theories of Crime and Delinquency: Problems and Prospects." *Criminology* 26(4): 519–52.

Burvill, P. W. 1998. "Migrant Suicide Rates in Australia and in Country of Birth." *Psychological Medicine* 28(1): 201–8.

Cacari-Stone, Lisa, and Magdalena Avila. 2012. "Rethinking Research Ethics for Latinos: The Policy Paradox of Health Reform and the Role of Social Justice." *Ethics and Behavior* 22(6): 445–60.

Caetano, Raul, and Catherine L. Clark. 2003. "Acculturation, Alcohol Consumption, Smoking, and Drug Use among Hispanics." Pp. 223–39 in *Acculturation: Advances in Theory, Measurement and Applied Research*, edited by Kevin M. Chun, Pamela B. Organista, and Gerardo Main. Washington, DC: American Psychological Association.

Caldwell, John C. 1982. *Theory of Fertility Decline*. New York: Academic Press.

Caldwell, John C. 2006. *Demographic Transition Theory*. London: Springer.

Camarota, Steven A. 2005. "Birth Rates among Immigrants in America: Comparing Fertility in the US and Home Countries." Research Report. Washington, DC: Center for Immigration Studies.

Camarota, Steven A. 2013. "How Many New Voters Would S.744 Create? A Look at the Electoral Implications of the Gang of Eight Immigration Bill." Washington, DC: Center for Immigration Studies. Available online at www.cis.org/how-many-new-voters-would-s744-create.

Campbell, Kristina M. 2011. "The Road to SB 1070: How Arizona Became Ground Zero for the Immigrants' Rights Movement and the Continuing Struggle for Latino Civil Rights in America." *Harvard Latino Law Review* 14: 2–21.

References

Capps, Randy, and Michael Fix. 2013. "Immigration Reform: A Long Road to Citizenship and Insurance Coverage." *Health Affairs* 32(4): 639–42.

Capps, Randy, Michael Fix, Julie Murray, Jason Ost, Jeffrey S. Passel, and Shinta Herwantoro. 2005. "The New Demography of America's Schools: Immigration and the No Child Left Behind Act." A report of the Urban Institute. Washington DC: The Urban Institute.

Carballo, Manuel, Jose J. Divino, and Damir Zeric. 1998. "Migration and Health in the European Union." *Tropical Medicine and International Health* 3(12): 936–44.

Card, David. 2001. "Immigrant Inflows, Native Outflows, and the Local Labor Market Impacts of Higher Immigration." *Journal of Labor Economics* 19(1): 22–64.

Card, David. 2005. "Is the New Immigration Really So Bad?" *Economic Journal* 115(507): F300–F323.

Card, David. 2007. "How Immigration Affects US Cities." CReAM Discussion Paper 11/07. London: University College London.

Card, David, and John DiNardo. 2000. "Do immigrant inflows lead to native outflows?" *The American Economic Review* 90(2): 360–7.

Card, David, and Ethan Lewis. 2007. "The Diffusion of Mexican Immigrants During the 1990s: Explanations and Impacts." Chapter 6 in *Mexican Immigration to the United States*, edited by George J. Borjas. Chicago: University of Chicago Press.

Card, David, and Stephen Raphael (eds.) 2013. *Immigration, Poverty, and Socioeconomic Inequality*. New York: Russell Sage.

Cardak, Buly A., and James Ted McDonald. 2001. "Neighbourhood Effects, Preference Heterogeneity and Immigrant Educational Attainment." School of Business Working Paper A02.02. Melbourne, Australia: La Trobe University.

Carlson, Elwood D. 1985a. "Increased Nonmarital Births among Foreign Women in Germany." *Sociology and Social Research* 70(1): 110–11.

Carlson, Elwood D. 1985b. "The Impact of International Migration upon Timing of Marriage and Childbearing." *Demography* 22(1): 61–72.

Carreón, Gustavo Pérez, Corey Drake, and Angela Calabrese Barton. 2005. "The Importance of Presence: Immigrant Parents' School Engagement Experiences." *American Educational Research Journal* 42(3):465–98.

Carter, Prudence L. 2003. "'Black' Cultural Capital, Status Positioning, and Schooling Conflicts for Low-income African American Youth." *Social Problems* 50(1): 136–55.

Castles, Stephen. 1985. "The Guests Who Stayed: The Debate on 'Foreigners Policy' in the German Federal Republic." *International Migration Review* 19(3): 517–34.

Castles, Stephen, Mark J. Miller, and Giuseppe Ammendola. 2003. *The Age of Migration: International Population Movements in the Modern World*. New York: The Guilford Press.

References

Castro, Felipe González, Judith A. Stein, and Peter M. Bentler. 2009. "Ethnic Pride, Traditional Family Values, and Acculturation in Early Cigarette and Alcohol Use among Latino Adolescents." *The Journal of Primary Prevention* 30(3–4): 265–92.

Catton, William R. 1980. *Overshoot: The Ecological Basis of Revolutionary Change.* Chicago: University of Illinois Press.

Caviglia-Harris, Jill L., Erin O. Sills, and Katrina Mullan. 2013. "Migration and Mobility on the Amazon Frontier." *Population and Environment* 34(3): 338–369.

Ceobanu, Alin M., and Xavier Escandell. 2008. "East is West? National Feelings and Anti-immigrant Sentiment in Europe." *Social Science Research* 37(4): 1147–70.

Ceobanu, Alin M., and Xavier Escandell. 2011. "Paths to Citizenship? Public Views on the Extension of Rights to Legal and Second-generation Immigrants in Europe." *The British Journal of Sociology* 62(2): 221–40.

Ceobanu, Alin, and Tanya Koropeckyj-Cox. 2013. "Should International Migration Be Encouraged to Offset Population Aging? A Cross-Country Analysis of Public Attitudes in Europe." *Population Research and Policy Review* 32(2): 261–84.

Chapman, Robert L. 2006. "Confessions of a Malthusian Restrictionist." *Ecological Economics* 59(12): 215–19.

Chattopadhyay, Arpita, Michael J. White, and Cornelius Debpuur. 2006. "Migrant Fertility in Ghana: Selection versus Adaptation and Disruption as Causal Mechanisms." *Population Studies* 60(2): 189–203.

Chavez, Leo. 1997. "Immigration Reform and Nativism: The Nationalist Response to the Transnationalist Challenge." Pp. 61–77 in *Immigrants Out! The New Nativism and the Anti-Immigrant Impulse in the United States*, edited by Juan F. Perea. New York: New York University Press.

Chavez, Leo R. 2008. *The Latino Threat: Constructing Immigrants, Citizens, and the Nation.* Stanford, CA: Stanford University Press.

Chertow, Marian R. 2001. "The IPAT Equation and its Variants: Changing Views of Technology and Environmental Impact." *Journal of Industrial Ecology* 4(4): 13–29.

Chiswick, Barry. 1978. "The Effects of Americanization on the Earnings of Foreign-born Men." *Journal of Political Economy* 86: 897–921.

Chiswick, Barry R., Yew Liang Lee, and Paul W. Miller. 2008. "Immigrant Selection Systems and Immigrant Health." *Contemporary Economic Policy* 26(4): 555–78.

Cho, Grace. 2000. "The Role of Heritage Language in Social Interactions and Relationships: Reflections from a Language Minority Group." *Bilingual Research Journal* 24(4): 369–84.

Chua, Amy, and Jed Rubenfeld. 2014. *The Triple Package: How Three Unlikely Traits Explain the Rise and Fall of Cultural Groups in America.* New York: The Penguin Press.

References

Citrin, Jack, Amy Lehman, Michael Murakami, and Kathryn Pearson. 2007. "Testing Huntington: Is Hispanic Immigration a Threat to American Identity?" *Perspectives on Politics* 5(1): 31–48.

Citrin, Jack, Beth Reingold, and Donald P. Green. 1990. "American Identity and the Politics of Ethnic Change." *Journal of Politics* 52(4): 1124–54.

Citrin, Jack, Beth Reingold, Evelyn Walters, and Donald P. Green. 1990. "The 'Official English' Movement and the Symbolic Politics of Language in the United States." *The Western Political Quarterly* 43(3): 535–59.

Clegg, Limin X., Marsha E. Reichman, Benjamin F. Hankey, et al. 2007. "Quality of Race, Hispanic Ethnicity, and Immigrant Status in Population-Based Cancer Registry Data: Implications for Health Disparity Status." *Cancer Causes and Control* 18(2): 177–87.

Cobb-Clark, Deborah A. 2003. "Public Policy and the Labor Market Adjustment of New Immigrants to Australia." *Journal of Population Economics* 16(4): 655–81.

Cochran-Smith, Marilyn, and Susan L. Lytle. 2006. "Troubling Images of Teaching in No Child Left Behind." *Harvard Educational Review* 76(4): 668–97.

Cohen, Sarit, and Chang Tai-Hsieh. 2001. "Macro-economic and Labor Market Impact of Russian Immigration in Israel." Working Paper 11-01. Ramat Gan, Israel: Bar Ilan University.

Cohen-Goldner, Sarit, and M. Daniele Paserman. 2006. "Mass Migration to Israel and Natives' Employment Transitions." *Industrial and Labor Relations Review* 59(4): 630–52.

Cole, Matthew A., and Eric Neumayer. 2004. "Examining the Impact of Demographic Factors on Air Pollution." *Population and Environment* 26(1): 5–21.

Coleman, David A. 1994. "Trends in Fertility and Intermarriage among Immigrant Populations in Western Europe as Measures of Integration." *Journal of Biosocial Science* 26(01): 107–36.

Coleman, David A. 2002. "Replacement Migration, or Why Everyone is Going to Have to Live in Korea: A Fable of Our Times from the United Nations." *Philosophical Transactions of the Royal Society B* 357(1420): 583–98.

Coleman, David A. 2004a. "Who's Afraid of Low Support Ratios?" *Population Bulletin of the United Nations* 44-5: 288–329.

Coleman, David A. 2004b. "Europe at the Crossroads: Must Europe's Population and Workforce Depend on New Immigration?" Pp. 19–33 in *International Migration*, edited by V. Iontzev. Moscow: Max.

Coleman, David. 2006. "Immigration and Ethnic Change in Low-Fertility Countries: A Third Demographic Transition." *Population and Development Review* 32(3): 401–46.

Coleman, David A. 2008. "The Demographic Effects of International Migration in Europe." *Oxford Review of Economic Policy* 24(3): 458–76.

References

Coleman, David A., and Robert Rowthorne. 2011. "Who's Afraid of Population Decline? A Critical Examination of its Consequences." *Population and Development Review* 37(s1): 217–48.

Coleman, James S. 1988. "Social Capital in the Creation of Human Capital." *American Journal of Sociology* 94: S95–S120.

Comer, James P., and Norris M. Haynes. 1991. "Parent Involvement in Schools: An Ecological Approach." *The Elementary School Journal* 91(3): 271–7.

Commissioner for Human Rights. 2010. "Criminalisation of Migration in Europe: Human Rights Implications." CommDH/IssuePaper. Strasbourg: Council of Europe. Available online at https://wcd.coe.int/ViewDoc. jsp?id=1579605.

Commoner, Barry, Michael Corr, and Paul J. Stamler. 1971. "The Causes of Pollution." *The Environment* 13(3): 2–19.

Congressional Budget Office (CBO). 2010. "Congressional Budget Office Cost Estimate: S. 3992 – Development, Relief, and Education for Alien Minors Act of 2010." Washington, DC: Congressional Budget Office.

Conley, Meghan. 2013. "Immigrant Rights in the Nuevo South: Enforcement and Resistance at the Borderlands of Illegality." Unpublished dissertation. Knoxville: The University of Tennessee.

Conley, Meghan, and Stephanie A. Bohon. 2010. "The Spectrum's Other End: Solidarity and Distrust in a New Latino Destination." *Journal of Latino – Latin American Studies* 3(4): 13–30.

Conzen, Kathleen Neils, David A. Gerber, Ewa Morawska, George E. Pozzetta, and Rudolph J. Vecoli. 1992. "The Invention of Ethnicity: A Perspective from the USA." *Journal of American Ethnic History* 12(1): 3–41.

Cortes, Patricia. 2008. "The Effect of Low-skilled Immigration on US Prices: Evidence from CPI Data." *Journal of Political Economy* 116(3): 381–422.

Cosman, Madeleine Pelner. 2005. "Illegal Aliens and American Medicine." *Journal of American Physicians and Surgeons* 10(1): 6–10.

Crimmins, Eileen M., Beth J. Soldo, Jung Ki Kim, and Dawn E. Alley. 2005. "Using Anthropometric Indicators for Mexicans in the United States and Mexico to Understand the Selection of Migrants and the 'Hispanic Paradox.'" *Social Biology* 52(3–4): 164–177.

Cunningham, Solveig Argeseanu, Julia D. Ruben, and K. M. Venkat Narayan. 2008. "Health of Foreign-born People in the United States: A Review." *Health & Place* 14: 623–35.

Currie, Janet and Enrico Moretti. 2003. "Mother's Education and the Intergenerational Transmission of Human Capital: Evidence from College Openings." *The Quarterly Journal of Economics* 118(4): 1495–532.

Crul, Maurice, Jens Schneider, and Fans Lelie (eds.) 2012. *The European Second Generation Compared: Does the Integration Context Matter?* Amsterdam: Amsterdam University Press.

Daily, Gretchen C., Anne H. Ehrlich, and Paul R. Ehrlich. 1995. "Response to

References

Bartlett and Lytwak (1995): Population and Immigration policy in the United States." *Population and Environment* 16(6): 521–6.

De Maio, Fernando G., and Eagen Kemp. 2010. "The Deterioration of Health Status among Immigrants to Canada." *Global Public Health* 5(5): 462–78.

DeJong, Gordon F., Brenda Davis Root, and Ricardo Abad. 1986. "Family Reunification and Philippine Migration to the United States: The Immigrants' Perspective." *International Migration Review* 20(3): 598–611.

Delvin, Bernie. 1997. *Intelligence, Genes, and Success: Scientists Respond to* The Bell Curve. New York: Springer.

DeNavas-Walt, Carmen, Bernadette D. Proctor, and Jessica C. Smith. 2010. *Income, Poverty, and Health Insurance Coverage in the United States: 2009*. (Current Population Reports P60-238.) Washington, DC: US Census Bureau.

Denktaş, Semiha. 2011. "Health and Health Care Use of Elderly Immigrants in the Netherlands: A Comparative Study." Thesis. Rotterdam: Erasmus University.

Desmond, Scott A., and Charis E. Kubrin. 2009. "The Power of Place: Immigrant Communities and Adolescent Violence." *The Sociological Quarterly* 50(4): 581–607.

Dewind, Josh, and Philip Kasinitz. 1997. "Everything Old is New Again? Processes and Theories of Immigrant Incorporation." *International Migration Review* 31(4): 1096–111.

Di Bartolomeo, Anna. 2009. "Educational Attainment of Second Generation Immigrants." *Journal of Identity and Migration Studies* 3(2): 63–80.

Dietz, Thomas, Amy Fitzgerald, and Rachael Shwom. 2005. "Environmental Values." *Annual Review of Environmental Resources* 30: 335–72.

Dietz, Thomas, and Eugene A. Rosa. 1994. "Rethinking the Environmental Impacts of Population and Technology." *Human Ecology Review* 1(Summer/Autumn): 277–300.

Dietz, Thomas, and Eugene A. Rosa. 1997. "Effects of Population and Affluence on CO_2 Emissions." *Proceedings of the National Academy of Science* 24: 175–9.

DinAlt, Jason. 1997. "The Environmental Impact of Immigration into the United States." *Focus* 4(2). An online publication of the Carrying Capacity Network. Available from www.carryingcapacity.org/DinAlt.htm.

Dixon, Lori Beth, Jan Sundquist, and Marilyn Winkleby. 2000. "Differences in Energy, Nutrient, and Food Intakes in a US Sample of Mexican-American Women and Men: Findings from the Third National Health and Nutrition Examination Survey, 1988–1994." *American Journal of Epidemiology* 152(6): 548–557.

Dohm, Arlene. 2000. "Gauging the Labor Force Effects of Retiring Baby-boomers." *Monthly Labor Review* 125: 17–25.

Domina, Thurston. 2005. "Leveling the Home Advantage: Assessing the

References

Effectiveness of Parental Involvement in Elementary School." *Sociology of Education* 78: 233–49.

Donato, Katharine M., Chizuko Wakabayashi, Shirin Hakimzadeh, and Amada Armenta. 2008. "Shifts in the Employment Conditions of Mexican Migrant Men and Women: The Effect of US Immigration Policy." *Work and Occupations* 35(4): 462–95.

Dong, Xiuwen, Sang D. Choi, James G. Borchardt, Xuanwen Wang, and Julie A. Largay. 2013. "Fatal Falls from Roofs among US Construction Workers." *Journal of Safety Research* 44: 17–24.

Dong, Xiuwen S. and James W. Platner. 2004. "Occupational Fatalities of Hispanic Construction Workers from 1992 to 2000." *American Journal of Industrial Medicine* 45(1): 45–54.

Driscoll, Anne K., Stephen T. Russell, and Lisa J. Crockett. 2008. "Parenting Styles and Youth Well-being across Immigrant Generations." *Journal of Family Issues* 29(2): 185–209.

Dunn, James R., and Isabel Dyck. 2000. "Social Determinants of Health in Canada's Immigrant Population: Results from the National Population Health Survey." *Social Science and Medicine* 51(11): 1573–93.

Dunne, Timothy, Mark J. Roberts, and Larry Samuelson. 1989. "Plant Turnover and Gross Employment Flows in the US Manufacturing Sector." *Journal of Labor Economics* 7(1): 48–71.

Durand, Jorge, and Douglas S. Massey. 2002. *Beyond Smoke and Mirrors: Mexican Immigration in an Age of Economic Integration.* New York: Russell Sage.

Ebin, Vicki J., Carl D. Sneed, Donald E. Morisky, Mary Jane Rotheram-Borus, Ann M. Magnusson, and C. Kevin Malotte. 2001. "Acculturation and Interrelationships between Problem and Health-Promoting Behaviors among Latino Adolescents." *Journal of Adolescent Health* 28(1): 62–72.

Eckstein, Zvi, and Yoram Weiss. 2004. "On the Wage Growth of Immigrants: Israel 1990–2000." *Journal of the European Economic Association* 2(4): 665–95.

Ehrlich, Paul R. 1968. *The Population Bomb.* San Francisco: Sierra Club / Ballantine Books.

Ehrlich, Paul R., and Anne E. Ehrlich. 2004. *One with Nineveh: Politics, Consumption, and the Human Future.* Washington, DC: Island Press / Shearwater.

Ehrlich, Paul R., and John P. Holdren. 1971. "Impact of Population Growth." *Science* 171: 1212–17.

Ehrlich, Paul R., and John P. Holdren. 1972. "Impact of Population Growth." Pp. 365–77 in *Population, Resources, and the Environment,* edited by R. G. Riker. Washington, DC: US Government Printing Office.

Ellguth, Peter, and Susanne Kohaut. 2007. "Tarifbindung und betriebliche Interessenvertretung – Aktuelle Ergebnisse aus den Betriebspanel 2006"

References

(Union coverage and work councils: Current evidence from establishment panel 2006). *WSI-Mitteilungen* 9: 511–14.

Elsby, Michael W., Bart Hobijn, and Aysegul Sahin. 2010. "The Labor Market in the Great Recession." NBER wWorking Paper 15979. Cambridge, MA: National Bureau of Economic Research.

Environmental Protection Agency. 2011. "Greenhouse Gas Emissions from a Typical Passenger Vehicle." Report EPA-420-F-11-041. Washington, DC: Office of Transportation and Air Quality.

Epstein, Jennifer A., Gilbert J. Botvin, and Tracy Diaz. 2001. "Linguistic Acculturation Associated with Higher Marijuana and Polydrug Use among Hispanic Adolescents." *Substance Use and Misuse* 36(4): 477–99.

Espenshade, Thomas J. 1994. "Can Immigration Slow US Population Aging?" *Journal of Policy Analysis and Management* 13(4): 759–68.

Espenshade, Thomas J. 1995. "Unauthorized Immigration to the United States." *Annual Review of Sociology* 21: 195–216.

Espenshade, Thomas J. 2001. "'Replacement Migration' from the Perspective of Equilibrium Stationary Populations." *Population and Environment* 22(4): 383–9.

Espenshade, Thomas J., and Maryann Belanger. 1998. "Immigration and Public Opinion." Pp. 365–403 in *Crossings: Mexican Immigration in Interdisciplinary Perspectives*, edited by Marcelo M. Suárez-Orozco. Cambridge, MA: Harvard University Press.

Espenshade, Thomas J., and Katherine Hempstead. 1996. "Contemporary American Attitudes Toward U.S. Immigration." *International Migration Review* 30(2): 535–70.

Ewing, Katherine Pratt. 2003. "Living Islam in the Diaspora: Between Turkey and Germany." *South Atlantic Quarterly* 102(2/3): 405–31.

Ewing, Reid H. 2008. "Characteristics, Causes and Effects of Sprawl: A Literature Review." Pp. 519–35 in *Urban Ecology: An International Perspective on the Interaction between Humans and Nature*, edited by John M. Marzluff et al. New York: Springer.

Faiola, Anthony. 2012. "Anti-immigrant Stance Gains Ground in Greece with Golden Dawn." *The Washington Post*. October 21.

Farley, Reynolds, and Richard Alba. 2002. "The New Second Generation in the United States." *International Migration Review* 36(3): 669–701.

Feagin, Joe R. 1997. "Old Poison in New Bottles: The Deep Roots of Modem Nativism." Pp. 13–43 in *Immigrants Out! The New Nativism and the Anti-Immigrant Impulse in the United States*, edited by Juan F. Perea. New York: New York University Press.

Feldmeyer, Ben. 2009. "Immigration and Violence: The Offsetting Effects of Immigration on Latino Violence." *Social Science Research* 38: 717–31.

Feliciano, Cynthia. 2005. "Educational Selectivity in US Immigration: How do Immigrants Compare to Those Left Behind?" *Demography* 42(1): 131–152.

References

Ferrer, Ana, and W. Craig Riddell. 2008. "Education, Credentials and Immigrant Earnings." *Canadian Journal of Economics* 41(1): 186–216.

Fetzer, Joel S. 2000. *Public Attitudes toward Immigration in the United States, France, and Germany.* Cambridge: Cambridge University Press.

Fischer, Claude S., Michael Hout, Martin Sánchez Jankowski, Samuel R. Lucas, Ann Swidler, and Kim Voss. 1996. *Inequality by Design: Cracking the Bell Curve Myth.* Princeton, NJ: Princeton University Press.

Fischer, Claude S., and Greggor Mattson. 2009. "Is America Fragmenting?" *Annual Review of Sociology* 35: 435–55.

Fischer-Kowalski, Marina, and Christof Amann. 2001. "Beyond IPAT and Kuznets Curves: Globalization as a Vital Factor in Analyzing the Environmental Impact of Socio-economic Metabolism." *Population and Environment* 23(1): 7–47.

Fix, Michael, and Jeffrey S. Passel. 1994. *Immigration and Immigrants: Setting the Record Straight.* Washington, DC: The Urban Institute.

Fix, Michael, and Jeffrey S. Passel. 1999. "Trends in Noncitizens' Use of Public Benefits Following Welfare Reform: 1994–97." Report. Washington, DC: The Urban Institute.

Flippen, Chenoa. 2012. "Laboring Underground: The Employment Patterns of Hispanic Immigrant Men in Durham, NC." *Social Problems* 59(1): 21–42.

Flores, Glenn, and Jane Brotanek. 2005. "The Healthy Immigrant Effect: A Greater Understanding Might Help Us Improve the Health of All Children." *Archives of Pediatric and Adolescent Medicine* 159(3): 295–6.

Florez, Karen R., Tamara Dubowitz, Naomi Saito, Guilherme Borges, and Joshua Breslau. 2012. "Mexico–United States Migration and the Prevalence of Obesity." *Archives of Internal Medicine* 172(22): 1760–2.

Foad, Hisham Salem. 2010. "Assimilation and Trade between the Middle East, Europe, and North America." *The Review of Middle East Economics and Finance* 6(2): 74–92.

Ford, Kathleen. 1990. "Duration of Residence in the United States and the Fertility of US Immigrants." *International Migration Review* 24(1): 34–68.

Fossett, Mark. 2006. "Ethnic Preferences, Social Distance Dynamics, and Residential Segregation: Theoretical Explorations using Simulation Analysis." *Journal of Mathematical Sociology* 30(3–4): 185–273.

Foster, John Bellamy. 2002. "Malthus' Essay on Population at Age 200." Pp. 137–54 in *Ecology against Capitalism*, edited by John Bellamy Foster. New York: Monthly Review Press.

Frank, Reanne. 2001. "A Reconceptualization of the Role of Biology in Contributing to Race/Ethnic Disparities in Health Outcomes." *Population Research and Policy Review* 20(6): 441–55.

Frank, Reanne, and Patrick Heuveline. 2005. "A Cross-over in Mexican and Mexican-American Fertility Rates: Evidence and Explanations for an Emerging Paradox." *Demographic Research* 12(4): 77–104.

References

Franzini, Luisa, and Maria Eugenia Fernández-Esquer. 2006. "The Association of Subjective Social Status and Health in Low-income Mexican-origin Individuals in Texas." *Social Science and Medicine* 63(3): 788–804.

Freeman, Richard B. 2006. "People Flows in Globalization." *Journal of Economic Perspectives* 20(2): 145–70.

Frey, William H. 1997. "Emerging Demographic Balkanization: Toward One America or Two?" PSC Research Report 97-410. Ann Arbor: Population Studies Center, University of Michigan.

Friedberg, Rachel M. 2001. "The Impact of Mass Migration on the Israeli Labor Market." *The Quarterly Journal of Economics* 116(4): 1373–408.

Friedberg, Rachel M., and Jennifer Hunt. 1995. "The Impact of Immigrants on Host Country Wages, Employment and Growth." *Journal of Economic Perspectives* 9(2): 23–44.

Friedlander, Dov, Zvi Eisenbach, and Calvin Goldscheider. 1980. "Family-size Limitation and Birth Spacing: The Fertility Transition of African and Asian Immigrants in Israel." *Population and Development Review* 6(4): 581–93.

Fry, Richard. 2007. "How Far Behind in Math and Reading are English Language Learners?" A report of the Pew Hispanic Center. Washington, DC: Pew Research Center.

Fu, Hongyun, and Mark J. VanLandingham. 2012. "Mental Health Consequences of International Migration for Vietnamese Americans and the Medicating Effects of Physical Health and Social Networks: Results from a Natural Experiment." *Demography* 49(2): 393–424.

Fuchs, Victor R. 2013. "How and Why US Health Care Differs from That in Other OECD Countries." *Journal of the American Medical Association* 309(1): 33–4.

Fulton, William, Rolf Pendall, Mai Nguyen, and Alicia Harrison. 2001. *Who Sprawls Most? How Growth Patterns Differ Across the US.* Washington, DC: The Brookings Institution.

Fung, Joey J., and Anna S. Lau. 2010. "Factors Associated with Parent–child (Dis) Agreement on Child Behavior and Parenting Problems in Chinese Immigrant Families." *Journal of Clinical Child and Adolescent Psychology* 39(3): 314–27.

Furuseth, Owen J., and Heather A. Smith. 2006. "From Winn-Dixie to Tiendas: The Remaking of the New South." Pp. 1–17 in *Latinos in the New South: Transformations of Place*, edited by H. A. Smith and O. J. Furuseth. Burlington, VT: Ashgate.

Gagnon, Alain, and Ryan Mazan. 2009. "Does Exposure to Infectious Diseases in Infancy Affect Old-Age Mortality? Evidence from a Pre-Industrial Population." *Social Science and Medicine* 68(9): 1609–16.

Galindo, Rene, and Jami Vigil. 2006. "Are Anti-Immigrant Statements Racist or Nativist? What Difference Does It Make?" *Latino Studies* 4(4): 419–47.

Gans, Herbert J. 1962. *The Urban Villagers: Groups and Class in the Life of Italian-Americans.* New York: Free Press of Glencoe.

References

Gans, Herbert J. 1992a. "Comment: Ethnic Invention and Acculturation: A Bumpy-Line Approach." *Journal of American Ethnic History* 11(1): 42–52.

Gans, Herbert J. 1992b. "Second-generation Decline: Scenarios for the Economic and Ethnic Futures of the Post-1965 American Immigrants." *Ethnic and Racial Studies* 15(2): 173–92.

Gans, Herbert J. 1997. "Toward a Reconciliation of 'Assimilation' and 'Pluralism': The Interplay of Acculturation and Ethnic Retention." *International Migration Review* 31(4): 875–92.

García, Eugene E. 2005. *Teaching and Learning in Two Languages: Bilingualism and Schooling in the United States.* New York: Teachers College Press.

Garling, Scipio. 1998. "Immigration Policy and the Environment: The Washington, DC Metropolitan Area." *Population and Environment* 20(1): 23–54.

Gentsch, Kerstin, and Douglas Massey. 2011. "Labor Market Outcomes for Legal Mexican Immigrants under the New Regime of Immigrant Enforcement." *Social Science Quarterly* 92: 875–93.

Germán, Miguelina, Nancy A. Gonzales, and Larry Dumka. 2009. "Familism Values as a Protective Factor for Mexican-origin Adolescents Exposed to Deviant Peers." *The Journal of Early Adolescence* 29(1): 16–42.

Gfroerer, Joseph C., and Lucilla L. Tan. 2003. "Substance Use among Foreign-born Youths in the United States: Does the Length of Residence Matter?" *American Journal of Public Health* 93(11): 1892–5.

Gibson, Campbell, and Kay Jung. 2006. "Historical Census Statistics on the Foreign-Born Population of the United States: 1850–2000." Population Division, Working Paper 81. Washington, DC: US Census Bureau. Available online at www.census.gov/population/www/documentation/twps0081/twps0081.pdf.

Gibson, Margaret A. 2001. "Immigrant Adaptation and Patterns of Acculturation." *Human Development* 44(1):19–23.

Gibson, Margaret A., and Silvia Carrasco. 2009. "The Education of Immigrant Youth: Some Lessons from the US and Spain." *Theory into Practice* 48(4): 249–57.

Gil, Andres G., Eric F. Wagner, and William A. Vega. 2000. "Acculturation, Familism, and Alcohol Use among Latino Adolescent Males: Longitudinal Relations." *Journal of Community Psychology* 28(4): 443–58.

Gilbert, M. Jean. 1987. "Alcohol Consumption Patterns in Immigrant and Later-Generation Mexican American Women." *Hispanic Journal of Behavioral Sciences* 9(3): 299–313.

Ginsburg, Paul B. 2008. *High and Rising Health Care Costs: Demystifying US Health Care Spending.* Research Synthesis Report 16. Princeton, NJ: The Robert Wood Johnson Foundation.

Givens, Terri E. 2007. "Immigrant Integration in Europe: Empirical Research." *Annual Review of Political Science* 10: 67–83

References

Gjerde, Jon, and Anne McCants. 1995. "Fertility, Marriage, and Culture: Demographic Processes among Norwegian Immigrants to the Rural Middle West." *The Journal of Economic History* 55(4): 860–88.

Glazer, Nathan. 1993. "Is Assimilation Dead?" *Annals of the American Academy of Political and Social Science* 530: 122–36.

Glennon, Robert. 2009. *Unquenchable: America's Water Crisis and What to Do about It*. Washington, DC: Island Press.

Glitz, Albrecht. 2012. "The Labor Market Impact of Immigration: A Quasi-experiment Exploiting Immigrant Location Rules in Germany." *Journal of Labor Economics* 30(1): 175–213.

Goldberg, David. 1959. "The Fertility of Two-Generation Urbanites." *Population Studies* 12(3): 214–22.

Goldenberg, Claude. 2010. "Reading Instruction for English Language Learners." Pp. 684–710 in *Handbook of Reading Research*, Volume IV, edited by Michael L. Kamil, P. David Pearson, Elizabeth Birr Moje, and Peter Afflerbach. New York: Routledge.

Goldman, Dana P., James P. Smith, and Neeraj Sood. 2006. "Immigrants and the Cost of Medical Care." *Health Affairs* 25(6): 1700–11.

Goldstein, Alice, Michael White, and Sidney Goldstein. 1997. "Migration, Fertility and State Policy in Hubei Province, China." *Demography* 34(4): 481–91.

Goldstein, Sidney. 1973. "Interrelations between Migration and Fertility in Thailand." *Demography* 10(2): 225–41.

Goldstein, Sidney, and Alice Goldstein. 1981. "The Impact of Migration on Fertility: An 'Own Children' Analysis for Thailand." *Population Studies* 35(2): 265–84.

Gonzales, Nancy A., Miguelina Germán, Su Yeong Kim, et al. 2008. "Mexican American Adolescents' Cultural Orientation, Externalizing Behavior, and Academic Engagement: The Role of Traditional Cultural Values." *American Journal of Community Psychology* 41(1–2): 151–64.

Gonzalez, Laura M., L. DiAnne Borders, Erik M. Hines, Jose A. Villalba, and Henderson. 2013. "Parental Involvement in Children's Education: Considerations for School Counselors Working with Latino Immigrant Families." *Professional School Counseling* 16(3): 185–93.

Goodell, Sarah, and Paul B. Ginsburg. 2008. "High and Rising Health Care Costs: Demystifying US Health Care Spending." Report. Washington, DC: Robert Wood Johnson Foundation.

Gordon, Milton M. 1964. *Assimilation in American Life: The Role of Race, Religion, and National Origins*. New York: Oxford University Press.

Gorodzeisky, Anastasia, and Moshe Semyonov. 2011. "Two Dimensions of Economic Incorporation: Soviet Immigrants in the Israeli Labor Market." *Journal of Ethnic and Migration Studies* 37(7): 1059–77.

Goss, Stephen, Alice Wade, J. Patrick Skirvin, Michael Morris, K. Mark Bye, and

References

Danielle Huston. 2013. "Effects of Unauthorized Immigration on the Actuarial Status of the Social Security Trust Funds." *Actuarial Note* 151: 1–5.

Gozdziak, Elzbieta, and Elizabeth A. Collett. 2005. "Research on Human Trafficking in North America: A Review of Literature." *International Migration* 43(1–2): 99–128.

Granovetter, Mark. 1974. *Getting a Job: A Study of Contacts and Careers.* Cambridge, MA: Harvard University Press.

Grant, Lindsey. 2001. "'Replacement Migration': The UN Population Division on European Population Decline." *Population and Environment* 22(4): 391–9.

Grasmuck, Sherri, and Patricia Pessar. 1991. *Between Two Islands: Dominican International Migration.* Berkeley: University of California Press.

Greenstone, Michael, and Adam Looney. 2010. "Ten Economic Facts about Immigration." A report of the Hamilton Project. Washington, DC: The Brookings Institution.

Greenstone, Michael, and Adam Looney. 2012. "What Immigration Means for US Employment and Wages." A report of the Hamilton Project. Washington, DC: The Brookings Institution.

Grieco, Elizabeth M., Yesenia D. Acosta, G. Patricia de la Cruz, et al. 2012. "The Foreign Born Population in the United States: 2010." American Community Survey Reports. Washington, DC: US Bureau of the Census. Available online at www.census.gov/prod/2012pubs/acs-19.pdf.

Gross, Stephen, Alice Wade, J. Patrick Skirvin, Michael Morris, K. Mark Bye, and Danielle Huston. 2013. "Effects of Unauthorized Immigration on the Actuarial Status of the Social Security Trust Funds." Actuarial Note 151. Baltimore, MD: Social Security Administration Office of the Chief Actuary.

Grossman, Jean B. 1982. "The Substitutability of Natives and Immigrants in Production." *Review of Economics and Statistics* 64: 596–603.

Grüber, C., S. Illi, A. Plieth, C. Sommerfeld, and U. Wahn. 2002. "Cultural Adaptation is Associated with Atopy and Wheezing among Children of Turkish Origin Living in Germany." *Clinical and Experimental Allergy* 32(4): 526–31.

Gryn, Thomas A., and Luke J. Larsen. 2010. "Nativity Status and Citizenship in the United States: 2009." American Community Survey Briefs. Washington, DC: US Census Bureau.

Guarnaccia, Peter J., and Steven R. Lopez. 1998. "The Mental Health and Adjustment of Immigrant and Refugee Children." *Child and Adolescent Psychiatric Clinics of North America* 7(3): 537–53.

Guest, Ross. 2007. "The Baby Bonus: A Dubious Policy Initiative." *Policy* 23(1): 11–15.

Gurak, Douglas T., and Fe Caces. 1992. "Migration Networks and the Shaping of Migration Systems." Chapter 9 in *International Migration Systems: A Global Approach*, edited by Mary M. Kritz, Lin Lean Lim, and Hania Zlotnick. Oxford: Clarendon Press.

References

Gushulak, Brian. 2007. "Healthier on Arrival? Further Insight into the 'Health Immigrant Effect.'" *Canadian Medical Association Journal* 176(10): 1439–40.

Gustin, Delancey, and Astrid Ziebarth. 2010. "Transatlantic Opinion on Immigration: Greater Worries and Outlier Optimism." *International Migration Review* 4(4): 974–91.

Haddad, Yvonne Yazbeck, and Michael J. Balz. 2006. "The October Riots in France: A Failed Immigration Policy or the Empire Strikes Back?" *International Migration* 44(2): 23–34.

Hagan, Jacqueline. 1998. "Social Networks, Gender and Immigrant Settlement: Resource and Constraint." *American Sociological Review* 63(1): 55–67.

Hagewen, Kellie J., and S. Philip Morgan. 2005. "Intended and Ideal Family Size in the United States, 1970–2002." *Population and Development Review* 31(3): 507–27.

Haller, William, Alejandro Portes, and Scott M. Lynch. 2011. "Dreams Fulfilled, Dreams Shattered: Determinants of Segmented Assimilation in the Second Generation." *Social Forces* 89(3): 733–762.

Hanushek, Eric A., and Ludger Woessmann. 2008. "The Role of Cognitive Skills in Economic Development." *Journal of Economic Literature* 46(3): 607–68.

Hao, Lingxin, and Richard W. Johnson. 2000. "Economic, Cultural, and Social Origins of Emotional Well-being: Comparisons of Immigrants and Natives at Midlife." *Research on Aging* 22(6): 599–629.

Harper, Candace A., Ester J. de Jong, and Elizabeth J. Platt. 2008. "Marginalizing English as a Second Language Teacher Expertise: The Exclusionary Consequence of *No Child Left Behind.*" *Language Policy* 7(3): 267–84.

Harris, Angel L. 2011. *Kids Don't Want to Fail: Oppositional Culture and the Black–White Achievement Gap.* Cambridge, MA: Harvard University Press.

Harris, Elizabeth K. 1993. "Economic Refugees: Unprotected in the United States by Virtue of an Inaccurate Label." *American University International Law Review* 9(1): 269–307.

Hartnett, Caroline Sten. 2012. "Are Hispanic Women Happier about Unintended Births?" *Population Research and Policy Review* 31(5): 683–701.

Hartney, Michael T., and Patrick Flavin. 2014. "The Political Foundations of the Black–White Education Achievement Gap." *American Politics Research* 42(1): 3–33.

Haubert, Jeannie, and Elizabeth Fussell. 2006. "Explaining Pro-Immigrant Sentiment in the U.S.: Social Class, Cosmopolitanism, and Perceptions of Immigrants." *International Migration Review* 40(3): 489–507.

Hayward, Mark D., Eileen M. Crimmins, Toni P. Miles, and Yu Yang. 2000. "The Significance of Socioeconomic Status in Explaining the Racial Gap in Chronic Health Conditions." *American Sociological Review* 65(6): 910–30.

Hendershot, Gerry E. 1971. "Cityward Migration and Urban Fertility in the Philippines." Paper presented at the annual meeting of the Population Association of America, April 22-24, Washington, DC.

References

Hendricks, Sarah E. 2008. "Skin Color Bias in the Immigration Process." Master's thesis. Knoxville: University of Tennessee.

Hernández-León, Rubén, and Victor Zúñiga. 2003. "Mexican Communities in the South and Social Capital: The Case of Dalton, Georgia." *Southern Rural Sociology* 19(1): 20–45.

Hernnstein, Richard J., and Charles A. Murray. 1994. *The Bell Curve: Intelligence and Class Structure in American Life.* New York: Free Press.

Herrmann, Michael. 2012. "Population Aging and Economic Development: Anxieties and Policy Responses." *Journal of Population Aging* 5(1): 23–46.

Hervitz, Hugo M. 1985. "Selectivity, Adaptation, or Disruption? A Comparison of Alternative Hypotheses on the Effects of Migration on Fertility: The Case of Brazil." *International Migration Review* 19(2): 293–317.

Higham, John. 1955. *Strangers in the Land: Patterns of American Nativism, 1860–1925.* New Brunswick, NJ: Rutgers University Press.

Himmelgreen, David A., Rafael Pérez-Escamilla, Dinorah Martinez, et al. 2004. "The Longer You Stay, the Bigger You Get: Length of Time and Language Use in the US are Associated with Obesity in Puerto Rican Women." *American Journal of Physical Anthropology* 125(1): 90–6.

Hing, Bill Ong. 2004. *Defining America Through Immigration Policy.* Philadelphia: Temple University Press.

Hirschman, Charles. 1983. "America's Melting Pot Reconsidered." *Annual Review of Sociology* 9: 397–423.

Hirschman, Charles. 2005. "Immigration and the American Century." *Demography* 42(4): 595–620.

Hitlin, Steven, J. Scott Brown, and Glen H. Elder, Jr. 2007. "Measuring Latinos: Racial vs. Ethnic Classification and Self-Understandings." *Social Forces* 86(2): 587–611.

Hjerm, Mikael. 2007. "Do Numbers Really Count? Group Threat Theory Revisited." *Journal of Ethnic and Racial Studies* 33(8): 1253–75.

Hjerm, Mikael. 2009. "Anti-immigrant Attitudes and Cross-municipal Variation in the Proportion of Immigrants." *Acta Sociologica* 52(1): 47–62.

Ho, Lintje, Vivian Bos, and Anton E. Kunst. 2007. "Differences in Cause-of-Death Patterns between the Native Dutch and Persons of Indonesian Descent in the Netherlands." *American Journal of Public Health* 97(9): 1616–18.

Hochschild, Jennifer L., and John H. Mollenkopf. 2009. *Bringing Outsiders In: Transatlantic Perspectives on Immigrant Political Incorporation.* Ithaca, NY: Cornell University Press.

Hoefer, Michael, Nancy Rytina, and Bryan Baker. 2012. "Estimates of the Unauthorized Immigrant Population Living in the United States." Report. Washington, DC: Department of Homeland Security Office of Immigration Statistics. Available online at www.dhs.gov/xlibrary/assets/statistics/publicat ions/ois_ill_pe_2011.pdf.

References

Hoem, Jan M. 2008. "The Impact of Public Policies on European Fertility." *Demographic Research* 19(10): 249–60.

Hogan, Joseph Daniel. 1992. "The Impact of Population Growth on the Physical Environment." *European Journal of Population* 8: 109–23.

Hollingworth, William, Annemarie Relyea-Chew, Bryan A. Comstock, Judge Karen A. Overstreet, and Jeffrey G. Jarvik. 2007. "The Risk of Bankruptcy before and after Brain or Spinal Cord Injury: A Glimpse of the Iceberg's Tip." *Medical Care* 45(8): 708–11.

Horowitz, Juliana Menasce. 2010. *Widespread Anti-Immigrant Sentiment in Italy*. Washington, DC: Pew Research Center.

Hotchkiss, Julie L., and Myriam Quispe-Agnoli. 2008. *The Labor Market Experience and Impact of Undocumented Workers*. Working Paper 2008-7c. Atlanta, GA: Federal Reserve Bank of Atlanta.

Howell, Embry M., and Dana Hughes. 2006. "A Tale of Two Counties: Expanding Health Insurance Coverage for Children in California." *The Milbank Quarterly* 84(3): 521–54.

Huang, Priscilla. 2008. "Anchor Babies, Over-Breeders, and the Population Bomb: The Reemergence of Nativism and Population Control in Anti-Immigration Policies." *Harvard Law and Policy Review* 2: 385–406.

Hudson, Kenneth. 2007. "The New Labor Market Segmentation: Labor Market Dualism in the New Economy." *Social Science Research* 36: 286–312.

Huijts, Tim, and Gerbert Kraaykamp. 2012. "Immigrant's Health in Europe: A Cross-Classified Multilevel Approach to Examine Origin Country, Destination Country, and Community Effects." *International Migration Review* 46(1): 101–37.

Humes, Karen R., Nicholas A. Jones, and Roberto R. Ramirez. 2011. "Overview of Race and Hispanic Origin." 2010 Census Briefs. Washington, DC: US Census Bureau.

Hunter, Lori M. 2000a. "The Spatial Association between US Immigrant Residential Concentration and Environmental Hazards." *International Migration Review* 32(2): 460–88.

Hunter, Lori M. 2000b. "A Comparison of Environmental Attitudes, Concern and Behaviors of Native and Foreign-born Residents." *Population and Environment* 21(6): 565–80.

Huntington, Samuel P. 2004a. "The Hispanic Challenge." *Foreign Policy* 141(2): 30–45. Huntington, Samuel P. 2004b. *Who Are We? The Challenges to America's National Identity*. New York: Simon & Schuster.

Hursh, David. 2007. "Assessing No Child Left Behind and the Rise of Neoliberal Education Policies." *American Educational Research Journal* 44(3): 493–518.

Hwang, Sean-Shong, and Rogelio Saenz. 1997. "Fertility of Chinese Immigrants in the US: Testing a Fertility Emancipation Hypothesis." *Journal of Marriage and the Family* 59(1): 50–61.

References

Institute on Taxation and Economic Policy (ITEP). 2013. "Undocumented Immigrants' State and Local Tax Contributions." Report. Washington, DC: ITEP.

Ironside, Andrew. 2007. "O'Reilly: Supporters of Liberalizing Immigration Bill Want to 'Change the Complexion' of America." *Media Matters*. Available online at http://mediamatters.org/video/2007/05/31/oreilly-supporters-of-liberalizing-immigration/138980.

Islam, Asadul. 2009. "The Substitutability of Labor between Immigrants and Natives in the Canadian Labor Market: Circa 1995." *Journal of Population Economics* 22(1): 119–217.

Jacobsen, Linda A., Mary Kent, Marlene Lee, and Mark Mather. 2011. "America's Aging Population." *Population Bulletin* 66(1): 1–16.

Jacobson, Robin. 2006. "Characterizing Consent: Race, Citizenship, and the New Restrictionists." *Political Research Quarterly* 59(4): 645–54.

Jäger, Jill, and Roger G. Barry. 1990. "Climate." Pp. 335–351 in *The Earth as Transformed by Human Action*, edited by B. L. Turner II et al. Cambridge: Cambridge University Press.

Jaret, Charles. 1999. "Troubled by Newcomers: Anti-Immigrant Attitudes and Action during Two Eras of Mass Immigration to the United States." *Journal of American Ethnic History* 18(3): 9–39.

Jasso, Guillermina. 1988. "Whom Shall We Welcome? Elite Judgments of the Criteria for the Selection of Immigrants." *American Sociological Review* 53(6): 919–32.

Jasso, Guillermina, Douglas S. Massey, Mark R. Rosenzweig, and James P. mith. 2004. "Immigrant Health: Selectivity and Acculturation." Chapter 7 in *Critical Perspectives on Racial and Ethnic Differences in Health in Late Life*, edited by Norman B. Anderson, Rodolfo A. Bulatao, and Barney Cohen. Washington, DC: National Academies Press.

Jasso, Guillermina, and Mark R. Rosenzweig. 1982. "Estimating the Emigration Rates of Legal Immigrants using Administrative and Survey Data: The 1971 Cohort of Immigrants to the United States." *Demography* 19(3): 279–90.

Jencks, Christopher, James Crouse, and Peter Mueser. 1983. "The Wisconsin Model of Status Attainment: A National Replication with Improved Measures of Ability and Aspiration." *Sociology of Education* 56(1): 3–19.

Jencks, Christopher, and Meredith Phillips. 1998. "The Black–White Test Score Gap: An Introduction." Chapter 1 in *The Black–White Test Score Gap*, edited by Christopher Jencks and Meredith Phillips. Washington, DC: Brookings Institution.

Jeynes, William H. 2007. "The Relationship between Parental Involvement and Urban Secondary School Student Academic Achievement: A Meta-analysis." *Urban Education* 42(1): 82–110.

Johnson, Kenneth M., and Daniel T. Lichter. 2008. "Natural Increase: A New

References

Source of Population Growth in Emerging Hispanic Destinations in the United States." *Population and Development Review* 34(2): 327–46.

Johnson, Kenneth M., Paul R. Voss, Roger B. Hammer, Glenn V. Fuguitt, and Scott McNiven. 2005. "Temporal and Spatial Variation in Age-specific Net Migration in the United States." *Demography* 42: 791–812.

Jones, Camara Phyllis. 2001. "'Race,' Racism and the Practice of Epidemiology." *American Journal of Epidemiology* 154(4): 299–304.

Jonsson, Stefan Hrafn, and Michael S. Rendall. 2004. "The Fertility Contribution of Mexican Immigration to the United States." *Demography* 41(1): 129–50.

Jung, Sven, and Claus Schnabel. 2011. "Paying More than Necessary? The Wage Cushion in Germany." *Labour* 25(2): 182–97.

Kahn, Joan R. 1988. "Immigrant Selectivity and Fertility Adaptation in the United States." *Social Forces* 67(1): 108–28.

Kahn, Joan R. 1994. "Immigrant and Native Fertility during the 1980s: Adaptation and Expectations for the Future." *International Migration Review* 28(3): 501–19.

Kahn, Matthew E. 2000. "The Environmental Impact of Surburbanization." *Journal of Policy Analysis and Management* 19(4): 569–86.

Kalleberg, Arne L. 2011. *Good Jobs, Bad Jobs: The Rise of Polarized and Precarious Employment Systems in the United States, 1970s–2000s.* New York: Russell Sage.

Kallen, Horace. 1924. *Culture and Democracy in the United States.* New York: Boni and Liveright.

Kandel, William A. 2008. *Profile of Hired Farmworkers: A 2008 Update.* (Economic Research Report 60.) Washington, DC: US Department of Agriculture.

Kandel, William A., and Katharine M. Donato. 2009. "Does Unauthorized Status Reduce Exposure to Pesticides? Evidence from the National Agricultural Workers Survey." *Work and Occupations* 36(4): 367–99.

Kaneda, Toshiko, Marlene Lee, and Kelvin Pollard. 2011. "SCL/PRB Index of Well-being in Older Populations." Final Report on the Global Aging and Monitoring Project. Washington, DC: Population Reference Bureau.

Kao, Grace. 1995. "Asian-Americans as Model Minorities: A Look at their Academic Performance." *American Journal of Education* 103(2): 121–59.

Kao, Grace. 2004. "Social Capital and its Relevance to Minority and Immigrant Populations." *Sociology of Education* 77(2): 172–5.

Kao, Grace, and Marta Tienda. 1995. "Optimism and Achievement: The Educational Performance of Immigrant Youth." *Social Science Quarterly* 76(1): 1–19.

Kao, Grace, Elizabeth Vaquera, and Kimberly A. Goyette. 2013. *Education and Immigration.* Cambridge: Polity.

Kaplan, Mark S., and Gary Marks. 1990. "Adverse Effects of Acculturation:

References

Psychological Distress among Mexican American Young Adults." *Social Science & Medicine* 31(12): 1313–19.

Karoly, Lynn A., and Gabriella C. Gonzalez. 2011. "Early Care and Education for Children in Immigrant Families." *The Future of Children* 21(1): 71–101.

Kasinitz, Philip, John H. Mollenkopf, Mary C. Waters, and Jennifer Holdaway. 2008. *Inheriting the City: The Children of Immigrants Come of Age.* New York: Russell Sage.

Kasl, Stanislav V., and Lisa Berkman. 1983. "Health Consequences of the Experience of Migration." *Annual Review of Public Health* 4: 69–90.

Kates, Robert W. 1997. "Population, Technology, and the Human Environment: A Thread through Time." Pp. 33–55 in *Technological Trajectories and the Human Environment,* edited by J. Ausubel and H. Langford. Washington, DC: National Academy Press.

Katz, Michael B. 1987. *Reconstructing American Education.* Cambridge, MA: Harvard University Press.

Kaufman, Phillip, Martha Naomi Alt, and Christopher D. Chapman. 2001. *Dropout Rates in the United States: 2000.* NCES 2002-114. Washington, DC: US Department of Education, National Center for Education Statistics.

Keely, Charles B. 2001. "Replacement Migration: The Wave of the Future?" *International Migration* 39(6): 103–10.

Keller, Ursula, and Katherine Harker Tillman. 2008. "Post-secondary Educational Attainment of Immigrant and Native Youth." *Social Forces* 87(1): 121–52.

Kennedy, Steven, James Ted McDonald, and Nicholas Biddle. 2006. "The Healthy Immigrant Effect and Immigrant Selection: Evidence from Four Countries." SEDAP Research Paper No. 164. Hamilton, Ontario, Canada: McMaster University.

Kesler, Christel. 2010. "Immigrant Wage Disadvantage in Sweden and the United Kingdom: Wage Structure and Barriers to Opportunity." *International Migration Review* 44(3): 560–92.

KewalRamani, Angelina, Lauren Gilbertson, Mary Ann Fox, and Stephen Provasnik. 2007. "Status and Trends in the Education of Racial and Ethnic Minorities." A report by the National Center for Education Statistics. Washington, DC: US Department of Education.

Khlat, M., and N. Darmon. 2003. "Is There a Mediterranean Migrants Mortality Paradox in Europe?" *International Journal of Epidemiology* 32(6): 1115–18.

Kim, Eunjung. 2002. "The Relationships between Parental Involvement and Children's Educational Achievement in the Korean Immigrant Family." *Journal of Comparative Family Studies* 33(4): 529–44.

Kirk, Dudley. 1996. "Demographic Transition Theory." *Population Studies* 50(3): 361–87.

Klatsky, Arthur L., Irene Tekawa, Mary Anne Armstrong, and Stephen Sidney. 1994. "The Risk of Hospitalization for Ischemic Heart Disease among Asian

References

Americans in Northern California." *American Journal of Public Health* 84(10): 1672–5.

Knickman, James R., and Emily K. Snell. 2002. "The 2030 Problem: Caring for Aging Baby Boomers." *Health Services Research* 37(4): 849–84.

Kogan, Irena. 2006. "Labor Markets and Economic Incorporation among Recent Immigrants in Europe." *Social Forces* 85(2): 697–721.

Kohler, Hans-Peter. 2000. "Social Interaction and Fluctuations in Birth Rates." *Population Studies* 54(2): 223–32.

Kohler, Hans-Peter, Francesco C. Billari and José Antonio Ortega. 2002. "The Emergence of Lowest-Low Fertility in Europe during the 1990s." *Population and Development Review* 28(4): 641–80.

Kohls, Martin. 2008. "Mortality of Immigrants in Germany." Paper presented at the European Population Conference, July 9–12, Barcelona, Spain.

Koopmans, Ruud, Paul Statham, Marco Giugni, and Florence Passy. 2005. *Contested Citizenship: Immigration and Cultural Diversity in Europe.* Minneapolis: University of Minnesota Press.

Kopczuk, Wojciech, Emmanuel Saez, and Jae Song. 2010. "Earning Inequality and Mobility in the United States: Evidence from Social Security Data since 1937." *Quarterly Journal of Economics* 125: 91–128.

Kossoudji, Sherrie A., and Deborah A. Cobb-Clark. 1996. "Finding Good Opportunities within Unauthorized Markets: US Occupational Mobility for Male Latino Workers." *International Migration Review* 30(4): 901–24.

Kraly, Ellen Percy. 1998. "Immigration and Environment: A Framework for Establishing a *Possible* Relationship." *Population Research and Policy Review* 17(5): 421–37.

Kreyenfeld, Michaela. 2002. *Employment and Fertility: East Germany in the 1990s.* Doctoral dissertation. Rostock, Germany: University of Rostock.

Kulu, Hill. 2005. "Migration and Fertility: Competing Hypotheses Re-Examined." *European Journal of Population* 21(1): 51–87.

Kuper, Alan. 2005. "Comment on Frederick Meyerson." *Population and Environment* 26(4): 369–70.

LaLonde, Robert J., and Robert H. Topel. 1992. "The Assimilation of Immigrants in US Labor Market." Pp. 67–92 in *Immigration and the Workforce: Economic Consequences for the United States and Source Areas*, edited by George J. Borjas and Richard B. Freeman. Chicago: University of Chicago Press.

Landsberg, H. E. 1955. "The Climate of Towns." Pp. 584–606 in *Man's Role in Changing the Face of the Earth*, edited by William Leroy Thomas. Chicago: University of Chicago Press.

Lareau, Annette. 2000. *Home Advantage: Social Class and Parental Intervention in Elementary Education.* Second edition. Lanham, MD: Rowman and Littlefield.

Leane, Geoffrey W. G. 2011. "Rights of Ethnic Minorities in Liberal Democracies: Has France Gone Too Far in Banning Muslim Women from Wearing the Burka?" *Human Rights Quarterly* 33(4): 1032–61.

References

Lee, Jaekyung. 2002. "Racial and Ethnic Achievement Gap Trends: Reversing the Process toward Equity?" *Educational Researcher* 13(1): 3–12.

Lee, Jennifer, and Frank D. Bean. 2004. "America's Changing Color Lines: Immigration, Race/Ethnicity, and Multiracial Identification." *Annual Review of Sociology* 30: 221–42.

Lee, Jennifer, and Frank D. Bean. 2007. "Reinventing the Color Line: Immigration and America's New Racial/Ethnic Divide." *Social Forces* 86(2): 561–86.

Lee, Jennifer, and Frank D. Bean. 2010. *The Diversity Paradox: Immigration and the Color Line in Twenty-First Century America.* New York: Russell Sage.

Lee, Jung-Sook, and Natasha K. Bowen. 2006. "Parent Involvement, Cultural Capital, and the Achievement Gap among Elementary School Children." *American Educational Research Journal* 43(2): 193–218.

Lee, Ronald. 2011. "The Outlook for Population Growth." *Science* 333: 569–73.

Lee, Stacey J. 2005. *Up Against Whiteness: Race, School, and Immigrant Youth.* New York: Teacher's College. Lewis, Ethan G. 2005. "Immigration, Skill Mix, and the Choice of Technique." Working Paper 05-8. Philadelphia, PA: Federal Reserve Bank of Philadelphia.

Lewis, Ethan. 2013. "Immigrant–Native Substitutability and the Role of Language." Chapter 3 in *Immigration, Poverty, and Socioeconomic Inequality*, edited by David Card and Steven Raphael. New York: Russell Sage.

Liebermann, Anne Juhasz, Christian Suter, and Katia Iglesias Rutishauser. 2014. "Segregation or Integration? Immigrant Self-Employment in Switzerland." *International Migration and Integration* 15: 93–115.

Lichter, Daniel T., Kenneth M. Johnson, Richard N. Turner, and Allison Churilla. 2012. "Hispanic Assimilation and Fertility in New US Destinations." *International Migration Review* 46(4): 767–91.

Light, Ivan, and Edna Bonacich. 1988. *Immigrant Entrepreneurs: Koreans in Los Angeles, 1965-1982.* Berkeley: University of California Press.

Lindstrom, David P., and Silvia Giorguli Saucedo. 2002. "The Short- and Long-Term Effects of US Migration Experience on Mexican Women's Fertility." *Social Forces* 80(4): 1341–68.

Lindstrom, David P., and Silvia Giorguli Saucedo. 2007. "The Interrelationship of Fertility, Family Maintenance, and Mexico–US Migration." *Demographic Research* 17(28): 821–58.

Linton, April. 2002. "Immigration and the Structure of Demand: Do Immigrants Alter the Labor Market Composition of US Cities?" *International Migration Review* 36(1): 58–80.

Lippard, Cameron D., and Charles A. Gallagher (eds.) 2010. *Being Brown in Dixie: Race, Ethnicity, and Latino Immigration in the New South.* Boulder: First Forum Press.

Livingston, Gretchen, and D'Vera Cohn. 2012. "US Birth Rate Falls to a Record Low; Decline is Greatest among Immigrants." Research report. Washington, DC: Pew Research Center.

References

Lleras-Muney, Adriana. 2005. "The Relationship between Education and Adult Mortality in the US." *Review of Economic Studies* 72(1): 189–221.

Lofstrom, Magnus. 2013. "Does Self-Employment Increase the Economic Well-Being of Low-Skilled Workers?" *Small Business Economics* 40(4): 933–52.

Lofstrom, Magnus, and Frank D. Bean. 2002. "Assessing Immigrant Policy Options: Labor Market Conditions and Postreform Declines in Immigrants' Receipt of Welfare." *Demography* 39(4): 617–37.

Lopez, Barbara, Wei Wang, Seth J. Schwartz, et al. 2009. "School, Family, and Peer Factors and Their Association with Substance Use in Hispanic Adolescents." *The Journal of Primary Prevention* 30(6): 622–41.

Lopez, Russell. 2014. "Urban Sprawl in the United States: 1970–2010." *Cities and the Environment (CATE)* 7(1): 1–19.

Lorant, Vincent, Herman Van Oyen, and Isabelle Thomas. 2008. "Contextual Factors and Immigrants' Health Status: Double Jeopardy." *Health and Place* 14(4): 678–92.

Louie, Vivian S. 2004. *Compelled to Excel: Immigration, Education, and Opportunity among Chinese Americans.* Stanford, CA: Stanford University.

Luedtke, Adam. 2005. "European Integration, Public Opinion and Immigration Policy: Testing the Impact of National Identity." *European Union Politics* 6(1): 83–112.

Lutz, Wolfgang, Brian C. O'Neill, and Sergei Scherbov. 2003. "Europe's Population at a Turning Point." *Science* 299(5615): 1991–2.

Lutz, Wolfgang and Christopher Prinz. 1992. "What Difference Do Alternative Immigration and Integration Levels Make to Western Europe?" *European Journal of Population* 8(4): 341–61.

Lynch, Robert, and Patrick Oakford. 2013. "The Economic Effects of Granting Legal Status and Citizenship to Undocumented Immigrants." A report. Washington, DC: Center for American Progress.

Macisco, John J., Jr., Leon F. Bouvier, and Martha Jane Renzi. 1969. "Migration Status, Education and Fertility in Puerto Rico, 1960." *The Milbank Memorial Fund Quarterly* 47(2): 167–86.

Macunovich, Diane. 2000. "Macunovich Response to Abernethy Rejoinder." *Population and Environment* 21(5): 473–6.

Malthus, Thomas. 1798. *An Essay on the Principle of Population.* London: St. Paul's Church.

Mandel, Ruth. 2008. *Cosmopolitan Anxieties: Turkish Challenges to Citizenship and Belonging in Germany.* Durham, NC: Duke University Press.

Marcelli, Enrico A. 2001. "From the Barrio to the 'Burbs: Immigration and Urban Sprawl in Southern California." Working Paper. San Diego: Center for Comparative Immigration Studies.

Markides, Kyriakos S., and Jeannine Coreil. 1986. "The Health of Hispanics in the Southwestern United States: An Epidemiological Paradox." *Public Health Reports* 101(3): 253–65.

References

Marks, Gary, Melinda Garcia, and Julia M. Solis. 1990. "Health Risk Behaviors of Hispanics in the United States: Findings from HHANES, 1982–84." *American Journal of Public Health* 80(12): 20–6.

Marmot, M. G., A. M. Adelstein, and L. Bulusu. 1984. "Lessons from the Study of Immigrant Mortality." *Lancet* 323(8392): 1455–7.

Marmot, Michael G., and S. Leonard Syme. 1976. "Acculturation and Coronary Heart Disease in Japanese-Americans." *Journal of Epidemiology* 103(3): 225–47.

Marrow, Helen. 2005. "New Destinations and Immigrant Incorporation." *Perspectives on Politics* 3(4): 781–99.

Martin, Daniel C. 2010. "Refugees and Asylees: 2009." Annual Flow Report. Washington, DC: US Department of Homeland Security.

Martin, Linda G. 1991. "Population Aging Policies in East Asia and the United States." *Science* 251(4993): 527–31.

Martin, Philip. 1994. "Germany: Reluctant Land of Immigration." Pp. 189–226 in *Controlling Immigration: A Global Perspective*, edited by Wayne Cornelius, Philip Martin, and James Hollifield. Stanford, CA: Stanford University Press.

Martin, Philip L., Anolo I. Abella, and Christiane Kuptsch. 2006. *Managing Labor Migration in the Twenty-First Century*. New Haven, CT: Yale University Press.

Martinez, Ramiro, and Abel Valenzuela. 2006. *Immigration and Crime: Race, Ethnicity, and Violence*. New York: New York University Press.

Massey, Douglas S. 1985. "Ethnic Residential Segregation: A Theoretical Synthesis and Empirical Review." *Sociology and Social Research* 39: 315–50.

Massey, Douglas S. 1987. "Understanding Mexican Migration to the United States." *American Journal of Sociology* 92(6): 1372–403.

Massey, Douglas S. 1994. "An Evaluation of International Migration Theory: The North American Case." *Population and Development Review* 20(4): 699–751.

Massey, Douglas S. 2005. "Backfire at the Border: Why Enforcement Without Legalization Cannot Stop Illegal Immigration." Trade Policy Analysis 29. Washington, DC: The CATO Institute.

Massey, Douglas S. (ed.) 2008. *New Faces in New Places: The Changing Geography of American Immigration*. New York: Russell Sage.

Massey, Douglas, and Katherine Bartley. 2005. "The Changing Legal Status Distribution of Immigrants: A Caution." *International Migration Review* 39: 469–84.

Massey, Douglas S., and Mary J. Fischer. 2005. "Stereotype Threat and Academic Performance: New Findings from a Racially Diverse Sample of College Freshman." *Du Bois Review* 2(1): 45–68.

Mattoo, Aaditya, Ileana Cristina Neagu, and _a_lar Özden. 2005. "Brain Waste? Educated Immigrants in the US Labor Market." *Journal of Developmental Economics* 87(2): 255–69.

References

Maxim, Paul S. 1992. "Immigrants, Visible Minorities, and Self-Employment." *Demography* 29(2): 181–99.

Mayda, Anna Maria. 2006. "Who is Against Immigration? A Cross-country Investigation of Individual Attitudes toward Immigrants." *The Review of Economics and Statistics* 88(3): 510–30.

Mayer, Jochen, and Regina T. Riphahn. 2000. "Fertility Assimilation of Immigrants: Evidence from Count Data Models." *Journal of Population Economics* 13(2): 241–61.

Mazur, Robert E., Grace S. Marquis, and Helen H. Jensen. 2003. "Diet and Food Insufficiency among Hispanic Youths: Acculturation and Socioeconomic Factors in the Third National Health and Nutrition Examination Survey." *The American Journal of Clinical Nutrition* 78(6): 1120–7.

McCall, Leslie. 2000. "Explaining Levels of Within-Group Wage Inequality in US Labor Markets." *Demography* 37(4): 415–30.

McCall, Leslie. 2001. "Sources of Racial Wage Inequality in Metropolitan Labor Markets: Racial, Ethnic, and Gender Differences." *American Sociological Review* 66(4): 520–41.

McConnell, Eileen Diaz, and Edward A. Delgado-Romero. 2004. "Latino Panethnicity: Reality or Methodological Construction?" *Social Focus* 37(4): 297–312.

McDaniel, Paul. 2014. *Revitalization in the Heartland of America: Welcoming Immigrant Entrepreneurs for Economic Development.* Research Report. Washington, DC: American Immigration Council.

McDonald, Peter. 2006. "Low Fertility and the State: The Efficacy of Policy." *Population and Development Review* 32(3): 485–510.

McFalls, Joseph A., Jr. 2007. *Population: A Lively Introduction.* Fifth edition. Washington, DC: Population Reference Bureau.

McHugh, Kevin E., Ines M. Miyares, and Emily H. Skop. 1997. "The Magnetism of Miami: Segmented Paths in Cuban Migration." *Geographical Review* 87(4): 504–19.

McKenzie, David and Hillel Rapoport. 2010. "Self-selection Patterns in Mexico–US Migration: The Role of Migration Networks." *The Review of Economics and Statistics* 92(4): 811–21.

McLaren, Lauren M. 2003. "Anti-Immigrant Prejudice in Europe: Contact, Threat Perception, and Preferences for the Exclusion of Migrants." *Social Forces* 81(3): 909–36.

Mehta, Neil K., and Irma T. Elo. 2010. "Migration Selection and the Health of US Immigrants from the Former Soviet Union." *Demography* 49(2): 425–47.

Menjívar, Cecilia. 2000. *Fragmented Ties: Salvadoran Immigrant Networks in America.* Berkeley: University of California Press.

Merida, Kevin. 1995. "Worry, Frustration Build for Many in the Black Middle Class." *Washington Post.* October 9. Pp. A1, A22–A23.

References

Mertz, Elizabeth A., and Len Finocchio. 2010. "Improving Oral Healthcare Delivery Systems through Workforce Innovations: An Introduction." *Journal of Public Health Dentistry* 70(s1): s1–s5.

Meyerson, Frederick A. B. 2001. "Replacement Migration: A Questionable Tactic for Delaying the Inevitable Effect of Fertility Transition." *Population and Environment* 22(4): 401–9.

Michielin, Francesca. 2002. "Lowest Low Fertility in an Urban Context: When Migration Plays a Key Role." MPIDR Working Paper 2002-050. Rostock: Max Planck Institute for Demographic Research.

Migration Policy Institute. 2012. "Anti-Immigrant Rhetoric Just One of Several Campaign Messages for Far-Right Parties." *Migration Information Source.* Washington, DC: Migration Policy Institute. Available online at www.migrationinformation.org/Feature/display.cfm?ID=918.

Milewski, Nadja. 2007. "First Child of Immigrant Workers and Their Descendants in West Germany: Interrelation of Events, Disruption, or Adaptation?" *Demographic Research* 17(29): 859–96.

Milewski, Nadja. 2010. "Immigrant Fertility in West Germany: Is There a Socialization Effect in Transitions to Second and Third Births?" *European Journal of Population* 26: 197–323.

Milner, H. Richard, III. 2013. "Analyzing Poverty, Learning, and Teaching through a Critical Race Theory Lens." *Review of Research in Education* 37(1): 1–53.

Mock, Brentin. 2013. "How the Sierra Club Learned to Love Immigration." *ColorLines: News for Action.* Available online at http://colorlines.com/archives/2013/05/.

Mogro-Wilson, Cristina. 2008. "The Influence of Parental Warmth and Control on Latino Adolescent Alcohol Use." *Hispanic Journal of Behavioral Sciences* 30(1): 89–105.

Mohanty, Sarita A., Steffie Wollhandler, David U. Himmelstein, Susmita Pati, Olveen Carrasquillo, and David H. Bor. 2005. "Health Care Expenditures of Immigrants in the United States: A Nationally Representative Analysis." *American Journal of Public Health* 95(8):1431–1438.

Mohl, Raymond A. 2003. "Globalization, Latinization, and the Nuevo New South." *Journal of American Ethnic History* 22(4): 31–66.

Montague, Ashley (ed.) 1999. *Race and IQ.* Second edition. New York: Oxford University Press.

Morehouse, Christal, and Michael Blomfield. 2011. "Irregular Migration in Europe." A Report of the Transatlantic Council on Migration. Washington, DC: Migration Policy Institute.

Morgan, S. Philip. 1996. "Characteristic Features of Modern American Fertility." *Population and Development Review* 22(Supplement): 19–63.

Mulder, Clara H., and Michael Wagner. 2001. "The Connections between Family Formation and First-Time Home Ownership in the Context of West

Germany and the Netherlands." *European Journal of Population* 17(2): 137–64.

Muradian, Roldan. 2006. "Immigration and the Environment: Underlying Values and Scope of Analysis." *Ecological Economics* 59(2): 208–13.

Murphy, John P. 2011. "Baguettes, Berets and Burning Cars: The 2005 Riots and the Question of Race in Contemporary France." *French Cultural Studies* 22(1): 33–49.

Mussino, Eleonora, and Salvatore Strozza. 2012. "The Fertility of Immigrants after Arrival: The Italian Case." *Demographic Research* 26(4): 99–130.

National Center for Health Statistics. 2004. *Health, United States, 2004.* Hyattsville, MD: National Center for Health Statistics.

National Research Council. 2007. "The Future of US Chemistry Research: Benchmarks and Challenges." Report in brief. Washington, DC: The National Academy of Sciences.

Nauck, Bernhard. 1987. "Individuelle und kontextuelle Faktoren der Kinderzahl in türkischen Migrantenfamilien." *Zeitschrift für Bevölkerungswissenschaft* 13(3): 319–44.

Neal, Micki, and Stephanie A. Bohon. 2003. "The Dixie Diaspora: Attitudes towards Immigrants in Georgia." *Sociological Spectrum* 23(2): 181–212.

Neckerman, Kathryn M., Prudence Carter, and Jennifer Lee. 1999. "Segmented Assimilation and Minority Cultures of Mobility." *Ethnic and Racial Studies* 22(6): 945–65.

Neuhouser, Marian L., Beti Thompson, Gloria D. Coronado, and Cam C. Solomon. 2004. "Higher Fat Intake and Lower Fruit and Vegetable Intakes are Associated with Greater Acculturation among Mexicans Living in Washington State." *Journal of the American Dietetic Association* 104(1): 51–7

Neumayer, Eric. 2006. "The Environment: One More Reason to Keep Immigrants Out?" *Ecological Economics* 59(2): 204–7.

Neupert, Kent E., and C. Christopher Baughn. 2013. "Immigration, Education and Entrepreneurship in Developed Countries." *Journal of Enterprising Communities* 7(3): 293–310.

Newman, Benjamin. 2013. "Acculturating Contexts and Anglo Opposition to Immigration in the United States." *American Journal of Political Science* 57(2): 374–90.

Newman, Benjamin, and Joshua Johnson. 2012. "Ethnic Change, Concern over Immigration, and Approval of State Government." *State Politics & Policy Quarterly* 12(4): 415–37.

Newman, Benjamin, Christopher Johnston, April A. Strickland, and Jack Citrin. 2012. "Immigration Crackdown in the American Workplace: Explaining Variation in E-Verify Adoption across the U.S. States." *State Politics & Policy Quarterly* 12(2): 160–82.

Ng, Edward, and François Nault. 1997. "Fertility among Recent Immigrant

References

Women to Canada, 1991: An Examination of the Disruption Hypothesis." *International Migration Review* 35(4): 559–80.

Nightingale, Demetra Smith, and Michael Fix. 2004. "Economic and Labor Market Trends." *The Future of Children* 14(2): 48–59.

Northcott, Herbert C. 1994. "Public Perceptions of the Population Aging 'Crisis.'" *Canadian Public Policy* 20(1): 66–77.

Ochocka, Joanna, and Rich Janzen. 2008. "Immigrant Parenting: A New Framework of Understanding." *Journal of Immigrant and Refugee Studies* 6(1): 85–111.

OECD. 2007. *Policy Coherence for Development: Migration and Developing Countries.* Paris: OECD Publishing.

OECD. 2010. *International Migration Outlook 2010.* Paris: OECD Publishing.

OECD. 2011. *Health at a Glance 2011: OECD Indicators.* Paris: OECD Publishing. Available online at http://dx.doi.org/10.1787/health_glance-2011-en.

OECD. 2013. "Immigrant and Foreign Population." In *OECD Factbook 2013: Economic, Environmental and Social Statistics.* Paris: OECD Publishing. Available online at http://dx.doi.org/10.1787/factbook-2013-6-en.

Office of Management and Budget (OMB). 2003. "Revisions to the Standards for the Classification of Federal Data on Race and Ethnicity." *Federal Register* notice.

Ogbu, John U. 1978. *Minority Education and Caste: The American System in Cross-Cultural Perspective.* San Diego, CA: American Press.

Ogbu, John U. 1991. "Cultural Diversity and School Experience." Chapter 2 in *Literacy as Praxis: Culture, Language and Pedagogy*, edited by Catherine E. Walsh. Norwood, NJ: Ablex.

O'Hare, William. 2004. *Trends in the Well-Being of America's Children.* New York and Washington, DC: Russell Sage and the Population Reference Bureau.

Okun, Barbara S., and Shlomit Kagya. 2012. "Fertility Change among Post-1989 Immigrants to Israel from the Former Soviet Union." *International Migration Review* 46(4): 792–827.

Oliver, Melvin and Thomas Shapiro. 1995. *Black Wealth / White Wealth: A New Perspective on Racial Inequality.* New York: Routledge.

Olzak, Susan. 1992. *The Dynamics of Ethnic Competition and Conflict.* Stanford, CA: Stanford University Press.

Omi, Michael, and Howard Winant. 1994. *Racial Formation in the United States: From the 1960s to the 1990s.* New York: Routledge.

Omran, Abdel R. 2005. "The Epidemiological Transition: A Theory of the Epidemiology of Population Change." *The Milbank Quarterly* 83(4): 731–57 (reprinted from original published in 1971).

Orellana, Marjorie Faulstich. 2008. *Translating Childhoods: Immigrant Youth, Language, and Culture.* Camden, NJ: Rutgers University Press.

Orenstein, Daniel E. 2004. "Population Growth and Environmental Impact:

References

Ideology and Academic Discourse in Israel." *Population and Environment* 26(1): 41–60.

Orenstein, Daniel E., and Steven P. Hamburg. 2010. "Population and Pavement: Population Growth and Land Development in Israel." *Population and Environment* 31: 223–54.

Orr, Amy J. 2003. "Black–White Differences in Achievement: The Importance of Wealth." *Sociology of Education* 76(4): 281–304.

Ortiz, Vilma. 1986. "Changes in the Characteristics of Puerto Rican Migrants from 1955 to 1980." *International Migration Review* 20(3): 612–28.

Ottaviano, Gianmarco I. P., and Giovanni Peri. 2005. "Cities and Cultures." *Journal of Urban Economics* 58(2):304–307.

Ottaviano, Gianmarco I.P. and Giovanni Peri. 2006. "Rethinking the Effect of Immigration on Wages." NBER Working Paper 12496. Cambridge, MA: National Bureau of Economic Research.

Ottaviano, Gianmarco I. P., and Giovanni Peri. 2007. "The Effect of Immigration on US Wages and Rents: A General Equilibrium Approach." CReAM Discussion Paper 13/07. London: University College London.

Ottaviano, Gianmarco I. P., and Giovanni Peri. 2008. "Immigration and National Wages: Clarifying the Theory and the Empirics." NBER Working Paper 14188. Cambridge, MA: National Bureau of Economic Research.

Owens, Jayanti, and Scott M. Lynch. 2012. "Black and Hispanic Immigrants' against Negative-ability Racial Stereotypes at Selective Colleges and Universities in the United States." *Sociology of Education* 85(4): 303–25.

Pablos-Méndez, Ariel. 1994. "Mortality among Hispanics": Letter to the Editor. *JAMA* 271(16): 1237–8.

Palmer, Anna, and Darren Samuelsohn. 2013. "Sierra Club Backs Immigration Reform." *Politico*. Available online at www.politico.com/story/2013/04.

Park, Robert, Ernest W. Burgess, and Roderick D. McKenzie. 1925. *The City*. Chicago: University of Chicago Press.

Park, Robert E. 1928. "Human Migration and the Marginal Man." *American Journal of Sociology* 33(6): 881–93.

Park, Robert E., and Ernest W. Burgess. 1921. *Introduction to the Science of Sociology*. Chicago: University of Chicago Press.

Parrado, Emilio A. 2011. "How High is Hispanic/Mexican Fertility in the United States? Immigration and Tempo Considerations." *Demography* 48: 1059–80.

Parrado, Emilio A., and S. Philip Morgan. 2008. "Intergenerational Fertility among Hispanic Women: New Evidence of Immigrant Assimilation." *Demography* 45(3): 651–71.

Parsons, Jack. 2000. "The Salience of Number-power: An Idea Whose Time Has Come?" *Population and Environment* 21(5): 477–508.

Passel, Jeffrey S. 2006. "The Size and Characteristics of the Unauthorized Migrant Population in the US." Research Report. Washington, DC: Pew Hispanic Center.

References

Passel, Jeffrey S., and D'Vera Cohn. 2010. "US Unauthorized Immigration Flows are Down Sharply since Mid-decade." A report of the Pew Hispanic Center. Washington, DC: Pew Research Center.

Passel, Jeffrey S., and D'Vera Cohn. 2011. *Unauthorized Immigrant Population: National and State Trends, 2010*. Washington, DC: Pew Hispanic Center.

Passel, Jeffrey, D'Vera Cohn, and Ana Gonzalez-Barrera. 2012. "Net Migration from Mexico Falls to Zero – and Perhaps Less." A report of the Pew Hispanic Center. Washington, DC: Pew Research Center.

Patten, Eileen. 2012. "Statistical Portrait of the Foreign-born Population in the United States, 2010." A report of the Pew Hispanic Center. Washington, DC: Pew Hispanic Center.

Pedace, Roberto. 2006. "Immigration, Labor Market Mobility, and the Earnings of Native-born Workers: An Occupational Segmentation Approach." *American Journal of Economics and Sociology* 65(2): 313–46.

Perea, Juan F. (ed.) 1997. *Immigrants Out! The New Nativism and the Anti-immigrant Impulse in the United States*. New York: New York University Press.

Perelli-Harris, Brienna. 2008. "Ukraine: On the Border between Old and New in Uncertain Times." *Demographic Research* 19(29): 1145–78.

Perez, Anthony Daniel, and Charles Hirschman. 2009. "The Changing Racial and Ethnic Composition of the US Population: Emerging American Identities." *Population and Development Review* 35(1): 1–51.

Pérez, Lisandro. 1992. "Cuban Miami." Chapter 5 in *Miami Now! Immigration, Ethnicity and Social Change*, edited by Guillermo J. Grenier and Alex Stepick III. Gainesville: University of Florida Press.

Pérez-Stable, Eliseo J., Gerardo Marín, and Barbara VanOss Marín. 1994. "Behavioral Risk Factors: A Comparison of Latinos and Non-Latino Whites in San Francisco." *American Journal of Public Health* 84(6): 971–76.

Peri, Giovanni. 2010. "The Effect of Immigrants on US Employment and Productivity." San Francisco Federal Reserve Board Report 2010–26. San Francisco: San Francisco Federal Reserve Board.

Peri, Giovanni. 2012. "The Effects of Immigration on Productivity: Evidence from the US States." *Review of Economics and Statistics* 94(1): 348–58.

Perlmann, Joel. 2005. *Italians Then, Mexicans Now: Immigrant Origins and Second-Generation Progress, 1890 to 2000*. New York: Russell Sage.

Petersen, William. 1999. *Malthus: Founder of Modern Demography*. New Brunswick, NJ: Transaction Publishers.

Pfeffer, Max J., and J. Mayone Stycos. 2002. "Immigrant Environmental Behaviors in New York City." *Social Science Quarterly* 81(1): 64–81.

Pinstrup-Andersen, Per, and Rajul Pandya-Lorch. 2001. "Meeting Food Needs in the 21st Century: How Many and Who Will Be At Risk?" Report. Washington, DC: International Food Policy Research Institute.

Plyler, Superintendent, Tyler Independent School District, et al. v. *Doe, Guardian, et al.* 1982. 457 US 202.

References

Population and Consumption Task Force. 1996. "Population and Consumption Task Force Report." Washington, DC: President's Council on Sustainability.

Population–Environment Balance, Inc. 1992. "Why Excess Immigration Damages the Environment." *Population and Environment* 13(4): 303–12.

Portes, Alejandro. 1997. "Immigration Theory for a New Century: Some Problems and Opportunities." *International Migration Review* 31(4): 799–825.

Portes, Alejandro. 1998. "Social Capital: Its Origins and Applications in Modern Sociology." *Annual Review of Sociology* 24: 1–24.

Portes, Alejandro, and József Böröcz. 1989. "Contemporary Immigration: Theoretical Perspectives on its Determinants and Modes of Incorporation." *International Migration Review* 23(3): 606–30.

Portes, Alejandro, Patricia Fernández-Kelly, and William Haller. 2005. "Segmented Assimilation on the Ground: The New Second Generation in Early Adulthood." *Ethnic and Racial Studies* 28(6): 1000–40.

Portes, Alejandro, and Leif Jensen. 1992. "Reply to Sanders and Nee: Disproving the Enclave Hypothesis." *American Sociological Review* 57(3): 418–20.

Portes, Alejandro, and Robert D. Manning. 1986. "'The Immigrant Enclave' Theory and Empirical Examples." Chapter 2 in *Competitive Ethnic Relations*, edited by Susan Olzak and Joane Nagel. Orlando, FL: Academic Press.

Portes, Alejandro, and Rubén G. Rumbaut. 2006. *Immigrant America: A Portrait*. Third edition. Berkeley: University of California Press.

Portes, Alejandro, and Alex Stepick. 1993. *City on the Edge: The Transformation of Miami*. Berkeley: University of California Press.

Portes, Alejandro, and Min Zhou. 1993. "The New Second Generation: Segmented Assimilation and Its Variants." *Annals of the American Academy of Political and Social Science* 530: 74–96.

Poston, Dudley L., Jr., Chiung-Fang Chang, and Hong Dan. 2006. "Fertility Differences between the Majority and Minority Nationality Groups in China." *Population Research and Policy Review* 25(1): 67–101.

Powles, John. 1990. "The Best of Both Worlds: Attempting to Explain the Persisting Low Mortality of Greek Migrants to Australia." Pp. 584–94 in *What We Know about Health Transition: The Cultural, Social and Behavioural Determinants of Health*, edited by J. Caldwell, S. Findlay, P. Caldwell and G. Santow. Canberra: Health Transition Center.

Prado, Guillermo, Shi Huang, Seth J. Schwartz, et al. 2009. "What Accounts for Differences in Substance Use among US-born and Immigrant Hispanic Adolescents? Results from a Longitudinal Prospective Cohort Study." *Journal of Adolescent Health* 45(2): 118–25.

Preston, Samuel H., Christine Himes, and Mitchell Eggers. 1989. "Demographic Conditions Responsible for Population Aging." *Demography* 26(4): 691–704.

Preston, Valerie, Ann Kim, Samantha Hudyma, Nancy Mandell, Meg Luxton, and Julia Hemphill. 2013. "Gender, Race, and Immigration: Aging and Economic Security in Canada." *Canadian Review of Social Policy* 2: 68–90.

References

Price, Carmel E., and Ben Feldmeyer. 2012. "The Environmental Impact of Immigration: An Analysis of the Effects of Immigrant Concentration on Air Pollution Levels." *Population Research and Policy Review* 31(1): 119–40.

Prislin, Radmila, Lucina Suarez, Diane M. Simpson, and James A. Dyer. 1998. "When Acculturation Hurts: The Case of Immunization." *Social Science and Medicine* 47(12): 1947–56.

Pudaric, Sonja, Jan Sundquist, and Sven-Erik Johansson. 2003. "Country of Birth, Instrumental Activities of Daily Living, Self-Rated Health and Mortality: A Swedish Population-Based Survey of People Aged 55-74." *Social Science and Medicine* 56(12): 2493–503.

Puentes, Robert, and David Warren. 2006. "One-fifth of America: A Comprehensive Guide to America's First Suburbs." A report of the Metropolitan Policy Program. Washington, DC: Brookings Institution.

Pumariega, Andrés J., Eugenio Rothe, and JoAnne B. Pumariega. 2005. "Mental Health of Immigrants and Refugees." *Community Mental Health Journal* 41(5): 581–97.

Quillian, Lincoln. 1995. "Prejudice as a Response to Perceived Group Threat: Population Composition and Anti-Immigrant and Racial Prejudice in Europe." *American Sociological Review* 60(4): 586–611.

Raijman, Rebeca, and Marta Tienda. 2000. "Immigrants' Pathways to Business Ownership: A Comparative Ethnic Perspective." *International Migration Review* 34(3): 682–706.

Ram, B., and M. V. George. 1990. "Immigrant Fertility Patterns in Canada, 1961–1986." *International Migration* 28(4): 413–26.

Ravitch, Diane. 2000. *The Great School Wars: A History of the New York Public Schools.* Baltimore, MD: Johns Hopkins University Press.

Razum, Oliver, and Dorothee Twardella. 2002. "Time Travel with Oliver Twist: Towards an Explanation for a Paradoxically Low Mortality among Recent Immigrants." *Tropical Medicine and International Health* 7(1): 4–10.

Razum, Oliver, Hajo Zeeb, H. Seval Akgün, and Selma Yilmaz. 1998. "Low Overall Mortality of Turkish Residents in Germany Persists and Extends into a Second Generation: Merely a Healthy Migrant Effect?" *Tropical Medicine International Health* 3(4): 297–303.

Read, Jen'nan Ghazal, Benjamin Amick, and Katharine M. Donato. 2005. "Arab Immigrants: A New Case for Ethnicity and Health?" *Social Science and Medicine* 61: 77–82.

Rees, William E. 1992. "Ecological Footprints and Appropriated Carrying Capacity: What Urban Economics Leaves Out." *Environment and Urbanisation* 4(2): 121–30.

Reichert, Josh, and Douglas S. Massey. 1979. "Patterns of US Migration from a Mexican Sending Community: A Comparison of Legal and Illegal Migrants." *International Migration Review* 13(4): 599–623.

Richardson, Scott, John Ruser, and Peggy Suárez. 2003. "Hispanic Workers in

References

the United States: An Analysis of Employment Distribution, Fatal Occupational Injuries, and Nonfatal Occupational Injuries and Illnesses." Pp. 43–82 in *Safety is Seguridad*, edited by the National Research Council. Washington, DC: National Academies Press.

Riphahn, Regina T. 2003. "Cohort Effects in the Educational Attainment of Second Generation Immigrants in Germany: An Analysis of Census Data." *Journal of Population Economics* 16(4): 711–37.

Rivkin, Steven G., Eric A. Hanushek, and John F. Kain. 2005. "Teachers, Schools, and Academic Achievement." *Econometrica* 73(2): 417–58.

Rist, Ray C. 1978. "The Guestworkers of Germany." *Society* 15(5): 81–90.

Roberts, Sam. 2011. "New York's Little Italy, Littler by the Year." *New York Times*. February 21.

Rodríguez, Clara E. 2000. *Changing Race: Latinos, the Census, and the History of Ethnicity in the United States*. New York: New York University Press.

Rogers, Richard G., Robert A. Hummer, and Charles B. Nam. 2000. *Living and Dying in the USA: Behavioral, Health, and Social Differentials in Adult Mortality*. San Diego, CA: Academic Press.

Roig Vila, Marta, and Teresa Castro Martín. 2007. "Childbearing Patterns of Foreign Women in a New Immigration Country: The Case of Spain." *Population – E* 62(3): 351–80.

Røpke, Inge. 2006. "Migration and Sustainability: Compatible or Contradictory?" *Ecological Economics* 59(2): 191–4.

Rosenbaum, Emily, and Samantha Friedman. 2007. *The Housing Divide: How Generations of Immigrants Fare in New York's Housing Market*. New York: New York University Press.

Rosenfeld, Michael J., and Marta Tienda. 1999. "Mexican Immigration, Occupational Niches, and Labor Market Competition: Evidence from Los Angeles, Chicago and Atlanta, 1970–1990." Chapter 2 in *Immigration and Opportunity: Race Ethnicity and Employment in the United States*, edited by Frank D. Bean and Stephanie Bell-Rose. New York: Russell Sage.

Rothenberg, Daniel. 1998. *With these Hands: The Hidden World of Migrant Farm Workers Today*. Berkeley: University of California Press.

Rothstein, Richard. 2008. "Leaving 'No Child Left Behind' Behind." *The American Prospect* 19(1): 50–4.

Rubalcava, Luis N., Graciela M. Teruel, Duncan Thomas, and Noreen Goldman. 2008. "The Healthy Migrant Effect: New Findings from the Mexican Family Life Survey." *American Journal of Public Health* 98(1): 78–84.

Rubia, Maria, Isabel Marcos, and Peter A. Muennig. 2002. "Increased Risk of Heart Disease and Stroke among Foreign-Born Females Residing in the United States." *American Journal of Preventive Medicine* 22(1): 30–5.

Rumbaut, Rubén G. 1994. "The Crucible Within: Ethnic Identity, Self Esteem, and Segmented Assimilation among Children of Immigrants." *International Migration Review* 28(4): 748–94.

References

Rumbaut, Rubén G. 1997a. "Paradoxes (and Orthodoxies) of Assimilation." *Sociological Perspectives* 40(3): 483–511.

Rumbaut, Rubén. 1997b. "Assimilation and its Discontents: Between Rhetoric and Reality." *International Migration Review* 31(4): 923–60.

Rumbaut, Rubén G. 2004. "Ages, Life Stages, and Generational Cohorts: Decomposing the Immigrant First and Second Generations in the United States." *International Migration Review* 38(3): 1160–205.

Rumbaut, Rubén G. 2005. "Turning Points in the Transition to Adulthood: Determinants of Educational Attainment, Incarceration, and Early Childbearing among Children of Immigrants." *Ethnic and Racial Studies* 28(6): 1041–86.

Ryan, Camille L., and Julie Siebens. 2012. "Educational Attainment in the United States: 2009." Population characteristics P20-566. Washington, DC: US Census Bureau.

Saczuk, Katarzyna. 2003. "A Development and Critique of the Concept of Replacement Migration." CEFMR Working Paper 4/2003. Warsaw: Central European Forum for Migration Research.

Salerno, Michael. 2006. "Reading is Fundamental: Why the No Child Left Behind Act Necessitates Recognition of a Fundamental Right to Education." *Cardozo Public Law, Policy and Ethics Journal* 5(2): 509–42.

Sampson, Robert J. 2008. "Rethinking Crime and Immigration." *Contexts* 7(1): 28–33.

Sánchez, George J. 1997. "Face the Nation: Race, Immigration, and the Rise of Nativism in Late Twentieth Century America." *International Migration Review* 31(4): 1009–30.

Sassen, Saskia. 1996. *Losing Control? Sovereignty in an Age of Globalization.* New York: Columbia University Press.

Schafer, Leslie E. 1998. "Population Implosion of the Developed World: Changing Attitudes toward Immigration to Support Aging Societies." *Indiana Journal of Global Legal Studies* 6(1): 357–69.

Schenk, Liane. 2007. "Migration und Gesundheit – Entwicklung eines Erklärungs – und Analysemodells für Epidemiologische Studien" (Migration and Health: Developing an Explanatory and Analytical Model for Epidemiological Studies). *International Journal of Public Health* 52(2): 87–96.

Schneider, Silke L. 2008. "Anti-immigrant Attitudes in Europe: Outgroup Size and Perceived Ethnic Threat." *European Sociological Review* 24(1): 53–67.

Schnittker, Jason. 2004. "Education and the Changing Shape of the Income Gradient inHealth." *Journal of Health and Social Behavior* 45(3): 286–305.

Schoeni, Robert F. 1997. "New Evidence on the Economic Progress of Foreign-bornMen in the 1970s and 1980s." *Journal of Human Resources* 32: 683–740.

Schoorl, J. J. 1990. "Fertility Adaptation of Turkish and Moroccan Women in the Netherlands." *International Migration* 28(4): 477–95.

Schuck, Peter H. 2003. *Diversity in America: Keeping Government at a Safe Distance.* Cambridge, MA: The Belknap Press of Harvard University.

References

Schwartz, Amber, and Don Soifer. 2012. "The Value of English Proficiency to the United States Economy." Arlington, VA: The Lexington Institute.

Schwartzman, Kathleen C. 2008. "Lettuce, Segmented Labor Markets, and the Immigration Discourse." *Journal of Black Studies* 39(1): 129–56.

Scribner, Richard. 1996. "Paradox as Paradigm: The Health Outcomes of Mexican Americans." *American Journal of Public Health* 86(3): 303–5.

Semyonov, Moshe, Rebecca Raijman, and Anastasia Gorodzeisky. 2006. "The Rise of Anti-Foreigner Sentiment in European Societies, 1988–2000." *American Sociological Review* 71(3): 426–49.

Semyonov, Moshe, Rebecca Raijman, Anat Yom-Tov, and Peter Schmidt. 2004. "Population Size, Perceived Threat, and Exclusion: A Multiple-Indicators Analysis of Attitudes toward Foreigners in Germany." *Social Science Research* 33: 681–701.

Şen, Faruk. 2003. "The Historical Situation of Turkish Immigrants in Germany." *Immigrants and Minorities* 22(2–3): 208–27.

Sevak, Puri, and Lucie Schmidt. 2008. "Immigrant–Native Fertility and Mortality Differentials in the United States." Working Paper 2008-181. Ann Arbor: Michigan Retirement Research Center.

Severance, Kristi. 2010. "France's Expulsion of Roma Migrants: A Test Case for Europe." Washington, DC: Migration Policy Institute. Available online at www.migrationinformation.org/Feature/display.cfm?ID=803.

Sewell, William H., Robert M. Hauser, and David L. Featherman. 1976. *Schooling and Achievement in American Society*. New York: Academic Press.

Shai, Donna, and Ira Rosenwaike. 1987. "Morality among Hispanics in Metropolitan Chicago: An Examination Based on Vital Statistics Data." *Journal of Chronic Diseases* 40(5): 445–51.

Shuey, Kim M., and Andrea E. Willson. 2008. "Cumulative Disadvantage and Black–White Disparities in Life-course Health Trajectories." *Research on Aging* 30(2): 200–25.

Shutika, Debra Latanzi. 2008. "The Ambivalent Welcome: *Cinco de Mayo* and the Symbolic Expression of Local Identity and Ethnic Relations." Pp. 274–307 in *New Faces in New Places: The Changing Geography of American Immigration*, edited by Douglas S. Massey. New York: Russell Sage Foundation.

Siddharthan, Kris, and Melissa Ahern. 1996. "Inpatient Utilization by Undocumented Immigrants without Insurance." *Journal of Health Care for the Poor and Underserved* 7(4): 355–63.

Sides, John, and Jack Citrin. 2007. "European Opinion about Immigration: The Role of Identities, Interests and Information." *British Journal of Political Science* 37: 477–504.

Singer, Audrey. 2004. *The Rise of New Immigrant Gateways*. Washington, DC: Brookings Institution.

Singer, Audrey. 2013. "Contemporary Immigrant Gateways in Historical

References

Perspective." *Dœdalus, The Journal of the American Academy of Arts and Sciences* 142(3): 76–91.

Singer, Audrey, Susan W. Hardwick, and Caroline B. Brettell, (eds.) 2008. *Twenty-First-Century Gateways: Immigrant Incorporation in Suburban America.* Washington, DC: Brookings Institution.

Singh, Gopal K., and Mohammad Siahpush. 2001. "All-cause and Cause-specific Mortality of Immigrants and Native Born in the United States." *American Journal of Public Health* 91(3): 392–9.

Singley, Susan G., and Nancy S. Landale. 1998. "Incorporating Origin and Process in Migration–Fertility Frameworks: The Case of Puerto Rican Women." *Social Forces* 76(4): 1437–64.

Smith, Craig S. 2005. "Immigrant Rioting Flares in France for Ninth Night." *The New York Times.* November 5.

Smith, N. R., Y. J. Kelly, and J. Y. Nazroo. 2009. "Intergenerational Continuities of Ethnic Inequalities in General Health in England." *Journal of Epidemiology and Community Health* 63(3): 253–8.

Sniderman, Paul M., Louk Hagendoorn, and Markus Prior. 2004. "Predisposing Factors and Situational Triggers: Exclusionary Reactions to Immigrant Minorities." *American Political Science Review* 98(1): 35–49.

Sobotka, Tomas. 2008. "The Rising Importance of Migrants for Childbearing in Europe." *Demographic Research* 19(9): 225–48.

Solé-Auró, Aïda, Montserrat Guillén, and Eileen M. Crimmins. 2012. "Health Care Usage among Immigrants and Native-born Elderly Populations in Eleven European Countries: Results from SHARE." *European Journal of Health Economics* 13(6): 741–54.

Solis, Julia M., Gary Marks, Melinda Garcia, and David Shelton. 1990. "Acculturation, Access to Care, and Use of Preventative Services by Hispanics: Findings from HHANES 1982–84." *American Journal of Public Health* 80 (Supplement): 11–19.

Sommers, Benjamin D. 2013. "Stuck Between Health and Immigration Reform: Care for Undocumented Immigrants." *New England Journal of Medicine* 369: 593–5.

Sorlie, Paul D., Eric Backlund, Norman J. Johnson, and Eugene Rogot. 1993. "Mortality by Hispanic Status in the United States." *JAMA* 270(20): 2464–8.

South, Scott J., Kyle Crowder, and Erick Chavez. 2005. "Migration and Spatial Assimilation among US Latinos: Classical versus Segmented Trajectories." *Demography* 42(3): 497–521.

Southern Poverty Law Center. 2006. "Immigration Fervor Fuels Racist Extremism." *Intelligence Report.* Available online at www.splcenter.org/get-informed/news/immigration-fervor-fuels-racist-extremism.

Soysal, Yasemin Nuhoqlu. 1994. *Limits of Citizenship: Migrants and Postnational Membership in Europe.* Chicago: University of Chicago Press.

References

Spickard, Paul. 2007. *Almost All Aliens: Immigration, Race and Colonialism in American History and Identity.* New York: Routledge.

Squalli, Jay. 2009. "Immigration and Environmental Emissions: A US County-level Analysis." *Population and Environment* 30(6): 247–60.

Squalli, Jay. 2010. "An Empirical Assessment of US State-level Immigration and Environmental Emissions." *Ecological Economics* 69(5): 1170–5.

Stamps, Katherine, and Stephanie A. Bohon. 2006. "Educational Attainment in New and Established Latino Metropolitan Destinations." *Social Science Quarterly* 87(1): 1225–40.

Stanley, William D. 1987. "Economic Migrants or Refugees from Violence? A Time Series Analysis of Salvadoran Migration to the US." *The Latin American Research Review* 22(1): 132–54.

Stanton-Salazar, Ricardo D. 2001. *Manufacturing Hope and Despair: The School and Kin Support Networks of US-Mexican Youth.* New York: Teachers College Press.

Steele, Claude M., and Joshua Aronson. 1995. "Stereotype Threat and the Intellectual Test Performance of African Americans." *Journal of Personality and Social Psychology* 69(5): 797–811.

Stephen, Elizabeth Hervey, and Frank D. Bean. 1992. "Assimilation, Disruption and the Fertility of Mexican-Origin Women in the United States." *International Migration Review* 26(1): 67–88.

Stephen, Elizabeth Hervey, Karen Foote, Gerry E. Hendershot, and Charlotte A. Schoenborn. 1994. "Health of the Foreign-Born Population: United States, 1989-90." (Advance Data no. 241.) Hyattsville, MD: National Center for Health Statistics.

Stevens, Mitchell L., Elizabeth A. Armstrong, and Richard Arum. 2008. "Sieve, Incubator, Temple, Hub: Empirical and Theoretical Advances in the Sociology of Higher Education." *Annual Review of Sociology* 34: 127–51.

Stier, Haya, and Varda Levanon. 2003. "Finding an Adequate Job: Employment and Income of Recent Immigrants to Israel." *International Migration* 41(2): 81–107.

Stowell, Jacob I. 2007. *Immigration and Crime: The Effects of Immigration on Criminal Behavior.* New York: LFB Scholarly Publishing.

Suárez-Orozco, Carola, Marcelo M. Suárez-Orozco, and Irina Todorova. 2008. *Learning a New Land: Immigrant Students in American Society.* Cambridge, MA: Harvard University Press.

Suárez-Orozco, Carola, Irina L. G. Todorova, and Josephine Louie. 2002. "Making Up for Lost Time: The Experience of Separation and Reunification among Immigrant Families." *Family Process* 41(4): 625–43.

Sue, Stanley, and Sumie Okazaki. 2009 [1990]. "Asian-American Educational Achievements: A Phenomenon in Search of an Explanation." *Asian American Journal of Psychology* S(1): 45–55.

Suro, Roberto, and Audrey Singer. 2002. *Latino Growth in Metropolitan*

References

America: Changing Patterns, New Locations. Washington, DC: Brookings Institution.

Takagi, Dana Y. 1998. *The Retreat from Race: Asian American Admissions and Racial Politics.* New Brunswick, NJ: Rutgers University.

Tarmann, Allison. 2000. "The Flap over Replacement Migration." *Population Today.* Available online at www.prb.org/Articles/2000/TheFlapOverRepla cementMigration.aspx.

Taylor, Jared. 2011. *White Identity: Racial Consciousness in the 21st Century.* Oakton, VA: New Century Foundation.

Teitelbaum, Michael S., and Myron Weiner (eds.) 1995. *Threatened Peoples, Threatened Borders: World Migration and US Policy.* New York: W. W. Norton.

Teitelbaum, Michael S., and Jay M. Winter. 1985. *The Fear of Population Decline.* Orlando, FL: Academic Press.

Thompson, Warren S. 1929. "Population." *American Journal of Sociology* 34(6): 959–75.

Toulemon, Laurent. 2004. "Fertility among Immigrant Women: New Data, a New Approach." *Population and Societies* 400: 1–4.

Toulemon, Laurent, and Magali Mazuy. 2004. "Comment prendre en compte l'âge à l'arrivée et la durée de séjour en France dans la mesure de la fécondité des immigrées?" [How Does Age at Arrival and Duration of Stay in France Account for the Fertility of Immigrants?]. Working Paper 120. Paris: Institut National d'Etudes Démographiques.

Tragaki, Alexandra, and Antonios Rovolis. 2012. "Immigrant Population in Italy During the First Decade of the 21st Century: Changing Demographics and Modified Settlement Patterns." *European Urban and Regional Studies* 21(3): 286–300.

Trovato, Frank. 2003. *Migration and Survival: The Mortality Experience of Immigrants in Canada.* Research report. Edmonton, Alberta: Prairie Centre of Excellence for Research on Immigration and Integration.

Turney, Kristin, and Grace Kao. 2009. "Barriers to School Involvement: Are Immigrant Parents Disadvantaged?" *Journal of Education Research* 102(4): 257–71.

Tyson, Karolyn, William Darity, Jr., and Domini R. Castellino. 2005. "It's not 'a Black Thing': Understanding the Burden of Acting White and Other Dilemmas of High Achievement." *American Sociological Review* 70(4): 582–605.

Tyyskä, Vappu. 2008. "Parents and Teens in Immigrant Families: Cultural Influences and Material Pressures." *Canadian Diversity* 6(2): 79–83.

Uhlenberg, Peter. 1992. "Population Aging and Social Policy." *Annual Review of Sociology* 18: 449–74.

United Nations. 2001. *Replacement Migration: Is It a Solution to Declining and Ageing Populations?* New York: United Nations Population Division.

United Nations. 2011. "International Migration Report 2009: A Global

References

Assessment." A report of the Department of Economic and Social Affairs, Population Division ST/ESA/SER.A/316. New York: United Nations.

United Nations. 2013. "The Number of International Migrants Worldwide Reaches 232 Million." (Population Facts 2013/2.) New York: United Nations Department of Economic and Social Affairs.

United Nations High Commissioner for Refugees (UNHCR). 2006. *Measuring Protection by the Numbers.* Geneva: United Nations High Commissioner for Refugees.

US Census Bureau. 2008. "An Older and More Diverse Nation by Midcentury." Press Release, August 14. Available online at www.census.gov/newsroom/releases/archives/population/cb08-123.html.

US Department of Education. 2002. "Executive Summary: The No Child Left Behind Act of 2001." Washington, DC: US Department of Education.

US Department of Education. 2004a. "Improving Teacher Quality State Grants Title II, Part A." Non-regulatory Guidance. Washington, DC: US Department of Education.

US Department of Education. 2004b. "Parental Involvement: Title I, Part A." Non-regulatory Guidance. Washington, DC: US Department of Education.

Valdez, Zulema. 2006. "Segmented Assimilation among Mexicans in the Southwest." *The Sociological Quarterly* 47(3): 397–424.

Valencia, Richard R., and Mary S. Black. 2002. "'Mexican Americans Don't Value Education!' On the Basis of the Myth, Mythmaking, and Debunking." *Journal of Latinos and Education* 1(2): 81–103.

Valenzuela, Abel, Jr., Nik Theodore, Edwin Meléndez, and Ana Luz González. 2006. "On the Corner: Day Labor in the United States." A report on the National Day Labor Study. Los Angeles: University of California–Los Angeles.

Valenzuela, Angela. 1999. *Subtractive Schooling: U.S.-Mexican Youth and the Politics of Caring.* Albany: State University of New York Press.

van Ours, Jan C., and Justus Veenman. 2003. "The Educational Attainment of Second-generation Immigrants in the Netherlands." *Journal of Population Economics* 16(4): 739–53.

van Tubergen, Frank. 2005. "Self-employment of Immigrants: A Cross-national Study of 17 Western Societies." *Social Forces* 84(2): 709–32.

Vaquera, Elizabeth, and Grace Kao. 2012. "Educational Achievement of Immigrant Adolescents in Spain: Do Gender and Region of Origin Matter?" *Child Development* 83(5): 1560–76.

Vasileva, Katya. 2011. "Population and Social Conditions." *Eurostat: Statistics in Focus.* Luxembourg: European Commission. Available online at http://epp.eurostat.ec.europa.eu/cache/ITY_OFFPUB/KS-SF-11-034/EN/KS-SF-11-034-EN.PDF.

Vega, William A., and Rubén G. Rumbaut. 1991. "Ethnic Minorities and Mental Health." *Annual Review of Sociology* 17: 351–83.

References

Vega, William A., and William M. Sribney. 2011. "Understanding the Hispanic Health Paradox through a Multi-Generation Lens: A Focus on Behavior Disorders." Pp. 151–68 in *Health Disparities in Youth and Families: Research and Applications*, edited by Gustavo Carlo, Lisa J. Crockett, and Miguel A. Carranza. New York: Springer.

Velez, Carmen Noemi, and Jane A. Ungemack. 1989. "Drug Use among Puerto Rican Youth: An Exploration of Generational Status Differences." *Social Science and Medicine* 29(6): 779–89.

Vernez, Georges, and Allan Abrahamse. 1996. *How Immigrants Fare in US Education*. Santa Monica, CA: RAND.

Viladrich, Anahí. 2012. "Beyond Welfare Reform: Reframing Undocumented Immigrants' Entitlement to Health Care in the United States: A Critical Review." *Social Science and Medicine* 74(6): 822–9.

Waldinger, Roger. 2007. "Did Manufacturing Matter? The Experience of Yesterday's Second Generation: A Reassessment." *International Migration Review* 41(1): 3–39.

Waldinger, Roger, and Cynthia Feliciano. 2004. "Will the New Second Generation Experience 'Downward Assimilation?' Segmented Assimilation Re-Assessed." *Ethnic and Racial Studies* 27(3): 376–402.

Ward, Colleen, and Anne-Marie Masgoret. 2008. "Attitudes toward Immigrants, Immigration, and Multiculturalism in New Zealand: A Social Psychological Analysis." *International Migration Review* 42(1): 227–48.

Ward, David. 1982. "Settlement Patterns and Spatial Distribution." Pp. 35–74 in *Immigration*, edited by Richard A. Easterlin, David Ward, William S. Bernard, and Reed Ueda. Cambridge, MA: Harvard University Press.

Warner, W. Lloyd, and Leo Srole. 1945. *The Social Systems of American Ethnic Groups*. New Haven, CT: Yale University Press.

Waters, Mary C. 1990. *Ethnic Options: Choosing Identities in America*. Berkeley: University of California Press.

Waters, Mary C., and Tomás R. Jiménez. 2005. "Assessing Immigrant Assimilation: New Empirical and Theoretical Challenges." *Annual Review of Sociology* 31: 105–5.

Waters, Mary C., Van C. Tran, Philip Kasinitz, and John H. Mollenkopf. 2010. "Segmented Assimilation Revisited: Types of Acculturation and Socioeconomic Mobility in Young Adulthood." *Ethnic and Racial Studies* 33(7): 1168–93.

Westman, Jeanette, Tuija Martelin, Tommi Härkänen, Seppo Koskinen, and Kristina Sundquist. 2008. "Migration and Self-Rated Health: A Comparison between Finns Living in Sweden and Finns Living in Finland." *Scandinavian Journal of Public Health* 36(7): 698–705.

White, Michael J., and Jennifer E. Glick. 2009. *Achieving Anew: How New Immigrants Do in American Schools, Jobs, and Neighborhoods*. New York: Russell Sage Foundation.

White, Michael J., Lorenzo Moreno, and Shenyang Guo. 1995. "The Interrelation of Fertility and Geographic Mobility in Peru: A Hazards Model Analysis." *International Migration Review* 29(2): 492–514.

White, Thomas J. 2007. "Sharing Resources: The Global Distribution of the Ecological Footprint." *Ecological Economics* 64(2): 402–10.

Williams, Belinda. 2003. "What Else Do We Need to Know and Do?" Pp. 13–24 in *Closing the Achievement Gap*, edited by Belinda Williams. Alexandria, VA: Association for Supervision and Curriculum Development.

Williams, David R., and Chiquita Collins. 1995. "US Socioeconomic and Racial Differences in Health: Patterns and Explanations." *Annual Review of Sociology* 21: 349–86.

Wirth, Louis. 1928. *The Ghetto*. Chicago: University of Chicago Press.

World Bank. 2012. "Data: India." Washington, DC: The World Bank Group. Available online at http://data.world-bank.org/country/india.

Xiao, Chenyang. 2013. "Public Attitudes toward Science and Technology and Concern for the Environment: Testing a Model of Indirect Feedback Effects." *Environment and Behavior* 45(1): 113–37.

Xie, Yu, and Margaret Gough. 2011. "Ethnic Enclaves and the Earnings of Immigrants." *Demography* 48(4): 1293–315.

Young, Christabel. 1994. "Beliefs and Realities about the Demographic Role of Immigration." *The Australian Quarterly* 66(4): 49–74.

Yuengert, Andrew M. 1994. "Testing Hypotheses of Immigrant Self-Employment." *Journal of Human Resources* 30(1): 194–204.

Zavodny, Madeline. 2011. "Immigration and American Jobs." A report of the American Enterprise Institute for Public Policy Research and the Partnership for a New American Economy. Washington, DC: American Enterprise Institute.

Zhang, Junfu. 2011. "Tipping and Residential Segregation: A Unified Schelling Model." *Journal of Regional Science* 51(1): 167–93.

Zhang, Wei, and Van M. Ta. 2009. "Social Connections, Immigration-related Factors, and Self-rated Physical and Mental Health among Asian Americans." *Social Science and Medicine* 68(12): 2104–12.

Zhou, Min. 1992. *New York's Chinatown: The Socioeconomic Potential of an Urban Enclave*. Philadelphia, PA: Temple University Press.

Zhou, Min. 1997a. "Segmented Assimilation: Issues, Controversies, and Recent Research on the New Second Generation." *International Migration Review* 31(4): 975–1008.

Zhou, Min. 1997b. "Growing Up American: The Challenge Confronting Immigrant Children and Children of Immigrants." *Annual Review of Sociology* 23: 63–95.

Zhou, Min, and Carl L. Bankston III. 1994. "Social Capital and the Adaptation of the Second Generation: The Case of Vietnamese Youth in New Orleans." *International Migration Review* 28(4): 821–45.

Zhou, Min and Carl L. Bankston III. 1998. *Growing Up American: How*

References

Vietnamese Children Adapt to Life in the United States. New York: Russell Sage.

Zlotnik, Hania, David Bloom, and Emmanuel Jiménez. 2011. "Seven Billion and Growing: The Role of Population Policy in Achieving Sustainability." United Nations Technical Paper 2011/3. New York: Department of Economic and Social Affairs.

Index

Index

Index

Index

Index

Index

Index

Index

CPSIA information can be obtained
at www.ICGtesting.com
Printed in the USA
LVOW10*1721190817
545630LV00011B/338/P